Dave Grant

The Longest Race

the Longest race

PETER COOK & BOB FISHER

David McKay Company, Inc.
New York

The Longest Race

Copyright © 1975 by Bob Fisher and Peter Cook

Library of Congress Catalog Card Number: 75-4438
ISBN 0 679 50564 4
Manufactured in Malta

First published in Great Britain by
Stanford Maritime, 12 Long Acre, London WC2E 9LP

One of the Italian entries, *CS e RB*, which was built by Nordcantieri as the prototype of the Robert Clark designed Koala 50 class.

To: *Paul Waterhouse*
Dominique Guillet
Bernard Hosking
Who lost their lives in the most
adventurous yacht race of all time.

Sir Alec Rose, singlehanded round-the-world voyager and member of the organising committee who fired the starting cannon at Southsea Castle on September 8th 1973.

Foreword

By Sir Alec Rose, Kt.

I am very pleased indeed to write a foreword in support of this book which describes every aspect of the Whitbread/RNSA Round the World Yacht Race.

A quick glance through the chapter headings should convince even the most critical reader how well the authors have done their job and the wealth of information they have compiled. It is written in language understood by the amateur and expert alike, and so will become a true life adventure story, gripping in intensity, combined with technical data that only became available as a result of this race. Remember that the distance sailed in this round the world epic is equivalent to that achieved in about fifteen years of normal ocean racing.

Every point of the race is covered starting with the organisation and the boats' preparation, and there are line drawings and descriptions of the yachts. The writers then go on to the actual race, and what stories there are to tell. Every condition of weather is met. There is the pleasant Trade Wind sailing with blue skies and warm sunshine; there are the calms in the Doldrums; and the boisterous, great South Atlantic Ocean that cost Eric Tabarly his mast. It was down in these waters, too, that one of the crew of *Great Britain II* had a miraculous escape when he fell overboard and was picked up again.

Then, after leaving Cape Town, the yachts enter the Roaring Forties on their way across the great Southern Ocean. I remember I had some of my worst weather of the whole trip down southeast of the Cape of Good Hope. Great hills of water rolling along with white, curling crests and the winds scream and howl incessantly. Strong hail squalls hit the decks like bullets and the cold is intense as one gets further south and near the ice belt.

All this is of course described in detail as the reader is taken along with this enthralling story. Safely in your armchair you may be, but even so, a cold shiver creeps down your spine with the description of conditions at times, unfolded in the pages of this exciting book. Several of the yachts almost capsized and freak waves constantly swept right across their decks. It was in these conditions that one of the French yachts, *33 Export*, lost her co-skipper overboard; in such weather there is little chance of survival. This was the case of the crew member of *Great Britain II* who again went overboard southeast of New Zealand. There is no second chance in these waters.

In all, three crew members were lost overboard in the race. But this will not deter others from pitting their skill against the great forces of nature. The danger is when they underestimate the strength of the elements against them. As with mountaineering or exploring, it is the element of danger that is stimulating and exciting. The achievement of success is the reward.

The authors conclude with comments on many aspects of the race and conclusions drawn on the problems that were met; valuable information that can only be obtained from the school of hard experience.

This is a great book, compiled from facts gathered from the skippers themselves and from their day by day signals. It is a great book for all lovers of an adventure story, for those planning similar voyages, and for architects designing deep water sailing craft.

Introduction

The Whitbread/RNSA Round the World Race was over for most of the participants: Vernon Creek in the Royal Navy's torpedo and anti-submarine establishment at Portsmouth was filled with yachts which had spent the previous seven or eight months battling their way across the oceans of the world in their various moods; through the most tempestuous and inhospitable seas; through tropical heat and Antarctic cold.

They had started in September 1973, some as close-knit crews, others newly recruited, each prepared to pit themselves against their adversaries and the elements. On the first leg to Cape Town they served their apprenticeships, discovering each other and producing a corporate identity, moulding themselves into teams with their yachts. At Cape Town they rested and identified their opponents, not as enemies but as fellow seafarers who had endured the same hardships, the same frustrations and finally achieved the satisfaction of arrival at a distant port.

The second leg from Cape Town to Sydney produced the worst weather and conditions, and two lives were lost. The reaction was in the best tradition of the sea – boats spoke to each other on their radio telephones whereas before they had even been reluctant to transmit their obligatory weekly position reports. Everyone was prepared to help the friends they had made in Cape Town.

At Sydney, the arrival of the Round the World fleet coincided with the Christmas and New Year Holiday and the top ocean racing events in the Southern Hemisphere, the Southern Cross Series and the Sydney-Hobart Race. Resources were stretched to the limit and the arrival of a dozen or two ocean voyagers and their crews could have passed almost un-noticed had it not been for the traditional hospitality of the Australians.

So, having exposed themselves to the rigours of that part of the Southern Ocean which lies between South Africa and Australia, they were now setting off again into high southerly latitudes and towards the dreaded passage round Cape Horn – most feared of all headlands. In the event this section of the course was comparatively gentle although it claimed one more life. And The Horn itself proved to be a mere doddle for many, but some found its reputation was well founded as they were struck by sudden squalls as they pranced along in front of the Royal Navy's Antarctic survey ship, HMS *Endurance*; the watching sailors were treated to at least one demonstration of a 90° knock down.

Rio at carnival time, the Mardi Gras, provided an unreal interlude for those lucky enough to be at the head of the fleet and, therefore, able to enjoy the maximum time in harbour between legs. But Rio added to the atmosphere and will forever be remembered by the crews; even the tail-enders had a few days there.

The last leg from Rio to Portsmouth was relatively uneventful – just a straightforward sail from Brazil to England, a mere 5,500 miles. Uneventful, that is, except for minor problems such as the parting of five of the nineteen strands of the forestay on the race winner *Sayula II* between the Canary Islands and the finish; a defective exhaust system on *Adventure*'s generator, necessitating the fabrication of a new exhaust pipe from cocoa tins soldered together; and the unscheduled call of the German tail-ender *Peter von Danzig* in the Azores to top up her almost depleted fresh water tanks. But these were relatively minor problems at this stage of the race.

At Portsmouth in the middle of April 1974 the post-race parties were in full swing. The editor of *Yachts and Yachting*, having safely driven his editorial desk for the previous eight months, participated in the post-race revelry. At a party given by the officers of HMS Vernon, in the best of naval tradition, he spoke to Rear Admiral Otto Steiner, the Race Committee Chairman, and it transpired that, whilst individual crew members had declared their intention of writing their own stories of the race, no one had indicated that they were going to write a book covering the overall picture. The seed was sown .... There followed a party on board *Grand Louis*, and someone even rode a bicycle round her deck!

The idea was slept on for a couple of nights and then Peter Cook telephoned Bob Fisher to ask if he was interested in joining forces to produce a book telling the story of the race. Bob, yachting correspondent of the British daily newspaper, *The Guardian*, and contributor to many English language yachting magazines had been in Portsmouth during the days leading up to the start of the race; had spent a month in Australia when the race passed through and had been waiting at Portsmouth when

Great Britain II was first across the finishing line. He was probably the best informed journalist on the race. Bob Fisher and Peter Cook decided to join forces and this book is the result.

In no way does the book tell the whole story of the race. Every crew member on every leg had enough material to write his own book – and that would mean three or four hundred books! The aim here has been to chronicle the events leading up to the start, the background organisation, a selection of the problems encountered and a few of the lessons learned. An attempt has been made to get over to the layman the atmosphere and difficulties facing someone who races a yacht round the world and to give at least a modicum of technical detail and analysis of the performance of the boats, crews and equipment for the serious student. The authors do not have personal experience of the conditions, neither will you unless you do it yourself. What is known is that this was one of the greatest sporting challenges facing man and to have left it unchronicled would have been an injustice to those many crews who took part.

The race was won by one of the largest yachts competing – a Swan 65 owned, equipped and skippered by a Mexican millionaire. The first yacht home was skippered by entrepreneur Chay Blyth, a professional adventurer, whose boat was paid for by a patriotic millionaire and who was given his £125,000 mount after the race. These were the boats which hit the headlines but the real heroes are those who sailed smaller, older, more basically equipped craft: the Poles in *Otago* and *Copernicus* and the Germans in *Peter von Danzig*. They spent 204 days at sea compared with the leaders' 144 days and sometimes had only a couple of days in harbour between legs. One Polish crew member remarked 'We have sailed round the world but we have not seen the world.' When considering the achievements of the leaders then, the effort of the back markers should not be overlooked for they played the game harder, in more difficult circumstances and for much longer than those in the leading boats.

Acknowledgements

It would have been impossible to write this book and compile all the necessary information without the generous help of many people. Our thanks must go first to the RNSA for their support and co-operation: we had access to all their records; walked in and out of the Race Office at all times of the day and night, seven days a week; and were always given a friendly welcome. The Race Secretary, Captain Dudley Norman, and his efficient assistant Mrs Betty Cripps spent many hours producing a vast amount of information which we called for, and never failed to bend over backwards to help us. Dudley Norman was also responsible for writing most of the chapter on the Race Organisation. The Race Chairman, Rear Admiral Otto Steiner, gave us help and encouragement and wrote the Organiser's Comments.

Butch Dalrymple-Smith, who was one of *Sayula II*'s crew, assisted us throughout the production of the book and was responsible for the chapters on Life on Board and the Performance of Boats and Gear, and wrote the vivid, first-hand account of *Sayula II*'s capsize. Adlard Coles has incorporated sections of this account in a new edition of his classic book *Heavy Weather Sailing*, and has added his comments to Butch's account of the incident, which are included in Chapter 10. Dr Robin Leach sailed the whole race in *Second Life* and provided the professional comment for the Medical chapter.

The chapter on Communications is based on an article by Bill Maconachie which appeared in *Motor Boat and Yachting* and we are indebted to the editor, Dick Hewitt, for permission to use it in this book.

There are comments by Alain Gliksman in the chapter on Navigation which are reproduced with the permission of the editor of *Neptune Nautisme*, and the remarks made by André Viant, Eric Tabarly and Jack Grout which are in Chapter 3 first appeared in another French magazine, *Bateaux*. For the translation of these and other French reports we are indebted to Claire Lines; the speed and accuracy with which she selected and produced the important items from these magazines was of particular help. Pat Godber, Secretary of the RNSA and editor of its *Journal*, has allowed us to quote from some of the articles about the race which were published in the *Journal*, and the information contained in these articles, together with accounts written by other members of *Adventure*'s crew, were most valuable. The Controller of Her Majesty's Stationery Office gave permission for us to publish extracts from *Ocean Passages for the World*.

Many of the designers of the yachts sent us notes and comments on their designs and provided the drawings from which Robert Humphreys produced the perspective lines and accommodation and sail plans. In particular we should like to thank Robert

Clark, Alan Gurney, André Mauric, Dominique Presles, John Sharp, E. G. van de Stadt, Sparkman and Stephens, and Raymond Wall of Camper and Nicholsons.

Many of the skippers and crew members answered our questions and we received considerable assistance from Lieutenant Commander Patrick Bryans, Major Niel Carlier, Wilhelm Grütter, Dick Kenny, Reinhard Laucht, the RN Sailing Coach Roy Mullender, and many others.

The photographs were taken by David Baker, Alastair Black, Butch Dalrymple-Smith, Keith Lorence, Jonathan Eastland, HMS *Endurance*, Christian Fevrier, Nick Rowe, Reinhard Laucht, Dr Robin Leach and the authors; others were supplied by the Ajax News and Feature Agency, *Paris Match* and the Director of Public Relations (Royal Navy).

Contents

1 Concept 19

2 Organisation 21

3 Boat Preparation 33

4 The Yachts 53

5 Leg One 83

6 Leg Two 91

7 Leg Three 101

8 Leg Four 111

9 Performance of
Boats and Gear 121

10 Capsize   130

11 Life on Board   135

12 Medical   142

13 Navigation   147

14 Communications   159

15 Organiser's Comments   163

16 Reflections   165

Appendices

I   Conditions of Entry   168

II   Sailing Instructions   173

III Crew List   178

IV   Results and Prizes   185

Index   189

Track Charts

Leg One   facing page 96

Leg Two   97

Leg Three   112

Leg Four   113

The track charts for each leg of the course show the daily positions of *selected* yachts taken from the records submitted by the yachts' navigators to the Race Organisers after the completion of each leg. The Organisers asked for the position of each yacht to be recorded for noon GMT each day but it is obvious that some yachts gave their noon position at local time because on the third leg, some of them recorded two noon positions for the same day, one either side of the international date line — 180°! Sometimes the position recorded was at neither noon GMT nor noon local time, also it was likely that an estimated position was given, based on a fix taken a number of hours or even days beforehand. So the positions shown for a particular day are not necessarily all for the same time, but the maximum error is unlikely to exceed twelve hours run.

It was not possible to check the track of each yacht by plotting positions and relating them to the prevailing weather conditions — this would have taken far too long even if all the necessary information had been available — but where a glaring anomaly was apparent the track was checked with the yacht's log and some errors were discovered and corrected this way.

1
Concept

The idea of a race around the world has been in the minds of yachtsmen for many years. Sailormen in the great days of the clipper ships had races, but they were to return with their cargoes to get the best price. Conor O'Brien, who went around the world in *Saiorse* in 1923/4, mooted the idea for yachts after his successful circumnavigation, but nothing was done to turn the idea into reality until 1967 when the *Sunday Times* proposed the Golden Globe event for the first man to complete a non-stop single handed circumnavigation in a sailing yacht. It was not a race in the true sense of the word, as there was no single starting time or place; but more a stimulatory competition to encourage the conquest of a sailing 'Everest'. In 1969 however, Anthony Churchill, then publisher of *Yachting & Boating Weekly*, together with Guy Pearse who had previously organised the Observer Singlehanded Transatlantic Race and the Observer/Daily Express Round Britain Race, produced a brochure at Cowes Week with details of a proposed race around the world, which largely followed the old clipper ship routes. It had stops at Cape Town, Sydney and Rio de Janeiro and was to be for yachts of Class I, IOR rating.

Churchill and Pearse were enthusiastic about the idea and plainly carried their own enthusiasm to others. By getting their concept over in the yachting magazines of the world, most of which were only too pleased to comment on the idea, they attracted many enquiries. Many of these naturally fell by the wayside, but a few firmed up as time went by and in March 1971 a list of the more important enquiries included the Royal Navy, the Army, Chay Blyth, Bruce Dalling with *Jakaranda* and a German yacht club with *Peter von Danzig*. Six months later, Chay Blyth in an interview with Gina Hunt reported in *Yachting & Boating Weekly*, spoke of his intention and suggested that the size should be limited together with the number of crew. Italian entries were confirmed by Churchill after a visit by him to Genoa in February 1972.

One problem stood in the way of Churchill and Pearse and their organising the race. It was going to be an expensive operation and they were having trouble finding sponsors. They had two concerns interested but neither was close to coming forward with the cash. The Royal Navy asked what the situation was concerning the race, as they had committed themselves to yachts for adventure training and wanted the race to go ahead as scheduled, rather than wait for another year whilst Churchill and Pearse raised the cash. Churchill had this race planned as the first of a trio of ideas and, whilst loath to part with the organisation, at this stage felt that the latter two, one of which was to be the one-stop Clipper Race sponsored by the *Financial Times*, were more important to him. He agreed that if he had not found a sponsor by April 1972 he would hand over the files on the race to the RNSA. The RNSA committee already had Whitbread interested in sponsoring the race and since they had their own public relations staff, both Churchill and Pearse were able to free themselves from further organisational activity in the race.

Pat Godber, the Secretary of the RNSA, was responsible for proposing that the club should take over the race and asking Whitbread to sponsor it. Whitbread had, some two years earlier, approached the Ministry of Defence (Navy), offering to support a prestigious yacht race and that information had filtered down to the RNSA. The handing over of the race took place officially at a meeting on May 8th 1972 and Captain Dudley Norman was appointed Secretary of the Race Committee, a job which was to last more than two years and take him all over the world. The RNSA Race Committee worked hard to produce the General Conditions of Entry, Safety Regulations and Preliminary Sailing Instructions and combined them in a brochure which was prepared for a press conference at Whitbreads' brewery on June 29th 1972 at which the Whitbread Round the World Race was announced. It gave the starting date as September 8th 1973 — just over 14 months away. It is a tribute to Dudley Norman and his staff (of one) that the race did start on time. But their problem was perhaps not as great as that facing those who were going to take part. From the conception, through the convincing to the competing is a long process involving time, money and considerable psychological adjustment. This race was conceived as an all time peak in the sport of ocean racing and as such was bound to be demanding.

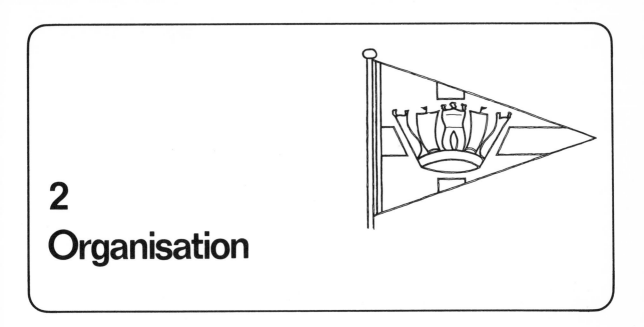

2
Organisation

Structure of the Race Committee

Once the decision had been taken by the committee of the Royal Naval Sailing Association to run the race, Rear Admiral Otto Steiner, the Vice Commodore, was invited to form a committee to organise it. The members of the committee were: Rear Admiral O. H. M. St J. Steiner, CB (chairman), Captain J. A. Hans Hamilton (vice chairman), Commander Errol Bruce, Sir Alec Rose, Alan Paul, John E. F. Fox, Commander F. A. Collins and Captain E. D. Norman. The committee was selected with a view to gathering together as wide a range of experience as possible, covering all aspects of the running of the race. Admiral Steiner had many years' experience of offshore sailing and was the first Navy Sailing Selector; Captain Hans Hamilton had considerable offshore sailing experience and was a member of the RORC Committee; Commander Errol Bruce has a lifetime of offshore sailing experience, he sailed Naval yachts in many offshore events and in longer races such as the Transatlantic, and after retiring from the Royal Navy he became editor of the magazine *Motor Boat and Yachting* and then a partner in the publishing company, Nautical Publishing. Sir Alec Rose was not an ocean racing expert, he had merely

sailed singlehanded round the world! Alan Paul, an honorary life member of the RNSA, was for many years the secretary of the Royal Ocean Racing Club; John Fox represented the sponsor, Whitbread, without whose financial help the race would not be possible; Commander Collins held the position of Deputy Director of Public Relations (Navy); and Captain Dudley Norman spent a period as secretary to the Royal Malta Yacht Club and was closely involved with the organisation of the first four Middle Sea Races. So the committee selected contained a wealth of experience covering every aspect of offshore sailing and the vital back-up support.

The RN and RNSA

The RNSA is an organisation with over 5,000 members. Many are serving in ships of the Royal Navy throughout the world and some 500 members live overseas, thus providing a wealth of world-wide sailing knowledge. Spread throughout the world are 120 honorary local officers and, backing up this organisation, close links are maintained with the sailing associations of the Commonwealth navies and the United States Navy.

Whilst the membership of the RNSA includes a hard core of active service Royal Navy men and women, there are a great many others who have finished their naval service but maintain a link with it through the RNSA. Thus it is not officially part of the Royal Navy, but an independent and self-supporting organisation, although it advises the Board of Admiralty officially on all aspects of sailing; this is a sport which gets full encouragement from the Navy and which also uses sailing as adventure training for its men and women, and indeed it is in this category that the Royal Navy entered their Nicholson 55 *Adventure* in the race.

The Association conducts and co-ordinates sailing activities in the fleet through 11 branches at home and abroad. Apart from open boats carried in RN ships, the Navy's official fleet consists of some 65 yachts and about 650 Bosun dinghies. The Association, independently of the official Naval fleet of sailing craft, owns for charter to its members seven modern cruising yachts, a Soling and numerous dinghies whilst its members have a fleet of over 2,000 privately owned boats.

RNSA Expertise and World-Wide Ramifications

Whilst the financing of the race was entirely independent of Naval funds, the experience, back-up facilities, expertise, and world-wide ramifications of the RNSA were valuable assets, readily to hand. The RNSA was in a position to approach the Naval authorities at Portsmouth and obtain the use of HMS Vernon for the start and finish of the race; in South Africa the Navy co-operated to the extent of opening up their Naval Reserve headquarters to act as a base; in Australia, the RANSA did their best to help the competitors, who found that their arrival over the Christmas holiday period co-incided with the Southern Cross Series and preparation for the Sydney–Hobart Race, stretching badly needed repair and re-storing facilities to the limit. Admiral Steiner, the Race Chairman, visited Cape Town, Sydney and Rio de Janeiro before the start of the race and in the first two ports was able to see naval flag officers whom he had known personally during his career; and in Rio, the arrival of an Admiral and Vice Commodore, later Commodore, of the RNSA to

With the first yachts secured in Vernon Creek after the finish, smiles from the two men who bore most of the responsibility for organising the race. Captain Dudley Norman, Race Secretary (left) and Rear Admiral Otto Steiner, Chairman of the Race Committee.

discuss race facilities had far more effect than if plain Mr Steiner had arrived!

Quite apart from sailing experience, the committee numbered in its ranks men experienced in writing orders for naval exercises, who could turn their talents equally to producing instructions for the race.

So although the organisers had no financial assistance from the Royal Navy, the 'fringe benefits' available were considerable.

The committee was backed up by a number of specialist advisers. Mr J. H. Froud of the Royal Corps of Naval Constructors to advise on construction and seaworthiness of entrants – a practical yachtsman himself; two round-the-world yachtsmen, Sir Francis Chichester (until his death) and Robin Knox-Johnston; and, later, Commander R.H.H. Brunner of the Coastguard.

Initial Planning

The committee met thirteen times before the start to discuss every aspect, to make policy decisions and to approve the detailed orders and instructions which resulted from their deliberations and which were prepared, in the main, by the Secretary, who was the only full time member of the committee.

At the first meeting of the Committee, which took place on May 10th 1972, the route and timing of the race was considered. Many different factors had to be taken into account: January for the best weather round Cape Horn; selecting suitable stop-over ports so that the legs of the race would be approximately equal in length; stops of sufficient length and frequency to ensure that enough food and water could be loaded and repair and rest facilities obtained at ports with adequate facilities to deal with 20 or more large Class I yachts at approximately the same time; the need to avoid conflict with other races at stop-over ports; the co-operation of yacht clubs of suitable standing.

Cape Town, Sydney and Rio de Janeiro were decided upon and cables sent to clubs inviting their co-operation, which was quickly forthcoming. September 8th was chosen as the starting date to leave a reasonable period clear after the Fastnet Race, which finishes around the middle of August, in case any of the Admiral's Cup boats wanted to race back to their home countries. It was also early enough to make a January passage round Cape Horn a virtual certainty. It was thought probable that the third leg would start from Sydney before the start of the Sydney–Hobart Race on Boxing Day, December 26th, and thus not clash with the Southern Cross Series. The arrival of the yachts in Rio would probably coincide with the finish of the Buenos Aires to Rio Race and so cause few extra problems as the local race organisation would be in full operation.

An organisation was set up to write the race rules which had to include specially strengthened sections on special regulations and safety equipment. These, together with the Provisional Sailing Instructions were included in a brochure printed just in time for a press conference on June 29th 1972 (Appendix II).

Predictions of Times and Weather Conditions

The prediction of the length of time yachts would be on passage between ports was made by HMS Dryad, the Royal Navy's school of navigation, which made very detailed calculations based on varying sizes of yacht and weather analysis. These predictions, in fact, turned out to be extremely accurate. *Burton Cutter*, the first yacht to arrive in Cape Town, being only a few hours early! When making these predictions, considerable reliance was placed on that remarkable publication, *Ocean Passages for the World*, which describes in great detail the type of weather that can be expected in all the oceans of the world together with information on the tides and currents, wind strengths and directions, the climatic conditions and the northern and southern limits of ice. The results of hundreds of years of sailing and steaming by the fighting and merchant navies of the world, but written for ships rather than for yachts. Although the yachts, whose design and structure was hardly dreamt of when much of the information in *Ocean Passages* was compiled and recorded, diverted considerably from the recommended routes and often found weather the direct opposite of what might have been expected, they nevertheless completed each leg very near the predicted dates.

Handicapping Explanation

The rules laid down that the race would be a handicap event and that yachts would be rated in accordance with the International Offshore Rule (1973). The IOR is a method by which monohull yachts of different size and type can be given a rating which enables a handicap to be levied so that they can race against each other on a more or less equal basis. One might compare a handicap yacht race with a golf competition. In the latter, different players have different handicaps and if they all play precisely to their handicap all would finish with the same score. In a yacht race, yachts are given a different time allowance to accord with their potential speeds and, if all the yachts sail exactly to their handicap, their times, when adjusted by their allowances will, like the golfers' scores, all be the same.

The rating of a yacht is expressed in feet (or metres) and from it, by means of a formula, can be calculated either a time correction factor (TCF) or a basic speed factor (BSF), providing two different methods of calculating the time allowance. In the case of TCF, the time taken by each yacht from start to finish, the elapsed time, is multiplied by the TCF to arrive at the corrected time. In the case of the BSF, the distance from the start to the finish is multiplied by the BSF (expressed in seconds per mile) to give a time allowance which is applied to the elapsed time to produce the corrected time.

Each of these two handicap systems has its protagonists; moreover, although there is only one IOR formula for calculating TCF, there are several for calculating BSF. After consultations with the International Offshore Rating Council, the Royal Ocean Racing Club's chief measurer and a number of others, a BSF formula was selected which fell part way between that favoured by the North American Yacht Racing Union (NAYRU) and that preferred by the RORC. This was not a bad choice as results showed that the handicap order of the first five yachts was always the same under either method, that on the second leg the handicap order of all the yachts was the same, and that on no leg would any yacht have moved up or down by more than one place, regardless of the system used.

The great advantage that the BSF system, often known as time on distance, has over TCF is that the handicap order of the yachts can be calculated at any period during the race according to the distance they have run and their elapsed time, whereas with the TCF (or time on time) system this cannot be calculated until a yacht has finished and established her elapsed time. The organisers insisted that yachts should report their positions each week, so that their handicap positions could be calculated and passed back to all of them. Thus the yachts themselves were able to follow the race and the report of the handicap order was always awaited eagerly. In fact this system was extremely accurate, although it came in for a certain amount of criticism after the start of the race because the reported order kept changing and the question was asked, 'How can so-and-so have dropped six places in a couple of days?' The answer was that this is precisely what had happened. The yacht in question had lost its wind for a few hours which the other had not and, because they were all so close together on handicap, had lost places. It was nearly always necessary to calculate the yachts' average corrected speeds to three places of decimals – that is to an accuracy of a thousandth of a knot – to sort out accurately their correct order.

The choice of route, the selection of ports, the prediction of speeds and the handicap system were the four fundamental factors which had to be decided by the organisers. All this information was, of course, passed on to the Cruising Association of South Africa at Cape Town, the Cruising Yacht Club of Australia in Sydney and the Iate Clube do Rio de Janeiro, all of which clubs were visited by the chairman of the Race Committee, Admiral Steiner, and which had formed committees to look after the race in their respective countries and waters.

Communications and Reports from Yachts

Meanwhile many other aspects of the race had to be planned and organised. Communications are dealt with in depth in Chapter 14 but the question of what action to take should a yacht fail to make its weekly position report called for careful thought. It was decided to take advice from the Coastguard, the Chamber of Shipping and Lloyds Intelligence. There were a number of problems to be considered: the safety of the yachts and crews; the fact that they would be in an area distant from the shore and shipping routes when they last reported; the probability that the lack of report was caused by radio failure; the weather conditions; and the need not to alarm relations and friends. HM Coastguard volunteered all possible help in coastal waters and offered to contact similar organisations along the route, though these proved to be fairly sketchy. The Chamber of Shipping was also very helpful, suggesting the publication of a suitable Notice to Mariners to draw attention to Notice to Mariners No. 4 which lays down the duties of ships at sea receiving information of a vessel in distress. Captain Baynham of the Chamber of Shipping added that a very large number of the ships at sea carry only one radio officer. If there was some way in which these officers could receive information about the race they might be of considerable help.

Mr Bingham of Lloyds Intelligence volunteered at once to pass information of any yacht, the whereabouts of which was in doubt, to all merchant shipping in the area. This was a great relief and it only remained to decide when to pass the message. It was agreed that this should go out on the day after the weekly report should have been received since, if disaster had struck, to delay longer was needlessly lessening the chance of survival. Obviously the probability was that the radio had failed. All the yachts were strongly built, seaworthy and fully crewed by competent yachtsmen. And so it turned out to be: several yachts experienced radio failures but when these occurred in or near shipping lanes, a report was very soon received via a merchant ship of their position. Not only the race organisation, but many friends and relatives were relieved of anxiety by this courteous service.

Reverting to the problem of alerting the lone radio officer, a meeting with the World Service of the BBC, which transmits regular programmes to the merchant service, produced a solution. Not only did the BBC undertake to include details of the race in their World Service sports programme, but they also agreed to mention those from whom position reports were overdue. This pattern of helpful co-operation was a feature in the planning throughout almost all the race.

Enquiries about the Race – Entry and Crew Register

Meanwhile, enquiries were coming in from all over the world, some for entry forms for the race, others applying to be placed on the crew register. This crew register eventually contained 179 names from 12 different countries and varying in age from 15 to 65 – in the event nearly all these hopefuls were doomed to disappointment as most of the skippers made up their own crews. There was only one withdrawal from the list and she became engaged to a member of the Committee!

Crew changes presented the organisers with a considerable problem. It was known that the Service boats, *Adventure* and *British Soldier*, were going to change their crews at each stop. It was thought that there could be many other crew changes as well, perhaps amounting to 40 or 50 at each place, and so companies operating charter aircraft were approached but could not help because International Air Traffic Association (IATA) rules do not permit them to take one group out and bring a different group back. The cost of transporting 40 crew members out to each port and 40 different ones back by scheduled flights would have been in the region of £60,000.

Sponsorship

The question of sponsorship and how it should be tackled arose early in the planning of the race. International Yacht Racing Union (IYRU) rules are very strict on this subject and limit advertising and the mention of company names to small areas on the sails and yacht, confined to the names of the sail makers and builders. No reference to a company's name or product is allowed in the name of the yacht. Whilst the organisers had no argument with these rules, they decided that they had to examine them in the context of a 27,000 mile, round the world race as opposed to a normal major offshore race such as the biannual 600 mile Fastnet. It was decided that to ban advertising completely, to the exclusion even of the brand name of the sponsor, would be to exclude several potential entries. The organisers, being the Royal Naval Sailing Association, were well aware that many would consider that the Royal Navy's own entry *Adventure*, and the Army entry *British Soldier*, were in effect sponsored by those Services. So it was agreed that no action would be taken by the organisers concerning IYRU Rule 26 if the name of any yacht entered for the race reflected that of a sponsor or his product, provided that the size of letters used to show the name on the boat and their position conformed to normal yachting practice and good taste.

Whales

Another of the smaller problems which faced the organisers was whales. Incidents connected with them were becoming all too frequent. Commander Bill King had nearly been sunk by a whale in the Australian Bight when sailing *Galway Blazer* singlehanded round the world and had only got back to harbour as a result of superb seamanship. The yacht *Pionier* was sunk by contact with a whale during the the first Cape-Rio Race in 1970. More recently, Dougal Robertson and his family survived 37 days in an open boat after their yacht *Lucette* had sunk after what they felt was a deliberate attack by a whale.

Consultations took place with Dr Fraser of the Department of Zoology at the British Museum who was most helpful. He wrote, in part, 'In the preface to *Tale of a Tub*, Jonathan Swift says "Seamen have a custom when they meet a whale to fling him out an empty tub by way of amusement, to divert him from laying violent hands on the ship." My experience is that it is usually so difficult when you want to get close to a cetacean that I just wouldn't think of including a deck cargo of tubs in my gear in order to keep them away.' It would appear very doubtful that whales deliberately attack, rather the reverse, and the recent encounters are more likely the result of increased yachting activity. However the race presented a wonderful opportunity for more information to be gathered and in co-operation with Dr Fraser a questionnaire was devised which each yacht was asked to complete. In the event very few whales were seen and, although one looked menacing, no attacks were recorded.

Forms

Forms, like those for reporting whales, proliferated as the planning proceeded despite efforts by the committee to keep them to the minimum. The last thing that a yachtsman, in the final throes of preparing for the longest yacht race ever, wants to be bothered with is forms. However, a few forms were essential.

Crew Form

A list of the crew carried on each leg together with a passport photograph of each member and a next of kin address to contact when he/she was at sea. Some difficulty was experienced with the forms identifying different members of the same family, or members with similar names. The organisers now admit that they should have insisted that the forms were typed or printed and all passport numbers included.

Special Equipment Form

A complete check list of all compulsory equipment which each yacht had to carry. All this equipment was inspected by a member of the Race Committee before the start of each leg. This examination was welcomed by the yachts as it ensured that they had not forgotten any compulsory item of equipment. (Appendix I)

Radio Equipment Form

Purely technical details of the type of equipment carried, frequencies etc. Useful to the organisers but not essential.

Noon Positions

A form to be completed at the end of every leg. Not compulsory but requested by the organisers and very useful for subsequent analysis. Extremely useful for plotting the actual track of yachts which were out of radio contact for relatively long periods.

Declaration Form

A form which had to be signed and handed in at the end of each leg by every competing yacht declaring that the rules had been obeyed (with exceptions if there were any) and the time of finish. It was on this form that the use of an engine in an emergency had to be declared – such as its use when recovering a man overboard.

Insurance

Insurance provided a minor problem. Not so much for the committee but for various insurance brokers and companies who had never before been asked to insure a yacht undertaking a race of such magnitude. Eventually Lloyds came up with a proposal form which was sent to all yachts but by the time they received it most of them had arranged their own insurance. The form was sent out rather late and the organisers feel that they could perhaps have been a little quicker off the mark in this respect.

Berthing Arrangements

From the start of the planning of the race a search was made for a suitable place to berth the competing yachts. It was anticipated originally that six yachts would make a race and if double figures were reached a tremendous response would have been achieved. Quite early on it became apparent that the total entry could exceed 20, some of which would be between 70 feet and 80 feet in length. Although Portsmouth is located centrally on the south coast of England in an area of very considerable yachting activity where almost every necessary facility exists, Portsmouth itself has very few berths for yachts as it is predominently a naval port. A number of places were investigated including the commercial docks in Old Portsmouth and Langstone Harbour, but none of the locations considered turned out to be entirely suitable. The organisers then approached, somewhat reluctantly, HMS Vernon, the Royal Navy's Torpedo and Anti Submarine School which lies just above the Old Portsmouth commercial docks on the east side of the harbour and includes a tidal dock known as Vernon Creek which was sufficiently large and sheltered to provide an ideal berthing site for the competitors. The captain of HMS Vernon, Captain Browning, immediately said that he would be delighted to welcome the yachts and to provide any facilities he could on the understanding that there would be absolutely no charge on Naval funds. This offer was accepted immediately by the organisers.

By this time the Portsmouth branch of the RNSA had been invited to act in a similar capacity in Portsmouth to the yacht clubs in Cape Town, Sydney and Rio, that is to say to be responsible for all local affairs. It was a happy coincidence that Captain Browning of HMS Vernon was due to take over as Portsmouth branch captain of the RNSA in the near future. So, under his chairmanship, a committee was set up to handle the 1,001 details connected with the arrival of about 20 yachts from 7 different nations, crewed by about 180 persons of 15 different nationalities, together with their families and supporters, to say nothing of the press and the public.

All yachts were told to report to HMS Vernon one week before the start of the race, that is by September 1st 1973, in order that the Committee could carry out their inspections and ensure that the yachts were fit and ready for the race. It so happened that HMS Vernon was closed for the summer leave period during this week which meant that plenty of space was available and that the public could visit HMS Vernon and look at the yachts – which they did by the thousand. A charge of 5p each was made on entry to HMS Vernon and race programmes were sold; the proceeds, over £1,000, went to the King George V Fund for Sailors.

Apart from providing pontoons and mooring lines, water and sometimes electricity to the yachts berthed at HMS Vernon, arrangements were made for banking facilities; for yacht chandlers to set up shop; for caterers to supply food; for Whitbread with the help and co-operation of the Customs to provide bonded stores; for sailmakers to repair sails; for radio sets to be installed, adjusted and repaired; for immigration authorities to operate; for medical and dental facilities; for telephones for the press; the presence of engineers, carpenters and riggers: the list is almost endless, but the space available for all these organisations coming in from outside was not and it soon looked as if HMS Vernon had been invaded, as indeed it had.

Liaison Officers

All this had been planned long before the first yacht was due to arrive at Portsmouth. Volunteer liaison officers were appointed, many with at least a working knowledge of one or more of the languages likely to be encountered amongst the competitors (with the exception of Polish). These liaison officers made themselves conversant with the sort of problems likely to arise and were provided with a wallet containing a mass of on-arrival information which took in everything from tourist maps of the area to the date, time and place of the all-important briefing meeting before the start. In addition a team of WRNS volunteered to man (if that is the right word!) an information office which proved its worth even though it was too small. With the detailed planning of the arrival and berthing of the yachts safely in the hands of the Portsmouth branch of the RNSA the Race Committee turned its attention to the start, an operation which had to be planned with meticulous detail.

Start Arrangements

It had originally been the organisers' intention to use the Royal Albert Yacht Club starting line at Southsea from which many RORC races are started but, as the entries increased, it was felt that this line would be too short. It was decided to start the race at noon, a suitable time for the yachts as the ebb out of Portsmouth Harbour would help them across the starting line and later help them on their way down Channel for a while, even if the wind was light and contrary. However, to avoid the risk of a yacht going aground on an ebb tide, it was decided to investigate a longer line, a little to seaward. A line joining Southsea Castle to Spitsand Fort offered sufficient length and a first class vantage point was available for spectators.

An approach was made to Portsmouth City Council who throughout the planning stage of the race were most helpful. The Council referred the organisers to the Director of Museums who is responsible for the Castle, it being not only an ancient monument, having been erected in 1539, but also one of the city's most important museums. The Director of Museums welcomed the idea but foresaw some difficulty in closing the museum to the public.

The Castle was an ideal place for the start. Inside its walls the ramparts afforded an ideal viewing area for the 300 or so guests who would be invited to the start – provided they were all over six feet tall or provided a platform could be erected. The 100-year old gun, ideally sited on the central bastion and built at Woolwich, would make an ideal starting gun, provided the bore could be cleared and it was still safe to fire. The central tower was perfect for the press and television crews and the area behind the ramparts perfect for the provision of refreshment – provided it did not rain!

The earthworks sloping up to the Castle walls outside the moat made excellent vantage points for the public. There were even positions for attaching the public address system so that everyone could be informed of progress.

The City Council was helpful as ever, the City Engineer agreed to put up a 2 foot high and 6 foot wide platform, the Director of Museums agreed to shut the Castle to the public until 1400 and also offered rooms inside the Castle for use as a VIP rest room, for press telephones and for refreshments if it rained. HMS Excellent, the Naval Gunnery Establishment, sent a team of ordnance inspectors who, with the help of museum staff, first drilled out the wooden tampion blocking the end of the barrel of the cannon, removed all the grit and gravel with which it was filled and finally inspected it thoroughly and passed it fit for action. They then offered to provide gunpowder charges made to approximately the same recipe as when the gun was built which would provide the ideal level of noise and smoke.

An approach to the Coastguard and the Parachute Regiment resulted in the promise of a display of rescue by lifeboat and helicopter from a burning yacht and a parachute drop on to the common behind the Castle by the Red Devils, the Army Parachute Regiment's display team. The Naval Commander-in-Chief Portsmouth lent his band and the Navy agreed to attempt to keep the starting line area clear of spectator craft.

Discussions took place with the Police and St John's Ambulance Brigade and the Council concerning crowd control and parking facilities. The Police expected that there would probably be about half the number of visitors that went to Portsmouth to welcome Sir Alec Rose on his return from his single-handed voyage round the world.

Starting the race was in the hands of the Royal Albert Yacht Club who decided to take one of their own small starting cannon as a stand-by in case of a misfire from the big gun, which was to be operated by a gun crew from HMS Excellent.

Overseas Organisation

The committees of the three yacht clubs – the Cruising Association of South Africa, the Cruising Yacht Club of Australia and the Iate Clube do Rio de Janeiro – each set up a sub-committee to deal with all aspects of the race that concerned them. The RNSA was fortunate in that branches of the South African Naval Sailing Association and the Royal

Petty Officers from the Royal Navy's gunnery establishment, HMS Excellent, sponge out the barrel of the 100 year old cannon at Southsea Castle after Sir Alec Rose had started the race.

Australian Naval Sailing Association were already operating in Cape Town and Sydney respectively and some of their members were invited to assist.

The preparations made and the organisation in Cape Town could hardly have been bettered. The experience gained in running two Cape – Rio Races was invaluable and the well earned reputation of the Cape for hospitality was much in evidence. However, as in the other two stop-over ports, Race Committee members found that there were many gaps in the information that had been passed out to them despite the fact that they had received copies of the minutes of all the meetings and a mass of other documents as well. These minor difficulties were soon overcome, sometimes by the local organisation, sometimes by the Committee members themselves, and generally, the crews were well satisfied.

Whilst the organisation in Cape Town had gone very smoothly, it was a different picture in Sydney. The problem was that the arrival of the yachts in the Round the World Race and their stop-over period in Sydney, coincided with the Australian Southern Cross series of offshore races, the last of which, the classic Sydney–Hobart, started on December 26th, Boxing Day. This meant that the Round the World yachts arriving in Sydney found that they were attempting to obtain repair and victualling services in a port in which these facilities were already stretched to the limit. Also, Christmas is the big mid-summer holiday period in Australia with many companies closed for a week or two. Those competitors who had themselves anticipated the situation, booked such services as slipping in advance and so were able to repair and re-stock relatively easily but those that arrived, literally, out of the blue found life more difficult. The Cruising Yacht Club of Australia (CYCA) already had its hands full with the climax of the Australian off-shore season but the RANSA came to the rescue by laying on extra berthing facilities, manning the finishing line and providing (at the expense of Whitbread) a steak and salad breakfast to each crew on arrival. The facilities at their small club were stretched to the limit but with the help of the CYCA nearby, who provided slipping and support, the yachts were received, repaired, rested and made ready for the start of the third leg on December 28th.

The Iate Clube do Rio de Janeiro must enjoy one of the finest locations and probably covers more acreage than any other yacht club in the world. It has been on the receiving end of the Buenos Aires – Rio Race for a number of years and twice for the Cape-Rio Race. The organisation for receiving the yachts – immigration, post office, banking, mail and information – worked very smoothly. It was not always best to ask how or why but to rely on an attractive (and very pregnant!) young Brazilian lady who spoke half a dozen languages fluently, never seemed to take a rest and almost always knew the answers. The club's repair facilities were excellent for the smaller yachts but could not cope with the larger ones, but the Brazilian Navy came to the rescue with their floating dock and carried out many repairs.

The finishing line was manned for the BA – Rio Race by two members of the club who lived on the line for ten days and nights and then continued to see the remaining Round the World yachts in – they were there for nearly a month. The Race Committee assisted by Alan Green, the Deputy Secretary of the RORC who happened to be in Rio, had to start the yachts on the last leg as nobody else was available. Rio in carnival time has to be seen to be believed and the hospitality of the club and its members will be a lasting memory for all those who were there.

Finishing Arrangements

As the end of the race approached, special preparations had to be made to receive the yachts back in Portsmouth. It had been decided that the last leg of the race should be a pursuit race involving a staggered start. A pursuit race is a handicap race in which the handicaps are applied at the beginning rather than at the end, thus the slowest boats start first and the fastest last. If the yachts had been started strictly in accordance with their handicap they would all have started at different times on different days and, as the wind in Rio dies away in the evening and does not get up again until late in the morning, this would not have given the boats an equal opportunity. During the first three legs of the race they had fallen roughly into three groups – the older and smaller, the small to middle size, and the three biggest. It was therefore decided to start

them in groups at intervals of two days. An objection from the biggest group that this was unfair was upheld and they were started only one day after the previous group.

Although the yachts experienced predominantly contrary winds during the final leg, they made better time than had been predicted and it became apparent that there was every likelihood of several yachts arriving back over Easter week end, a purely fortuituous circumstance for which the organisers claimed no credit! However, this did pose a few problems. HMS Vernon (enjoying their Easter leave period) again agreed to berth the yachts in Vernon Creek and a volunteer team consisting of motor boat and crew to tow the yachts in if necessary, berthing party, chefs to cook steaks, WRNS to man the information office and sundry other helpers prepared themselves for action day or night. A press office, banking facilities, and dining room were installed and a volunteer barman prepared to open the bar at any time.

The Royal Albert Yacht Club finishing team prepared themselves for some all night vigils at Southsea. Coastguards on various headlands on the Isle of Wight and on points to the west were given details of the yachts and subsequently reported nearly all of them which proved a great help in keeping track of progress during the closing stages. One thing was fairly evident: there were some eight hours of darkness each day and therefore a 2:1 chance that the leading yacht would arrive at a time which would not suit the waiting photographers and television crews. This particular problem was resolved by tracing a firm making rocket flares which sent a 100,000 candlepower flare, which burnt for a period of 30 seconds, to a height of 1,000 feet.

In the event, the leading yacht *Great Britain II* was the first to cross the line at 1330 on April 11th – a glorious, sunny day – watched by large crowds and followed during the next two days by five more yachts. An unexpected Easter holiday bonus for Portsmouth Easter holiday makers!

Race Control

The real backroom boys were the Race Control Officers who were directed by Lieutenant Commander Morty Drummond and consisted largely of retired officers and gentlemen. They operated from the billiard room of the Royal Naval and Royal Albert Yacht Club at Southsea which housed an enormous chart – 20 ft long and 12 ft high.

The Race Control volunteers, about 20 of them, had been told that their duties would consist of checking race positions twice a day and dealing with any messages that might come through. Once a week they were to plot all the positions on the chart and pass the information to the computer which had been made available by Captain Murphy of HMS

Collingwood, the Navy's electrical establishment at Portsmouth, for about an hour each week. In fact the race officers found themselves answering two telephones at once as enquiries flooded in from all over the world.

As with every other aspect of this race, it would be possible to write a full book on the work of Race Control alone but suffice it to say that without their continual efforts far from the scene of action, the smooth running of the race would have been impossible.

CS e RB seen here slipping away from the starting line. She was provided with an interior steering position beneath a double glazed clear dome.

Second Life, a van de Stadt designed Ocean 71, received no sponsorship and was financed by her crew who all contributed to the costs.

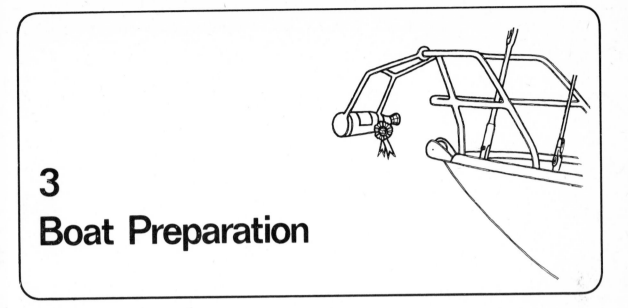

3
Boat Preparation

Build-Up

The announcement of the Whitbread Round the World Race sparked off a steady stream of enquiries from all the corners of the earth. The prospect of racing a yacht round the world; of pitting one's skills of seamanship, navigation and endurance against those of others; of exchanging the ever increasing man-made pressures of everyday life, with their attendant frustrations and lack of real reward, for a simple, tough challenge had very wide appeal. Here was a problem which was easy to identify, the goal was there for all to see; to win the race would be magnificent, merely to complete the course would be the achievement of a lifetime. Whilst there would be a strong element of competition between the boats which would build up as the race progressed, and certain individual rivalries would appear, the main adversary would be the elements.

To complete the course successfully would call for mastery of conditions ranging from the sultry and frustrating calms of the Doldrums near the Equator, where tempers can fray and the pressures of living in close quarters with the rest of the crew are all too apparent, to the continuous gales raging in the Roaring Forties where for days on end the wind may never drop below 30 knots, where squalls with a 20

knot increase can slam down and catch even the most wary unawares, where minds become dulled and bodies numbed from continuous exposure to temperatures near freezing and when every step and movement must be planned to prevent one's body being thrown around or even overboard by the incessant rolling, pitching, surging and bucking of the chosen means of transport.

Books have been written about sailing round the world and in the lonely Southern Oceans from the time of Captain Cook's voyages of exploration in the 1700s, through the great clipper era in the late 19th century to the recent singlehanded voyages of such people as Sir Francis Chichester, Sir Alec Rose and Robin Knox-Johnston. But no book can ever give the true feeling of experiencing these conditions – only personal involvement will do this.

The prospect of the race sparked the imagination of sailors throughout the world, in all over 100 enquiries were received from people interested in entering. Some came from those with no chance of getting anywhere near the starting line, from those living a dream which could never be realized, with no chance of tapping the necessary resources of time and money; some had money but not the time, more had time but not the money. Apart from the cost of providing a large yacht and equipping it for the race there was the cost of feeding a crew of say ten for up to eight months to be considered; and also there should be financial reserves to provide for repairs and replacements after damage sustained during the race. Sailors are nothing if not resourceful and the determined efforts of a few hundred men and a handful of women of widely varying ages resulted in 16 yachts entering for the whole race of which 14 actually completed all four legs; in addition three yachts sailed one leg each.

Some boats were built specially for the race, some owners ordered new stock boats, whilst others entered boats they already owned. They varied from the German entry, *Peter von Danzig*, which had been built in 1936, to *Burton Cutter* which was still being finished during the race. Some boats were paid for by a sponsor, some were financed jointly by sponsors and private funds, some relied solely on contributions from their crew whilst others were paid for completely by their owners. There were three entries crewed by Service personnel – two from the British Army and one from the Royal Navy – but even these were prepared, crewed and financed in different ways. A whole book could be written about the selection, and preparation of each boat and its crew for the race, but we only have room here to look briefly at some of the more interesting entries.

Adventure

The Royal Navy showed an interest in entering the race right from the word go. It was decided that a yacht of around 55 ft overall would be about the right size and that the accent should be on IOR handicap performance rather than on aiming to achieve line honours. The thinking behind this decision was that there was plenty of experience in the design and building of a yacht of this size available in Britain and that stock items of equipment could be obtained from British manufacturers to fit out a yacht of this size. Existing British winches could be used and the size of the bagged sails would not be too inconvenient. It was a happy coincidence that a joint Services study group had just decided that an order should be placed with Camper and Nicholsons for a number of their stock Nicholson 55s fitted out to a special specification for Services

adventure training. And so the first of the Services' yachts named *Adventure* went to the Royal Navy and became their entry in the race.

Crew selection for *Adventure* was the complete opposite to that for *Sayula*, for instance. With a few changes, *Sayula* shipped the same crew for the whole race. This was the sensible thing to do for it meant that after the first leg the crew had shaken down and their experience of working as a team could be put to good effect in the second and subsequent legs; it resulted in a build-up of experience throughout the race; also it avoided the expense of air-lifting relief crews. The skipper of *Sayula* was footing the bill and he could make his own crew selection; the exercise facing the Royal Navy was considerably more difficult. The prime consideration was that *Adventure* was a Naval yacht maintained for adventure training and paid for from public funds, as opposed to many of the yachts sailed by the Royal Navy which are owned and administered by Naval yacht clubs having the same status as any other yacht club. So, to provide the maximum training value, the crew had to be changed at the end of every leg and the question of expense was not so important because the crews could often be air-lifted by scheduled Service trooping flights.

About 300 responded to the Navy's call for volunteers to sail in the race. Of these some 100 officers and ratings dropped out for one reason or another and the remaining 200 together with ten RAF personnel were put through a practical selection procedure. Under *Adventure*'s work-up skipper, Chief Petty Officer Roy Mullender, who was to skipper her on the last leg of the race, a new crew joined each week. They spent a couple of days of solid sail drills, often sailing round a triangular course, a few miles across, near the Nab Tower in the eastern approaches to The Solent just off Portsmouth, for hours on end. After this they set off into the western approaches to the English Channel for three or four days under racing conditions.

Adventure's crew selection trials ran from October 1972 until April 1973, so early on in her training programme valuable experience was being gained of sailing in foul weather conditions. A score sheet carrying over 100 questions, most of which called for a marked assessment, was completed for each person who took part in the trials. There were sections headed: Practical Ability (on deck); Physical Abilities; Personality; Below Deck Skills and General Considerations; all of which called for a points scoring, and at the head of the form the most important of all 'Suitable for Further Consideration – Yes, No'. Apart from *Adventure*, two of the Navy's 100 Square Metre yachts *Merlin* and *Marabu* were used for the trials. The operation of any selection procedure has its problems and this one was no exception, but the task of the selectors was helped in many cases by the aspirant being asked to complete sections of his own form when it often became all too apparent to him that he was not suitable for the job and so he gracefully 'eliminated' himself. The completed forms together with the skipper's comments were sent to a committee known as SAG, (Sailing Advisory Group) who produced a short list of 60 from whom the final 37 were selected.

Volunteers had originally been invited to apply for selection in a DCI – a Defence Council Instruction – which is a weekly publication covering a wide range of subjects and circulated to all Naval ships and establishments. Applicants had to be recommended by their commanding officers as suitable for consideration. Having got the 300 names, the selectors were keen to ensure that the trials were carried out as fairly as possible so that every applicant whether or not he was selected felt that he had a fair test. This was important to ensure that the Navy thought of *Adventure* as their entry in the race rather than that of a select few.

Although sailing experience was not a prerequisite for application, it is interesting to note that previous sailing experience proved a great asset. In fact most on the final crew list had considerable previous offshore experience and many had sailed with each other before. This was reflected in the age of the crews – the average being about $32\frac{1}{2}$. Only one of the final 37 had no previous sailing experience.

At the beginning of July the Royal Navy announced the names of the four skippers who had been selected for the race. Leg 1 – Lieutenant Commander Patrick Bryans aged 40, who had sailed all his life and had raced and cruised to many European countries. He had taken the trouble to learn and practice morse, a help to *Adventure* as it meant that they were one of

the few crews which could read the CANAL morse weather forecasts. Leg 2 – Lieutenant Commander Malcolm Skene, aged 48 with 35 years sailing experience. Finished second in the 1971 Middle Sea Race. Leg 3 – Commander George Vallings, aged 41 and to be promoted to the rank of Captain during the leg, had sailed during the whole of his naval career and his experience included sailing in *Noryema* in the victorious British Admiral's Cup team in 1965. Leg 4 – Chief Petty Officer Roy Mullender, aged 42 and the Royal Navy's Sailing Coach, had been involved with the choice of *Adventure* and the selection and training of the crew from the start and it was particularly appropriate that he should be given the last leg.

Once the crews had been selected, a work-up period was planned for each culminating with a RORC race. This worked well for three of the crews but the fourth leg crew sailed together for only four days before they took over *Adventure* in Rio as she had to be taken out of commission for urgent work when they were due to do their training. The work-up period was not devoted just to sailing but included the establishment of radio, navigation and maintenance routines, listing the spare parts required and working out a ship's routine. Finally it was decided that the crew of ten should be divided into three watches of three with the skipper out of the watch routine. A three day cycle was worked in which each watch worked watch-and-watch on deck for two days and then spent one day as 'mother' watch. The 'mother' watch took care of cooking, washing up, cleaning and maintenance and were also stand-by watch on deck for sail changing. This system proved to be most popular as it allowed the 'mother' watch to get a good night's sleep, sometimes all night, and the watch below remained undisturbed.

While ashore, manufacturers' courses were arranged for crew members with individual responsibilities for radio, spars, rod rigging, wire rigging, engine, electrics, and sail and hull repairs. Skippers and navigators visited the Royal Navy's Hydrographic Department at Taunton for briefings on the special navigational and meteorological problems likely to be encountered on their legs of the course. Everyone attended sail trimming seminars given by Hood Sailmakers which had proved so popular when they were first introduced for the British Admiral's Cup contestants.

One of the great advantages of the intense training programme undertaken by *Adventure* was that it brought to light weak points and potential sources of trouble – she had sailed over 15,000 miles, or half the distance round the world, between October 1972 and the start of the race. It was found that the glassfibre deck flexed beneath the steering gear and so this had to be strengthened; the forehatch came away in someone's hand one day and so it was refastened, more securely; there were a number of small leaks and minor snags which required attention. At the end of August, *Adventure* went back to her builders, Camper and Nicholsons, for a final refit before the start of the race.

One of the most worrying troubles was the breaking of two of the intermediate shrouds and of the forestay; luckily however, on no occasion did the mast suffer damage. Rod rigging had been decided upon rather than galvanized plough steel or stainless steel wire and when the rigging parted the protagonists of wire rigging, who are always ready to decry solid rod rigging, were only too keen to say 'I told you so'. But extensive tests and calculations were made and it was decided to stick with rod rigging but to ship out a spare set to Sydney so that the rigging could be changed half way through the race. This was done and there was no trouble at all during the race. In fact the cause of the failure of the intermediate shrouds appeared to be that they were subjected to a kink of about 7° or 8° where they emerged from the mast – they were anchored internally to reduce windage – which produced local stresses that resulted in fatigue and subsequent failure. The same happened to the forestay but this was caused by the omission of a toggle when re-rigging on one occasion.

Some competitors, the French in particular, if not actually jealous of the fact that *Adventure* was apparently financed entirely out of public funds certainly commented on the fact and felt that the British Navy's representative in the race had a distinct advantage. No one would deny that to have a boat paid for and the facility of being able to choose a crew from 300 volunteers, any of whom could

obtain release from their employment on full pay, was a desirable situation. However there were some drawbacks, the greatest of which was that the crew had to change at every stop-over port. The other problem was that, as *Adventure* was a Service Training Yacht, sponsorship could not be accepted in any form – and that included equipment provided free or at a discount – solicited or otherwise! So although the basic requirements were provided, when it came down to the refinements there was no way that a snap decision could be made to buy a last-minute piece of equipment, for the financing of *Adventure* was a committee operation – and we all know the story of how the camel was a horse designed by a committee! This problem was overcome by the setting up of an *Adventure* fund by the RNSA which produced £6,000, and all the crew members contributed something apart from what it cost them as individuals.

There is a saying that the three most useless items aboard a yacht are a wheelbarrow, an umbrella and a naval officer. After the performance put up by *Adventure* on the Round the World Race the list of useless items can be reduced to two. One great advantage that *Adventure* had over the other competitors was the fact that she was backed up by the Royal Navy, an organisation which has a wealth of experience of keeping things running efficiently at sea in the extremes of weather likely to be encountered from the tropics to the Southern Ocean – just the conditions facing the yachts on this race. *Adventure*'s campaign of preparation has been dealt with in some detail and although no two yachts were prepared in the same way, it does give an indication of the amount of work involved before a yacht could hope to complete such a course. If one book tells the story of each boat in the race, a book could be written about each leg for *Adventure* because, being an official Service entry, complete records had to be kept for submission to higher authority and this meant that all the details of the planning and execution of the venture were fully chronicled. Comprehensive accounts of each leg of the course have been published in the *Journal* of the Royal Naval Sailing Association quite apart from the many official reports which were produced.

British Soldier, the British Army's entry for the race, at Gosport after her re-naming ceremony on 31st July 1973. She was previously called *British Steel* and used by Chay Blyth for his singlehanded round the world voyage in 1971.

British Soldier

The British Army showed an interest in the race right from the beginning and, in order to ensure that they had a boat available, cabled Chay Blyth whilst he was still at sea in *British Steel* on his single-handed 'Round-the-World-Backwards' voyage. They received an affirmative reply and it was agreed that if Chay could not find a sponsor for his own individual entry, he would skipper the boat. In the event, of course, Chay found his sponsor.

British Steel had been designed by Robert Clark specially for Chay Blyth's singlehanded round the world voyage and was therefore fitted out for one man to sail; a considerable amount of conversion work was therefore called for before she would be suitable for a fully crewed race. So the Army started basically with a shell and had to raise money to pay for the conversion. To start with the deck was cut open and a new coachroof fitted – this gave 6ft 4in of headroom below and the foam sandwich construction was designed to combat condensation. The cockpit was enlarged, and new winches purchased; below, eight bunks were constructed, a new chart table and galley area built, the sail stowage was modified and the whole yacht was completely re-wired. The *pièce de résistance* was a tilting installation for the WC; it could be angled in the athwartship direction to compensate for the angle of heel, and a 'strain' bar clipped into place in front of the user thus securing him relatively comfortably in a natural position for his daily 'constitutional'. The strain bar was similar to that which clips across the front of a fun fair big wheel, and the angle of the WC could be adjusted in use in the event of the boat coming more upright or heeling further as a result of a change of wind strength.

The arrangement with Chay Blyth was that the Army had the free use of the yacht for two years but would pay for the alterations, which had to meet with Chay's approval. As it happened, Chay let the Army get on in their own way as he became more and more immersed in preparing *Great Britain II* for the race. The alterations were to remain when the boat was handed back.

Financing the project was a problem as no Treasury funds were available. Major Niel Carlier was appointed project manager with the job of raising funds and supervising the alterations to the yacht. It was estimated that between £20,000 and £30,000 would be needed – £4,000 came from regimental funds and the Nuffield Trust; Scott Bader provided the resin needed for the new coachroof.

The initial coachroof and cockpit job was done by Philips of Dartmouth, who had built the yacht, and she was then moved to Portsmouth where carpenters, hired by the hour, completed the interior work. ICI produced £1,000 and then the insurance brokers Stewart Wrightson offered to provide the insurance, worth £2,500, and a further £5,000 in cash. This allowed an order to be placed for a taller mast to increase the size of the rig. £7,000 was raised by contribution, mainly from Army personnel, and a scheme to send First Day Covers signed by the skipper from ports of call raised another £3,000. In all over £30,000 was raised which left a balance in hand at the end of the race which has gone towards paying for an entry in the next round the world race.

British Steel was renamed *British Soldier* after the name had been obtained from BP who had a tanker of that name which had been sold to Cyprus. The name, *British Soldier*, had been retained for possible future use on a supertanker. The name will revert to BP at the end of the yacht's life.

There were over 400 volunteers for the crew from many regiments. A short list of 60 was selected who all sailed aboard the Army's Nicholson 55, *Sabre*. Of the final crews, each man did at least a month's work-up of which two weeks was aboard *British Soldier*. Crews were changed at the stop-over ports.

Participation in the race proved to be a great shot in the arm for Army sailing and plans are now afoot to campaign *Great Britain II* in the Financial Times Clipper Race in 1975 and to build a special boat to win the next round the world race.

Great Britain II

A totally different method was adopted by Chay Blyth to select a crew of tough paratroopers for his 77 foot ketch *Great Britain II*. Blyth was a Paratroop Regiment sergeant when he rowed across the Atlantic in 1966 with Captain John Ridgeway. He entered for the Sunday Times Golden Globe Round-the-World Race but withdrew after passing the Cape of Good Hope after experiencing trouble with his self steering gear. Subsequently he sailed round the world from east to west against the prevailing winds in *British Steel* – a successful singlehanded voyage which was sponsored by the British Steel Corporation. Now out of the Army, Blyth was putting his faith in a big ketch designed by Alan Gurney, an expatriate Englishman with a New York design office and previous experience of designing big yachts to the IOR limit. Chay Blyth's venture was this time being backed by Jack Hayward, the patriotic Englishman who was responsible for bringing *Great Britain*, the first iron ship, back from her resting place in the Falkland Islands to Bristol Docks for renovation; hence the race challenger was called *Great Britain II*. Hayward also bought Lundy Island in the Bristol Channel to prevent it falling into the hands (by legal purchase!) of an American. Designed in America, *Great Britain II* was built of foam sandwich construction by Derek Kelsall at Sandwich in Kent. (Foam sandwich construction is so called because the hull is made of a layer of pvc foam sandwiched between inner and outer skins of glassfibre; it is purely coincidental that Derek Kelsall chose to specialize in this form of construction at Sandwich in Kent!)

Being a paratrooper himself, who had achieved notable success in two previous successful ocean voyaging ventures by guts and determination, it is not surprising that Chay went to the Paratroop Regiment for his crew. They were happy to co-operate in the venture and it was up to Blyth to select them.

A notice was sent to all divisions of 16 Para. Brigade which produced 200 volunteers. Blyth devised a novel method of sorting the keen from the not-so-keen. Selected volunteers were told at 1600 on a Wednesday to report to a crofter's hut in Scotland by Friday evening using their own resources. Having reached the hut they were subjected to a weekend of initiative and compatability tests. A few weekends of this programme whittled the field down to about 50 of which 20 or so could not be spared from their Army jobs, which left 30 for the final selection.

The short list of 30 were again told to report to Scotland with no help, financial or otherwise, and were given ingenuity tests – e.g. given a couple of hours to prepare a lecture on a particular aspect of sailing – a subject of which few of the aspirants had any previous knowledge! This reduced the number to about two dozen. Alan Gurney, *Great Britain II*'s designer, reckoned that the boat needed a crew of 15 but in the end only a dozen were taken; of these one left at Cape Town for compassionate reasons, one retired hurt with a broken arm and one was lost overboard leaving only nine at the end of the race – Chay Blyth admitted afterwards that this was definitely too few.

There was only one officer in the crew – Captain Alec Honey. There was no particular significance in this except that of those on the short list for final selection, the officers could not be spared from their regimental jobs for the full period of the race and it had been decided that the crew must go all the way round as there were no funds available for changing them between legs. The only members of the crew who had sailed before were Mike Thomson, Len Price and, of course, the skipper Chay Blyth, but he lacked previous experience of skippering a crew in offshore racing.

The crew members selected were sent off to do courses to familiarize themselves with the gear and equipment on *Great Britain II* – a couple went to Ratsey and Lapthorn the sailmakers at Cowes and two were sent to Spencers the riggers, also at Cowes, whilst two more were sent to Sparlight to help with the final construction of the spars. John Powell, who was then the managing director at Sparlight, mentioned that the two Paras who were sent to him were a definite asset – they understood engineering and could therefore be a real help, as opposed to the usual situation when, on occasion, owners had sent crew members to Sparlight to assist in the completion of a spar but they seldom proved to be any help at all.

Whilst Jack Hayward, backed by his millions, paid for Chay Blyth's Gurney-designed flyer – Chay Blyth told the French magazine *Neptune Nautisme* that he had a budget of £130,000 to pay for the boat – the money for the race itself came from other sources. In November 1972 all those involved

paid £4 per head into a fund which produced an initial £200. Later, those remaining in the scheme paid £4 per month from their own resources and there was also some money from Derek Kelsall the builder for help he received in completing the boat from the crew of *Great Britain II*. The crew drew their full Army pay during the race and received victualling and overseas allowances but these totalled only about £40 per man for the whole race. The hat was passed round the Parachute Regiment which produced about £900 – mainly from special Regimental funds rather than from contributions from individuals. At the three stop-over ports, Cape Town, Sydney and Rio, the crew benefitted from the world-wide esprit de corps which ties paratroopers of whatever nationality and although this did not mean financial assistance it did produce hospitality and help in kind.

There was a feeling amongst the crew of *Great Britain II* that they had got the rough end of the deal when it came to receiving their share of official Service funds. Both the Royal Navy's entry *Adventure* and the official Army entry, Chay Blyth's own *British Steel*, on loan for the race and renamed *British Soldier*, received grants from the Combined Services Adventure Training Fund but there was only £700 available for *Great Britain II*. This £700 was spent on oilskins for the crew and a dinghy. But it should be remembered that both *British Soldier* and *Adventure* were official Service entries committed to a training requirement and having to change crews at the end of each leg, whereas *Great Britain II* was a privately entered yacht sponsored commercially which happened to draw its crew from an Army regiment.

Out of the funds available the crew had to pay all the running expenses for the trip including food but with the exception of the replacement mizzen mast which was paid for by Jack Hayward. In the end Blyth was left with a deficit of £1,300 – but he was given the boat by Jack Hayward and immediately after the race got to work converting it to a charter yacht to run trips for overworked executives!

Great Britain II was launched on May 21st by Princess Anne and it was the intention to sail her in the 1973 Fastnet Race as a work-up for the Round the World, but the boat was nowhere near ready in

Burton Cutter, being launched at Poole a few weeks before the race as *Windward Spirit*. She was renamed *Burton Cutter* when Burton Menswear produced sponsorship at the eleventh hour.

time for this classic event. So instead, the crew moved to Sandwich to Derek Kelsall's yard and worked on it to accelerate completion. The crew was divided into two shifts – one shift took over when the yard knocked off at 5.30 pm and worked through till midnight when they were relieved by the other shift which worked through until the yard started work again in the morning.

Burton Cutter

Burton Cutter started life with a built-in handicap. She was a compromise since after the race she had to join Leslie Williams' charter fleet. Designed by John Sharp, who had previously worked for Illingworth and Primrose, she was his first major yacht commission. Williams and his partner Alan Smith were in search of all the honours in the race from the first mutterings of its possibility. They knew the public could only understand the first boat home and insisted that Sharp put all his efforts into that. He did, but also kept the 80 footer rating low.

Leslie Williams (right) and his partner Alan Smith on board *Burton Cutter* at Portsmouth before the race.

Burton Cutter was built in aluminium by Windward Marine at Poole. They had had only minimum experience with this material and at the same time were under-capitalized in their business. Progress on the hull was delayed for various reasons and finally stopped altogether over a disputed bill. It was only court action that released the boat to her owners.

Originally she was named *Windward Spirit*, but changed a week before the race started when the Burtons menswear shops came in with a £10,000 offer of sponsorship. That liaison was happy, but the rush to try to finish the yacht left her little chance in the race. She left Portsmouth for the start with shavings on the deck and most of her interior in 'kit form' down below.

Second Life

Second Life realized a dream for her skipper Roddie Ainslie. A cruising man from the Menai Straits area, Ainslie was caught by the idea of going round the world and the race seemed too good an opportunity to miss. He gathered together some friends who

Wendy Hinds, the only girl among eleven men on board *Second Life*, photographed before the start with her parrot Beaky who was to have sailed on the voyage but was put ashore at the last moment.

agreed to go and jointly finance the trip. He spent much time looking for a boat and was all set to buy *Second Life* when she was sold from under him. He approached the new owner and organised a charter.

Second Life was built in glassfibre by Southern Ocean Shipyard at Poole as was one of a production series of 71 footers, the largest production glassfibre yachts in the world. She was built for Gerard Djikstra with a ketch rig for the 1968 Singlehanded Transatlantic Race. Subsequently she returned in a record west-east crossing time. In many ways *Second Life* was ideally suited for the big race but she was not well fitted out, particularly with her deck hardware.

The French Challengers

The French are keen followers of marathon ocean races – they have competed successfully in the Observer Singlehanded Transatlantic Races and also in the Transpacific Races and entered four yachts for the Whitbread Race, three of them specially built. Leading the challenge with the latest of a line of *Pen Duicks* – this one numbered VI – was Eric Tabarly.

Pen Duick VI

Eric Tabarly is probably the best known of all French yachtsmen. Aged 41 and a lieutenant in the French Navy, who give him plenty of leave to satisfy his appetite for sailing, he first gained fame in 1964 when he won the Singlehanded Transatlantic Race in *Pen Duick II*. With *Pen Duick III* he took the Class I RORC championship in 1967 and in the same year took line honours and Class I in the Sydney-Hobart Race. In 1969 he won the singlehanded San Francisco to Tokyo Race and in 1972 won the Los Angeles to Tahiti Transpac Race. For the Whitbread race he chose to build a new *Pen Duick*.

Tabarly went to the well known French designer André Mauric for his boat. His brief was for a design which would be capable of winning the Round the World Race and also of competing successfully in offshore races in both Europe and North America with the ability to take line honours and win on corrected time. Mauric applied much of the knowledge he gained in researching his Twelve Metre design *France* and came up with a ketch 74 feet overall with a relatively long waterline length of 62 feet and an IOR rating of around 63 feet. Whilst Mauric was given a free hand with the hull design, Tabarly designed the deck layout which included four separate cockpits. A ketch rig was chosen rather than schooner because it was more versatile and certainly better suited for normal offshore courses which would be sailed after the Round the World Race. The most unusual feature, in a yacht of this size, was the provision of a tiller for steering rather than a wheel and it was calculated

that to apply 10 degrees of rudder at a speed of 14 knots a force of 286 lb would have to be applied to the end of the tiller – there was provision in the steering cockpit right aft for two helmsmen and it certainly looked as if both would be needed in heavy weather! But Tabarly was obstinate and, despite advice from all quarters, refused to consider a wheel.

Pen Duick VI was built in aluminium by the French Naval Dockyard in Brest. Unlike some of the other boats in the race she did not have a main sponsor but financial backing and help in kind was solicited from a number of sources. Mickaël Le Berre, head of a public relations firm, devised one clever financing scheme – the creation of a Pen Duick logo – which manufacturers were allowed to apply to their equipment if it stood the test of the race. The Brest dockyard supplied the labour to build the boat, aluminium was provided for the hull, uranium ballast for the keel, Goïôt winches, Nord-Aviation coffee grinders, Tonnerre sails, Nirvana masts, a Renault engine … the list was almost unending but many companies were prepared to back the man they thought had the best chance of winning the race.

A big publicity operation was launched to support Tabarly and the *Pen Duick VI* operation. There were all sorts of money-raising methods – the sale of T-shirts, posters, story and photos. It was, however, reported in *Bateaux* that he owed the French Navy a million francs which had to be paid eventually either in cash, by selling the boat perhaps, or through services such as youth training, lectures etc.

The sixth *Pen Duick* was launched by crane at Brest on July 28th 1973, allowing little over a month for working up before the start of the race. On her first trials she achieved a speed of over 10 knots and impressed the many spectators who had gathered to see in action the yacht which they believed would carry the honour of France in this important event. Tabarly was obviously pleased with his new boat and frightened some of the watching dignitaries by aiming straight for them and tacking only a few metres from the jetty where they were standing. The tiller steering seemed to work better than the experts had predicted and in moderate conditions Tabarly could steer using only two fingers – but adjustments to the steering kept *Pen Duick VI* in Brest until August 9th.

Eric Tabarly's entry, *Pen Duick VI* being 'launched' by crane in Brest dockyard at the end of July 1973.

Pen Duick VI nearing completion in the French Naval dockyard at Brest. She was built entirely of aluminium alloy and most of the fabrication is welded.

The helmsman's and crew's cockpits on *Pen Duick VI* before the race showing the tiller which was replaced by a wheel when she went into Rio on the first leg after her main mast was lost for the first time.

Tabarly chose his crew mainly from young men – many of them given time off from their military service – but all with previous sailing experience. Also on board was Marc Pajot, France's silver medallist crew in the Flying Dutchman class at the 1972 Kiel Olympic Regatta. The majority of the crew stayed together for the whole race because Tabarly believed that this would pay dividends in terms of increased experience as the race wore on and would save the cost of air fares for replacement crews.

Grand Louis

André Viant is one of France's most experienced offshore racing skippers and a Rear Commodore of the RORC. A 53-year-old businessman, he owned his first boat at the age of 12 and has been sailing ever since. In 1967 he won the RORC Class II championship with *Esprit de Rueil* with five firsts which included the Fastnet Race. He repeated his success in 1968, again with five firsts. When the Round the World Race was announced, Viant was just ready for such an event so he went to Dominique Presles who designed him a 60 foot staysail schooner which he called *Grand Louis*; the name was chosen because his first grandson is known as Petit Louis.

Grand Louis was built of foam sandwich construction by Tecimar at Saint-Nazaire. Although at first glance she appeared to be a cruising yacht her displacement was only 21 tons. She was not designed solely for the race but also for long ocean cruises which André Viant intends to undertake in the future. For protection from the elements she had an interior steering position as well as the wheel on deck – no tiller in this yacht. And the crew probably fed better than any other on the race for the traditional high priority that the French put on gastronomic affairs was backed up by a refrigerator and a freezer which meant that the crew could eat fresh meat for the whole race whilst others were committed to tinned meat throughout. *Grand Louis* also had a seawater distillation plant which could produce 12 litres of fresh water per hour.

Viant was able to call on some pretty experienced offshore racing hands to crew his schooner – but it was not his intention to retain the same crew for the whole race although he meant to remain skipper throughout. He felt that it was important to give the maximum number of young people the opportunity to take part, but in the event only 15 different people made up his crew of 10 and many were from his own family. Amongst them were Michel and Sylvie Vanek, Viant's son-in-law and daughter, who had had experience sailing *St Papa*, a similar yacht to *Grand Louis*, on charter work in the West Indies, and a Belgian, Franck van Beuningen of the successful and well known Class II yacht *Hestia* which always puts up a good performance during her annual visits to The Solent. *Grand Louis* was the only French entry not to receive sponsorship – the whole cost of the venture being borne by Viant – and the best prepared for the race, having been launched on June 16th 1973 in time to work up in France before enjoying Cowes Week in August.

Kriter

Jack Grout, a 48-year-old Paris businessman who owns underground car parks in Paris, decided to go for a wooden yacht built specially for the race. Grout had sailed since he was 23, and most of his early experience was of ocean cruising including many trans-Atlantic trips especially to the West Indies. For the five years before the race, however, he had concentrated on ocean racing and had been on board *Narragansett* with Alain Colas for the 1970 Transatlantic Race and was on *Striana* with Alain Maupas in the 1971 Cape-Rio Race. He was not such a well known racing skipper as Tabarly or Viant but had raced his yacht *Leopard Norman* and intended to name the new £100,000 boat *Leopard Norman II* until the Beaune firm of Patriarche Père et Fils, owners of G. Kriter et Cie, came along with £40,000 worth of sponsorship in return for which the boat was re-named *Kriter*, to promote the sparkling champagne-type wine of that name.

Kriter, a 75 foot ketch, was designed by Georges Auzépy-Brenneur and Georges Commarond and built in record time by Yves Désbordes who had one of the last remaining yards in France capable of first class construction in wood. She was beautifully built – cold moulded on a laminated keel and 20 laminated frames, 15 of which are completely circular running right round the yacht without a break. Such was the quality of finish and attention to detail below by Georges Commarond, who was responsible for the accommodation plan, that the French yachting press showed some scepticism concerning *Kriter*'s suitability for racing – 'We suspect that more thought has gone into her suspended galley than into the sails required' was just one comment. But her centre cockpit with ready access below made sense for round the world racing giving good protection to the helmsmen and avoiding a perilous journey across relatively open deck which was a feature of some boats in the race.

Jack Grout selected a formidable team to form the crew of *Kriter* – skipper on the first leg was to be Michel Malinovsky, Alain Gliksman would take over for the second, Grout himself would skipper on the third. In all 21 Frenchmen and one Englishman filled the 12 crew places during the race so there was a fair amount of crew changing at the stop-over ports.

33 Export

The only French entry not to be built specially for the race was *33 Export*. This André Mauric design had been built for the 1968 Transatlantic Race and was the result of co-operation between Mauric and Alain Gliksman who was then editor of *Neptune Nautisme* and named her *Raph*. She had been laid up for two years at Deauville and was bought by two young but very experienced offshore sailors Jean-Pierre Millet and Dominique Guillet who, together with four other young crew members, formed a six-man limited company called ORPIF (L'Office des Relations Publiques Internationales Flottates). The company – and the boat – were then literally floated on an interest free loan of 50,000 francs (about £5,000) from the French brewers of 33 Export, Les Brasseries et Glacières d'Indochine. Considerable help was also received from many suppliers of materials and equipment.

Originally Dominique Presles, the designer of *Grand Louis*, had been involved in the design and building of *Raph*, for André Mauric was very involved at that time with design work on a Twelve Metre for Baron Bich. Presles, therefore, was to a great extent responsible for the sail plan, deck layout and accommodation design and also supervised the building of the boat. *Raph* was a $57\frac{1}{2}$ foot ketch with a sail plan designed specifically for ease of handling singlehanded and had been built in aluminium by ACNAM. After the 1968 Singlehanded Transatlantic Race she had gone to St Raphael on the Mediterranean coast of France where Eric Tabarly and Alain Gliksman ran her as an exclusive training yacht for offshore sailing, numbering among their clients Brigitte Bardot.

33 Export carried a crew of eight and at the start of the race their average age was less than 25. But in no way did they lack experience; Jean-Pierre Millet, one of the co-skippers, had already sailed round the world before joining Eric Tabarly in *Pen Duick III* for the 1971 Cape to Rio Race. The other skipper, the ill fated Dominique Guillet who was lost overboard on the second leg in the south Indian Ocean, was a member of Baron Bich's Twelve Metre crew and had sailed in *Pen Duick III*, *Coriolan* and *Gitana*; he had also helped Jean-Yves Terlain with *Vendredi Treize*. There was Jaques Redier, a merchant navy officer and his 20-year-old brother Yves, a sailing instructor. One who tragically did not make it was Dominique Rulhe, a Brazilian who was on his way to join the yacht when he was killed in the Varig Boeing crash at Orly Airport; Jorg Bruder the World Finn Champion was also killed in the same crash. Also in the crew were a couple of Rhodesian Fireball sailors – Tom and Peter-John Addeson.

Special preparation work was carried out on *33 Export* at St Malo during the summer of 1973, converting her from a yacht designed primarily for singlehanded trans-Atlantic sailing to one which would more readily withstand the rigours of a round the world course when driven by a tough crew of eight. In particular the hull was stiffened and the accommodation re-organised. The crew of *33 Export* were given a special mission by CERBOM (Centre d'Etudes et de Recherches Biologie, Océanographie Médicale) to take water samples for the estimation of the degree of pollution existing in the oceans of the world.

Moksha

With four well prepared yachts, crewed by experienced offshore sailors, France was mounting a strong challenge for top honours in the race. There was, however, a fifth French entry – *Moksha*. This 51 foot ketch designed by Gwénaël Marchand was built in St Malo using an unusual aluminium alloy/glass fibre composite construction method devised by her skipper Georges Faux. *Moksha* was a late starter and did not slip into the water until the middle of August. Some sponsorship had been obtained from Honywell-Bull but one French yachting magazine described her as 'the boat of tomorrow' – referring not so much to her construction as to the money that had yet to be found to pay for her. In fact the French yachting press had been sceptical about the whole project for some months before *Moksha* was launched, and their suspicions were confirmed when *Moksha* slipped away from St Malo taking four days to reach Deauville where she was

Eric Tabarly, skipper and owner of *Pen Duick VI* – one of the favourites at the beginning of the race but who broke her main mast twice and finally sailed directly home to France, not bothering to go to Portsmouth.

reported to have been seized by her creditors with the mysterious Faux nowhere to be found.

Bateaux reported a discussion with the three French skippers, Eric Tabarly of *Pen Duick VI*, André Viant of *Grand Louis* and Jack Grout of *Kriter*, and it is interesting to record a summary of some of the points they discussed especially when these are considered in the light of subsequent events.

Q. Why did you take part?

Tabarly: This is an exceptional competition; if one loves ocean racing as I do, one cannot abstain from a possibility such as this.

Grout: I compare it to mountain climbing. It is the Annapurna of the mountaineers; the best there is in our sport.

Viant: Conventional racing no longer presents any real difficulties to me and my crew. This is an extraordinary event posing many problems, such as finding the right crew, from different backgrounds, making them live together and arranging relays of crews at the stop-over ports. It does not seem reasonable to me to keep the same crew from beginning to end; one must try and let the maximum number of young people take part.

Tabarly: I will retain the same crew as this simplifies the problem of finding air fares to change crews for each stage. And they will then be well worked up especially for the second half of the race.

Grout: Our participation is a project planned by friends. Of the 12 crew planned, six will be permanent – the friends – and the others will be changed for each leg.

Viant: We will be ten, ideally a skipper-navigator and three watches of three people each.

Tabarly: We will normally be two watches of five plus a cook and the skipper.

Q. No apprehensions?

Grout: Not really; if I leave as I would like to, I will be very pleased.

Tabarly: I cannot say that I haven't any. When running or with the wind free it is no holiday. One is tempted to carry maximum sails because one is convinced that they are doing the same on other boats and that is when accidents happen. There is a definite danger.

Q. Have you any thought that you may lose a member of the crew?

Tabarly: It is obvious that in extreme conditions anything can happen.

Q. Will you be fastened on board?

Tabarly: Maybe. On my boat I let people decide for themselves.

Viant: With me they must be attached. That is an order.

Grout: And the same with me.

Q. André Viant, you once lost a man overboard?

Viant: Yes, it was on a Fastnet, but we retrieved him within four minutes.

Q. What effect does such an accident have on the skipper?

Viant: It is a terrible thing. That is why I consider that the skipper should order the wearing of safety harnesses and that no one should dispute this order.

Three men, three personalities, three different approaches to the problem. Tabarly was described as the go-getter, Viant, the humanist, and Grout, the romantic.

The Mexican Entrant

Race winner Ramon Carlin, a 50 year old Mexican washing machine millionaire, first took an interest in sailing only five years before the race. His first offshore racing yacht was a Cal 40 which he named *Sayula* after the town in which his wife was born – Sayula is Indian for 'town of flies'. He soon became deeply interested in offshore racing and clocked up three wins in the annual Honolulu Race across the Pacific. When he heard of the Round the World Race he ordered a Sparkman and Stephens-designed Swan 65 from Nautor OY at Pietarsaari in Finland and took delivery of the yacht in time to sail in the 1973 Cowes Week and Fastnet Race which enabled him to iron out any snags and get the yacht worked up into racing trim.

Sayula II was a privately financed entry and the crew were collected together in a somewhat offhand manner compared with the meticulous approach of some of the Services entries. But this did not mean that they were in any way a scratch crew – there was Butch Dalrymple-Smith, a widely experienced

sailor, who knew the offshore racing circuits in both Europe and Australia; Keith Lorence, another experienced offshore crew and the sailmaker on board; Ray Conrady, the navigator – another American who, although lacking wide offshore racing experience, was a qualified merchant navy navigator; there was a Dutchman with a Fastnet Race or two to his credit, a South African, a Canadian and a couple of Mexicans apart from members of Carlin's own family. He did not carry out involved selection and aptitude tests but just used his judgement to collect together a professional and compatible team which in the event proved to be just what was wanted.

During the race the story went out that *Sayula* was not taking matters particularly seriously – just cruising round the world drinking cocktails from a silver tray each evening before the four-course dinner was served. This may or may not have been the case but any relaxed atmosphere which ensued was due not to indifference but more to competence.

The Italian Entries

The Italians fielded three yachts in the race, two existing boats, *Guia* and *Tauranga*, both designed by Sparkman and Stephens of New York, and *CS e RB*, the first of the Koala 50 class designed by Robert Clark for Nordcantieri of Turin.

Guia

Guia at 45.39 feet overall was the second smallest yacht in the race and only marginally longer than the Polish *Copernicus*. She was built of wood by Craglietto of Trieste in 1970, a sister ship of Miss Serena Zaffagni's *Mabelle* which had been built the previous year specifically to meet the requirements of the Two Ton Cup racing in Italian waters. In 1969 *Mabelle* won all five selection races for the Italian Admiral's Cup team and followed this with an impressive record in England. Giorgio Falk, *Guia*'s owner and skipper, had raced extensively in offshore races in the Mediterranean and, with *Guia*, won the Italian Class I offshore championship in 1971. Falk made a number of changes to the original Sparkman and Stephens design, the most

As well as her radical articulated rudder, *Guia* had a bendy wood boom – the type of feature to be found on a One Tonner perhaps but unusual in a deep sea ocean racer.

significant of which was the installation of a three-section, articulated rudder which he reported gave excellent control, particularly in heavy weather conditions; he also fitted *Guia* with a bendy boom of a type not normally used in yachts above One Ton size; it was about eight inches wide and less than two inches thick and could be bent down in the middle to flatten the mainsail.

Tauranga

Tauranga was a Swan 55 designed by Sparkman and Stephens in 1969 to the IOR and built of glassfibre in Finland by Nautor OY who also built the race winner, *Sayula II*. The design was produced both for fast cruising in the Mediterranean and West Indies and as a competitive racing yacht. The skipper for the race was Eric Pascoli and some sponsorship was received, including finance from the Italian publishers Epoca.

CS e RB

The third Italian entry *CS e RB* was built specially for the race although she was intended to be the first of a line of production Koala 50s from the Nordcantieri yard at Turin. The sponsor of this entry was the firm of furniture makers whose initials gave *CS e RB* her name. This ketch was designed by Robert Clark who also designed *British Soldier*. One of the features of the design was an interior steering position beneath a clear dome which gave the helmsman a view of the sails and over the deck whilst protected from the elements. The dome was 'double glazed' to prevent condensation and specially treated to filter the sun's rays. There were six in the crew for each leg and 16 took part altogether, which meant quite a lot of crew changing at each stop. Doi Malingri, a 36-year-old company director from Turin who had sailed *Koala Tre* in the Cape–Rio Race, remained the skipper throughout; amongst the 16 crew, eight had sailed in Cape–Rio Races and seven had sailed across the North Atlantic, two of whom took part in the 1972 Observer Singlehanded Transatlantic Race (OSTAR). One of the crew was Alberto Passi who had sailed with Malingri in the 1973 Cape–Rio Race; this 24-year-old student of philosophy examined the

Doi Malingri di Bagnolo, skipper of the Italian yacht *CS e RB*.

behaviour of the crew as a basis for his final thesis. A journalist from *La Stampa*, Paolo Bertoldi, was on board for the first leg. *CS e RB* was launched at the beginning of August and sailed to England via Gibraltar and Lisbon, providing a first class shakedown cruise to sort out any snags.

The Lone German

The only German starter in the race was also the oldest to complete the course. *Peter von Danzig* was built in 1936 at Danzig – then under German control – by students of the Danziger Werft (Danzig Shipyard) for the Akademischer Segler-Verein and underwent a major refit below in 1957. She is a 59 foot steel-built yawl designed by Henry Gruber and a typical design of her period – relatively narrow in the beam and thus lacking space below when compared with more modern designs of similar length. She was the only yacht in the race with a non-masthead rig.

Peter von Danzig started her career as an ocean voyager soon after her launching, for in the autumn of 1936 she took part in a race before the Olympic Games from Hamilton in Bermuda to Cuxhaven in Germany and then raced regularly in offshore events in the North Sea until the Second World War when she became a training ship for the German Navy. In 1945 she was sailed from Danzig to Denmark and then to Flensburg just across the border in Germany, to escape from the advancing Russians.

After the war the Akademische Segler-Vereine of Danzig, Rostock and Kiel united at Kiel and they succeeded in securing the release of *Peter von Danzig* from the Allies. Since then she has been used extensively for sail training cruises and has taken part in many sail training races, crossing the Atlantic a number of times.

The crew of *Peter von Danzig* were all students or graduates from Kiel with a strong representation from medicine and dentistry. Initially there were a large number of volunteers to crew her for the race but as time went by most of them fell out for one reason or another leaving just enough to form the all male crew. Nine sailed all the way round the world, one did the first leg only, one the second and third only, one the third only and three the fourth

only whilst one, Aki Mullër-Deile, was landed at Bluff Harbour in New Zealand with a broken foot and rejoined in Rio. All the crew were members of the Akademischer Segler-Verein at Kiel, a club open to students over the age of 18, which owned the boat.

Before the race the members of the Akademischer Segler-Verein put in something between 3,000 and 4,000 hours' work on *Peter von Danzig* preparing her for the race but there was a general shortage of money to pay for extra equipment and new materials. The cost to those actually sailing in the race was about £500 each.

Because the boat had a full cruising programme and had to be prepared for the race, there was little or no time for special training – only the trip from Kiel to Portsmouth as a work-up period. The crew however had all had previous cruising experience in the boat and the skipper, 30-year-old Reinhard Laucht, and watch captains held German Ocean Navigation Certificates, the equivalent of the British Yachtmaster Certificate.

Poland – Otago

There were two Polish yachts entered for the race and, like *Peter von Danzig*, they were both owned and crewed by clubs. The older of the two was *Otago*, owned by the Yacht Club Stoczni Gdanskiej, a sail-

Skipper Reinhard Laucht at the wheel of *Peter von Danzig* at Portsmouth after the race. Note the new spokes which were fitted in Sydney.

ing club for workers at a Gdansk shipyard. She was a 55 foot ketch, built in steel in 1959 to designs by H. Kujawa, a member of the club. The Polish town of Gdansk where *Otago* was built in 1959 is the 1936 German town of Danzig where *Peter von Danzig* was built 23 years earlier and, by coincidence, both yachts were built of steel at the same yard. Although *Otago* was built nearly a quarter of a century after *Peter von Danzig*, both have a similar hull shape and relatively narrow beam.

There were eight men and one girl in the crew of *Otago* ranging in age from 19 to 50. The men were all workers at the Gdansk shipyard who were given time off for the race; the girl, 19-year-old Iwona Pienkawa, a student of architecture, who acted as cook, was the daughter of the skipper Zdzislaw Pienkawa. Throughout the race they worked in two watches with the skipper and the navigator, Witold Ciecholewski, as watch captains.

None of the crew had any previous ocean racing experience but most of them had cruised extensively on *Otago*'s regular trips in the Baltic and North Sea and some had been in her as far afield as Iceland,

Greenland, Spitzbergen and the Canary Islands. There was no time for special crew training as *Otago* had only finished her previous cruise, in the North Atlantic, a couple of weeks before departure from Gdansk for Portsmouth. This period was taken up in preparing the yacht for the race and included shipping new sails, to make 25 in all, and installing a Marconi Falcon II ship to shore radio and Brookes and Gatehouse D/F.

Copernicus

The other Polish boat *Copernicus* came from Gdynia just along the coast from Gdansk and, at just under 45 feet overall, was the smallest yacht in the race; she was also the lowest rated. *Copernicus* was owned by the sailing club of a Gdynia shipyard and the all-male crew of five came from the shipyard. Like the crew of *Otago*, they had no previous off-shore racing experience but had all cruised extensively; the skipper was Zygfryd Perlicki who, the previous year, had been Poland's representative in the Soling class at the Kiel Olympic Regatta.

Copernicus, a ketch designed by Liskiewicz and Rejewski, was of conventional carvel wood construction and had been completed only just before the race. There was, therefore, no time for any specific crew training or work-up apart from the passage from Gdynia to Portsmouth.

Other Entrants

One of the reasons for selecting September for the start of the race was that it was thought that this might attract Australian and South African yachts which had been competing in England in offshore races, Cowes Week and the Admiral's Cup. In the event only one such yacht took the bait – the South African *Jakaranda*, a 57 foot Sparkman and Stephens design built in glassfibre sandwich construction by the Dutch yard of Frans Maas in 1970 as a yawl and subsequently changed to a sloop.

Jakaranda had been one of the South African Admiral's Cup team and had been skippered by a veteran South African offshore sailor, Bobby Bongers. She was, therefore, a well tuned boat when

Zdzislaw Pienkawa, skipper of the Polish yacht *Otago* whose 19 year old daughter Iwona was also in the crew.

the new crew took over just before the Round the World Race. The complete new crew, under skipper John Goodwin, only managed to sail together a couple of times before the start of the race. In her crew were Wilhelm Griitter and Gerhard Last, who were planning to sail Last's Hillyard cruiser to Cape Town when the opportunity to sail in *Jakaranda* presented itself, Warrant Officer Mike Avery of the South African Navy and Vice- Commodore of the South African Naval Sailing Association, Bill Damerell, a Cape Town Harbour pilot and former square-rigger man, Peter Koehorst, a keen round-the-buoys sailor from Cape Town and Charles Smith, a hockey star from the Transvaal. Making up the eight crew was Yvonne van de Byl, an English-woman from Lymington who had originally planned to sail in the German *Nai Ut* and whose son, a lieutenant in the Royal Navy, was in the crew of *Adventure* for the first leg.

Jakaranda was built in 1970 for Theunis Bester whose company, the Bester Organisation of Pretoria, financed the project. A company called Ocean Racing International (Pty) Ltd manages the project, the aim of which is to enter *Jakaranda* for prestige offshore races round the world. *Jakaranda*'s skipper on many of these races has been the well known Bruce Dalling.

The oldest actual entry in the race was the 79 foot Swedish ketch *Keewaydin* built at Rye in Sussex in 1913. She carried a square sail on her mainmast and her skipper, David Sundbaum, had sailed in a three-masted barque on the wheat trade runs. *Keewaydin* arrived late in Portsmouth and, after being inspected by the race officials and arranging last minute insurance, started on September 25th, two and a half weeks behind the other starters. She reached the Canary Islands on October 14th and having signalled her intention to sail again on November 7th for the Cape Verde Islands sent a further message on November 4th stating that she could no longer continue the race and requesting her insurance certificate. So although *Keewaydin* actually started the race as a competitor, she saw nothing of the rest of the fleet and withdrew without completing the first leg.

Nai Ut, a 45 foot steel yawl designed by Horst Glacer and built by Lubbe Voss in 1969, was entered by her 60-year-old skipper Herbert Lupke and arrived at Portsmouth at the end of August but was not allowed to compete in the race because she failed to reach the minimum 33 foot rating. However, she started with the rest of the fleet on September 8th, put into Lisbon on September 19th for radio repairs, and sailed on October 21st from the Canary Islands for Cape Town and then cruised home via Rio de Janeiro.

With sail trimmer Keith Lorence casting a professional eye at the leech of the genoa and a lookout posted in the eyes, *Sayula II* picks her way between the scores of spectator craft just after the start of the race.

4
The Yachts

Seventeen yachts started the race from Portsmouth with the intention of completing all four legs of the course. As one of these, *Keewaydin*, started over a fortnight late and got no further than the Canary Islands, there were really only 16 serious competitors trying to go all the way round. Of these, 14 managed to complete all four legs – a credit to the preparation, determination and sailing skill of their crews.

All 16 completed the first leg from Portsmouth to Cape Town, although *Pen Duick VI* arrived only just in time for the start of the second leg having gone in to Rio to have a new mast shipped. She went on to take line honours on the second leg to Sydney, but *Burton Cutter* dropped out of this leg due to hull weaknesses and missed the third leg as well. Fifteen of the original 16 started from Sydney and all completed the leg, but the ill-fated *Pen Duick VI* again lost her mast and had to return to Sydney for repairs. Although she completed leg 3 eventually, the rest of the fleet had left Rio for the final leg home before she arrived. With *Burton Cutter* back in the fray, 15 of the original 16 started the last leg on time, even the late starting *Pen Duick VI* tried but a spreader failure forced her to abandon the race when approaching the Bay of Biscay.

Three other yachts took part in the race. The South African *Jakaranda* sailed the first leg, the French *Concorde* the second and the French *Pen Duick III* the last.

All the yachts which took part in the race except two were of the modern fin keel and skeg-hung rudder configuration. Only the 1936 built German entry *Peter von Danzig*, and the Polish *Otago*, built in 1960, had rudders hung on long keels. Eleven of the 16 were ketches, there were two yawls, one cutter, one sloop and one schooner. The most popular construction material was glassfibre with five boats built by the single skin method and two of sandwich construction; there were three yachts each built of wood, steel and aluminium alloy. Eight of the entries were already built when the race was announced whilst the other eight were built with the race in mind.

Of the boats built for the race, the British Navy's *Adventure* was probably the best prepared, having been launched in 1972 and been sailed over 15,000 miles before the start. The yachts which were launched before the middle of July certainly seemed to benefit from their six to eight weeks' work-up period. The three largest yachts – those that were being tipped to win – were the least prepared because they were short of time. Chay Blyth's *Great Britain II* was being worked on frantically well into August; Eric Tabarly's sophisticated *Pen Duick VI* had teething troubles and suffered as a result;

whilst *Burton Cutter* was still being completed as she sailed south through the Atlantic. Whilst these three giants shared line honours, they could not save their time on handicap and *Pen Duick VI* and *Burton Cutter* suffered disastrously as the result of structural failures.

The yachts were measured to IOR Mark III, 1973 and the data given in this chapter for each yacht was taken from the IOR Rating Certificates lodged with the race organisers. Imperial units have been quoted which means that the dimensions are given in feet with the exception of RSAT which is given in square feet. CGF, the centre of gravity factor, and EPF, the engine and propeller factor, remain the same for imperial and metric units. To convert the data into metric units multiply feet by 0.305 to obtain metres and square feet by 0.0929 to give square metres.

CONCORDE

Designer:	Georges Auzépy-Brenneur
Builder:	Nautic Saintonge
Owner:	Pierre Chassin
Nationality:	French
Rig:	Sloop
Construction:	Glassfibre
Dimension:	lwl 32·05 ft (9·77 m)
Launched:	1972
Sail number:	56
Crew on race:	5

Concorde took part in only the second leg of the race from Cape Town to Sydney. She started with a crew of five but this was reduced to four when she had to return to South Africa to land one with appendicitis. She was the slowest yacht on this leg.

COPERNICUS

Type:	One of a number built to the same design.
Designer:	Liskiewicz and Rejewski
Builder:	Gdynia Boatyard
Owner:	Stal Gdynia Club
Nationality:	Polish
Rig:	Ketch
Construction:	Wood, single skin.
Dimensions:	Loa 45·00 ft (13·73 m)
	beam 12·25 ft (3·74 m) draft 7·00 ft (2·14 m)
Launched:	1973
Sail number:	VII PZ30
Crew on race:	5
IOR Data:	L 40·1586; B 12·004; BWL 11·752; D 5·5190; DC − 0·0636; FC − 0·0922; CGF 0·9812; EPF 0·9716; I 51·902; J 16·962; LPG 25·229; P 40·780; E 13·346; RSAT 854·554; MR 34·6325. RATING 33·00 ft

The smallest yacht in the race and completed only in time to take on her crew and stores before the passage to Portsmouth for the start. Like the other Polish entry, *Otago*, she was run on a shoestring but the boat and crew earned the respect and admiration of all the competitors for their pluck and perseverence.

JAKARANDA

Type:	One off
Designer:	Sparkman and Stephens
Builder:	Frans Maas, Breskens, Holland
Owner:	Theunis Bester
Nationality:	South African
Rig:	Sloop
Construction:	Glassfibre sandwich
Dimensions:	Loa 56·83 ft (17·33 m) lwl 40·00 ft (12·20 m)
	beam 14·38 ft (4·39 m) draft 8·31 ft (2·53 m)
	displacement 37,150 lb (16,866 kilo)
	ballast 18,200 lb (8,263 kilo)
Launched:	1970
Sail number:	SA7
Crew on race:	8
IOR Data:	L 45·4492; B 14·193; BWL 13·025; D 6·5691; DC −0·0059; FC −0·0220; CGF 0·9854; EPF 0·9919; I 64·993; J 22·998; LPG 34·481; P 58·234; E 20·013; MR 33·7787; RATING 42·8 ft

Built to show the South African flag, *Jakaranda* is a familiar sight at the major international offshore events and has represented South Africa in the Admiral's Cup. Originally a yawl, the mizzen mast was removed and she sailed the first leg of the race as a sloop.

OTAGO

Type:	One off
Designer:	H. Kujaw
Builder:	Stocznia Gdanska, Gdansk, Poland
Owner:	Yacht Klub Stoczni Gdanskiej
Nationality:	Polish
Rig:	Ketch
Construction:	Steel
Dimensions:	Loa 55·00 ft (16·78 m)
Launched:	1960
Sail number:	XIV PZ3
Crew on race:	8
IOR Data:	L 50·0224; B 13·018; BWL 12·956; D 8·4835; DC −0·0889; FC 0·1145; CGF 0·9755; EPF 0·9794; I 61·974; J 18·700; LPG 30·675; P 55·117; E 18·799; RSAT 1442·484; MR 42·6255; RATING 41·7 ft

A very similar yacht to *Peter von Danzig* and built in the same shipyard. An old design, narrow in the beam, lacking accommodation space and equipped to a very basic level but kept going by the skill and determination of her crew.

One of the two Polish entries, *Otago*, slipping away from the starting line. She was built of steel in 1960.

ADVENTURE

Type:	Nicholson 55
Designer:	Raymond Wall
Builder:	Camper and Nicholsons Limited, Gosport, Hampshire, England
Owner:	Ministry of Defence (NAVY)
Nationality:	British
Rig:	Cutter
Construction:	Glassfibre
Dimensions:	Loa 55·50 ft (16·93 m) lwl 39·17 ft (11·95 m)
	beam 14·38 ft (4·38 m) draft 8·25 ft (2·52 m)
	displacement 39,820 lb
	ballast 19,770 lb
Launched:	1972
Sail number:	K3138
Crew on race:	10 or 11
IOR Data:	L 42·9057; B 14·140; BWL 12·830; D 5·9714; DC 0·0094; FC −0·0490; CGF 0·9839; EPF 0·9781; I 62·330; J 20·600; LPG 33·000; P 54·980; E 18·560; RSAT 1453·198; MR 41·4506. RATING 40·2 ft

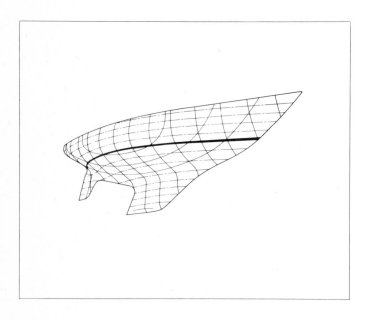

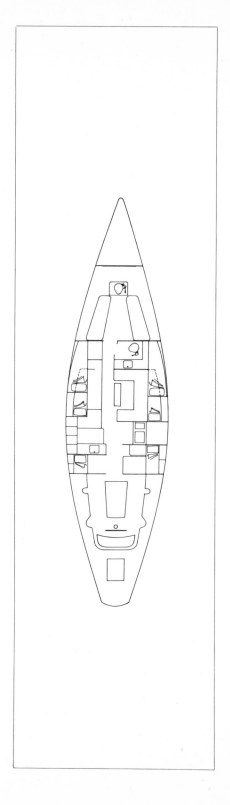

The Nicholson 55 is one of the most successful of Camper and Nicholsons' designs. Among the earlier yachts built to this basic design, which is offered with sloop, cutter or yawl rig, are *Lutine* and the British Admiral's Cup Team boat, *Quailo III. Adventure* was the first of an order of eight Nicholson 55s completed to a special specification for use by the British Services Adventure Training Scheme. For this race the deck and steering mounting were specially strengthened and a particularly rugged rig was adopted. MOD (NAVY) also decided to alter the standard method of securing the rudder stock in the glassfibre rudder and it was this which failed on the second leg of the race.

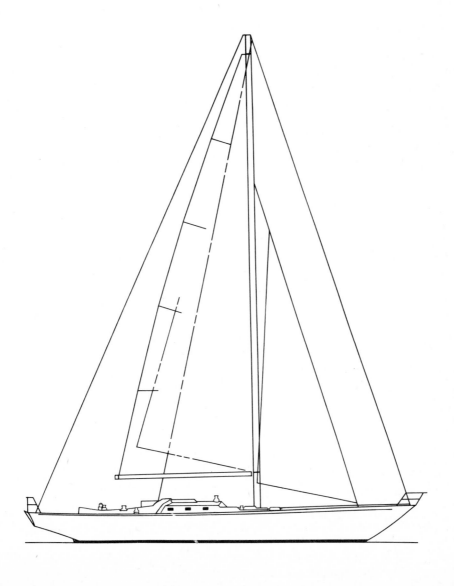

BRITISH SOLDIER

Type:	One off
Designer:	Robert Clark
Builder:	Phillip and Son Limited, Dartmouth, Devon, England
Owner:	Chay Blyth (chartered to the British Army)
Nationality:	British
Rig:	Ketch
Construction:	Steel
Dimensions:	Loa 59·00 ft (18·00 m) lwl 43·50 ft (13·26 m)
	beam 12·80 ft (3·91 m) draft 8·00 ft (2·44 m)
Launched:	1970
Sail number:	K3388
Crew on race:	10
IOR Data:	L 49·1982; B 12·900; BWL 12·890; D 7·1219; DC −0·1849; FC −0·0699; CGF 0·9693; EPF 0·9910; I 61·000; J 22·000; LPG 35·400; P 54·600; E 16·200; RSAT 1492·082; MR 45·5486. RATING 43·8 ft

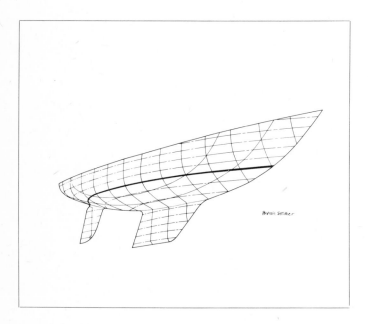

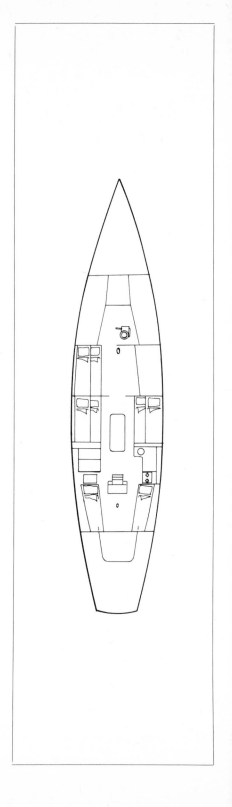

British Soldier was built as *British Steel* for Chay Blyth's single handed, non-stop round the world voyage from east to west which he completed in August 1971 in a, then, record time of 292 days. The British Army chartered the boat from Chay Blyth for the Round the World Race and re-named her *British Soldier*. Modifications were carried out to the rig and accommodation to suit the role of a fully crewed yacht.

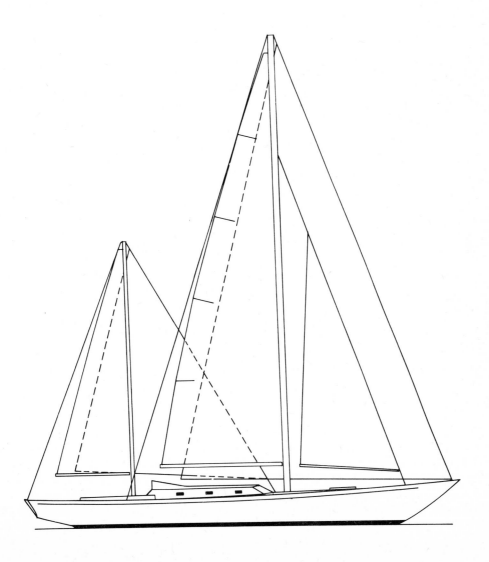

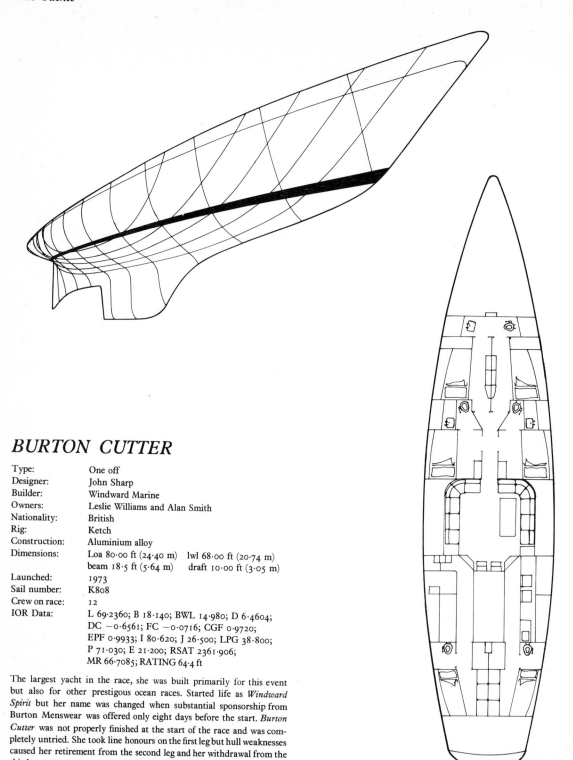

BURTON CUTTER

Type:	One off
Designer:	John Sharp
Builder:	Windward Marine
Owners:	Leslie Williams and Alan Smith
Nationality:	British
Rig:	Ketch
Construction:	Aluminium alloy
Dimensions:	Loa 80·00 ft (24·40 m) lwl 68·00 ft (20·74 m)
	beam 18·5 ft (5·64 m) draft 10·00 ft (3·05 m)
Launched:	1973
Sail number:	K808
Crew on race:	12
IOR Data:	L 69·2360; B 18·140; BWL 14·980; D 6·4604;
	DC −0·6561; FC −0·0716; CGF 0·9720;
	EPF 0·9933; I 80·620; J 26·500; LPG 38·800;
	P 71·030; E 21·200; RSAT 2361·906;
	MR 66·7085; RATING 64·4 ft

The largest yacht in the race, she was built primarily for this event
but also for other prestigous ocean races. Started life as *Windward
Spirit* but her name was changed when substantial sponsorship from
Burton Menswear was offered only eight days before the start. *Burton
Cutter* was not properly finished at the start of the race and was completely untried. She took line honours on the first leg but hull weaknesses
caused her retirement from the second leg and her withdrawal from the
third.

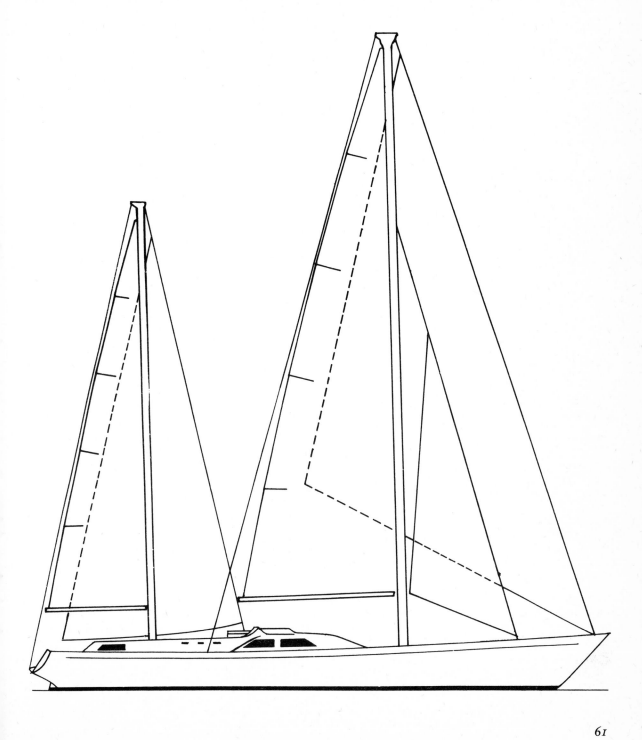

CS e RB

Type:	Prototype Koala 50
Designer:	Robert Clark
Builder:	Nordcantieri s.a.s., di Nicolotti G & C,
	Via Pontetto 79, 10051 Avigliana (Lago Grande),
	Torino, Italy
Owner:	Nordcantieri
Nationality:	Italian
Rig:	Ketch
Construction:	Glassfibre
Dimensions:	Loa 50·39 ft (15·36 m) lwl 40·39 ft (12·31 m)
	beam 13·12 ft (4·00 m) draft 7·38 ft (2·25 m)
	displacement 29,228 lb (16,000 kilo)
	ballast 13,228 lb (6,000 kilo)
Launched	1973
Sail number:	15905
Crew on race:	6
IOR Data:	L 41·3922; B 13·123; BWL 11·562; D 6·4743;
	DC −0·1496; FC −0·2182; CGF 0·9972;
	EPF 1·000; I 55·905; J 17·913; LPG 29·691;
	P 49·540; E 13·943; RSAT 1118·857;
	MR 37·1787; RATING 37·1 ft

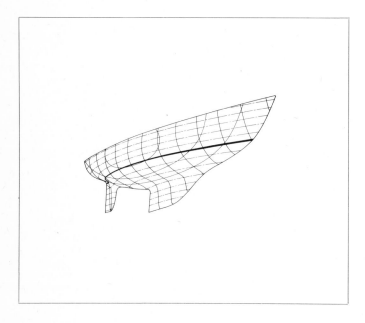

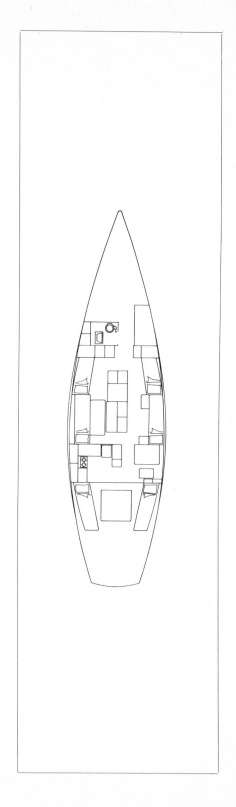

CS e RB, named after the initial letters of her sponsor, the furniture designers and manufacturers Centro Studi e Richerche Busnelli, was the prototype of a line of production offshore cruisers built by Nordcantieri – the Koala 50. She was well equipped for protection against the elements and crew comfort – there was an interior steering position beneath a clear dome and heating and drying facilities below. One of the three boats in the race without an engine – the others were *Peter von Danzig* and *Guia*.

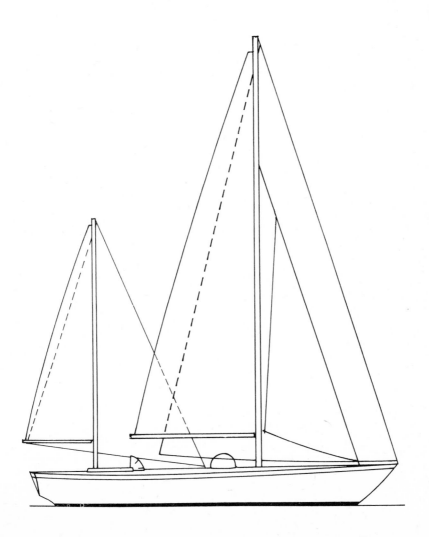

GRAND LOUIS

Type:	One off but similar to previous designs
Designer:	Dominique Presles
Builder:	Tecimar, St Nazaire, France
Owner:	André Viant
Nationality:	French
Rig:	Schooner
Construction:	Glassfibre sandwich
Dimensions:	Loa 60·37 ft (18·40 m) lwl 43·31 ft (13·20 m)
	beam 15·09 ft (4·60 m) draft 8·20 ft (2·50 m)
	displacement 46,300 lb (21,000 kilo)
	ballast 14,329 lb (6,500 kilo)
Launched:	1973
Sail number:	F5959
Crew on race:	10
IOR Data:	L 48·1198; B 15·121; BWL 13·815; D 6·2381;
	DC −0·2110; FC −0·1699; CGF 0·9717;
	EPF 0·9795; I 51·981; J 20·702; LPG 33·300;
	P 50·360; E 16·831; RSAT 1617·722;
	MR 46·7504; RATING 44·5 ft

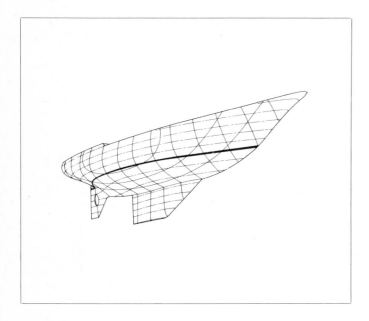

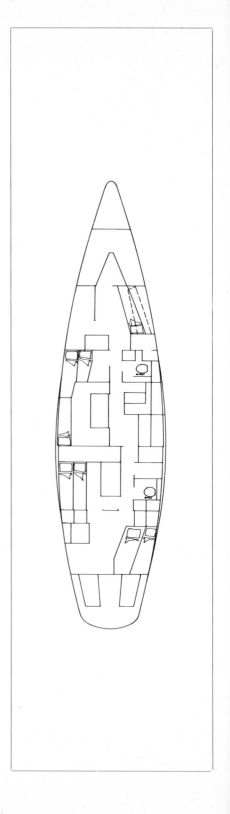

This yacht was designed, and construction had started before the conditions and rules for the race were announced. She is primarily a superbly comfortable family cruiser and was probably the most comfortable and happy yacht on the race. Her owner, André Viant, is an extremely experienced offshore sailor, and was completely unsponsored. She was one of the few yachts to be equipped with a deep freeze and so the crew enjoyed fresh food for much of the time.

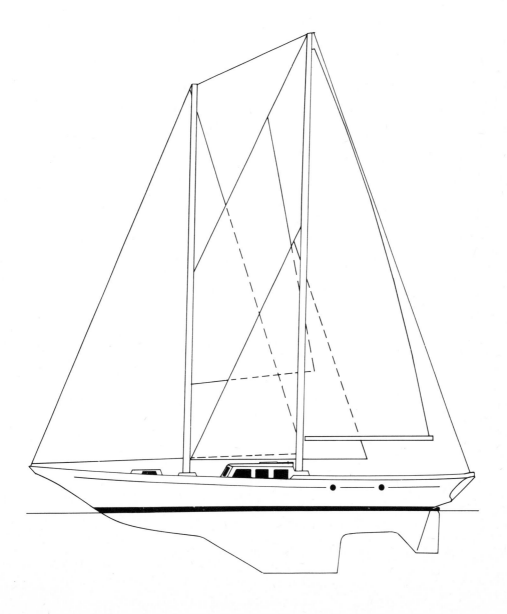

GREAT BRITAIN II

Type:	One off
Designer:	Alan P. Gurney
Builder:	Bayside Marine, Sandwich, Kent, England
Owner:	Chay Blyth/Jack Hayward
Nationality:	British
Rig:	Ketch
Construction:	Glassfibre sandwich
Dimensions:	Loa 77·16 ft (23·53 m) lwl 68·16 ft (20·18 m)
	beam 18·42 ft (5·62 m) draft 9·00 ft (2·75 m)
	displacement 73,000 lb (33,142 kilo)
	ballast 34,313 lb (15,578 kilo)
Launched:	1973
Sail number:	K3566
Crew on race:	9 to 12
IOR Data:	L 70·4036; B 17·800; BWL 16·310; D 7·0509;
	DC −0·6832; FC −0·0949; CGF 0·9824;
	EPF 0·9865; I 82·000; J 33·250; LPG 52·500;
	P 75·000; E 23·000; RSAT 2883·870;
	MR 71·4356; RATING 62·9 ft

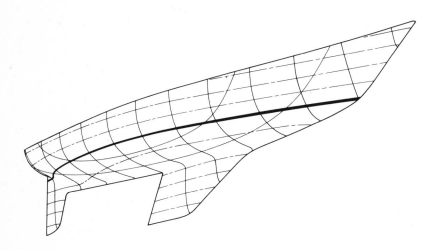

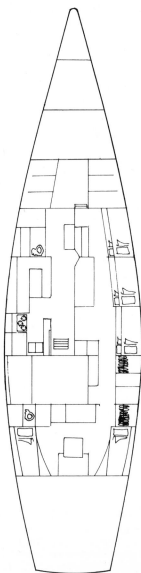

Chay Blyth asked Alan Gurney, an Englishman with his office in New York, to design this boat specially for the race. Gurney had previous experience of designing large ocean racing yachts, the most famous of which was *Windward Passage*. *Great Britain II* needed a crew of 15 but she started with only 12 and ended the race with a mere 9. Undercrewed and never properly tuned, she did not achieve her full potential.

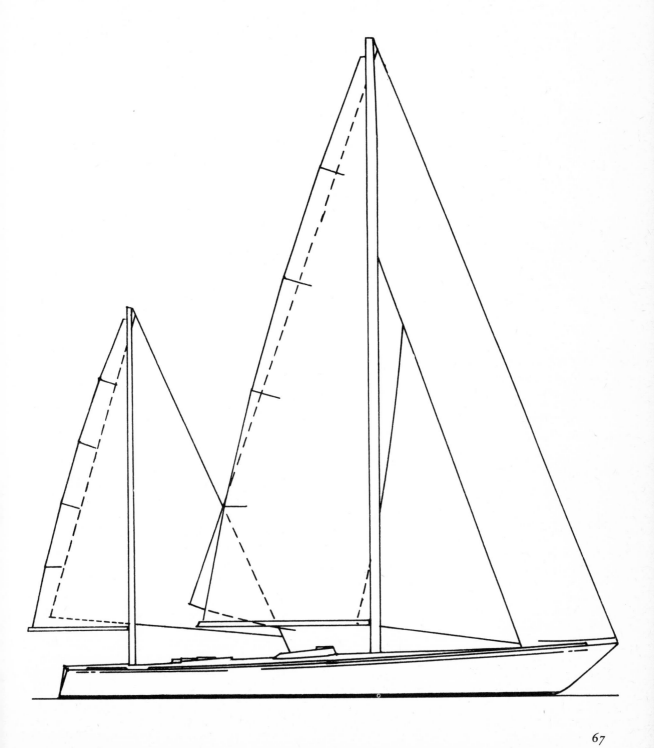

GUIA

Type:	Custom built stock design
Designer:	Sparkman and Stephens
Builder:	Craglietto, Trieste, Italy
Owner:	Giorgio Falck
Nationality:	Italian
Rig:	Sloop
Construction:	Wood, single skin.

Dimensions: Loa 45·39 ft (15·06 m)   lwl 33·33 ft (10·17 m)
beam 12·75 ft (3·89 m)   draft 7·25 ft (2·21 m)
displacement 24358 lb (11,059 kilo)
ballast 12,500 lb (5,675 kilo)

Launched:	1970
Sail number:	4371
Crew on race:	6
IOR Data:	L 37·3512; B 12·693; BWL11·155; D 5·3956;
	DC −0·0079; FC −0·0722; CGF 0·9838;
	EPF 1·000; I 56·220; J 18·471; LPG 27·887;
	P 48·621; E 14·107; RSAT 1088·088;
	MR 35·2076; RATING 34·9 ft

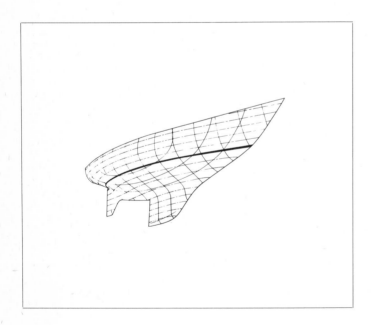

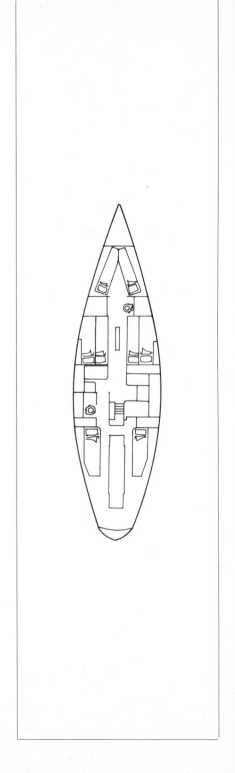

Built to the same design as *Mabelle*, *Guia* enjoyed a most successful offshore racing record in the Mediterranean. Her owner, Giorgio Falck, made a number of changes to the original design including an articulated rudder and a bendy boom. She was designed to the old RORC rule.

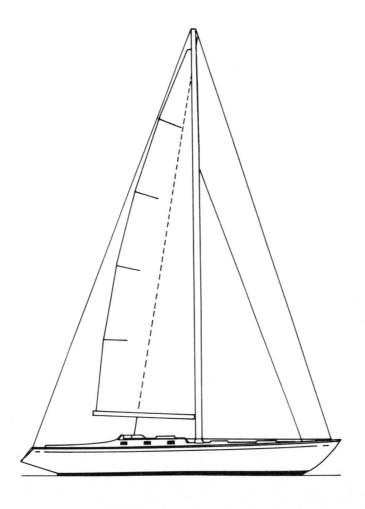

KRITER

Type:	Custom built sister ship to *Wild Rocket*
Designer:	Georges Auzépy-Brenneur
Builder:	Nautic Saintonge
Owner:	Jack Grout
Nationality:	French
Rig:	Ketch
Construction:	Cold moulded wood.
Dimensions:	Loa 66·50 ft (20·27 m)
	beam 16·40 ft (5·00 m) draft 8·20 ft (2·50 m)
	displacement 49,603 lb (22,500 kilo)
	ballast 19,840 lb (9,000 kilo)
Launched:	1973
Sail number:	F5784
Crew on race:	12
IOR Data:	L 56·5941; B 16·059; BWL 14·436; D 6·3513;
	DC −0·3865; FC −0·0577; CGF 0·9721;
	EPF 0·9851; I 66·351; J 22·605; LPG 37·565;
	P 59·251; E 16·929; RSAT 1778·428; MR 52·8324;
	RATING 50·6 ft

Kriter was built specially for the race. The only cold moulded wood yacht in the race, she was beautifuly built with a wealth of lamination work. She took her name from her sponsor who produces the sparkling champagne-type wine called Kriter.

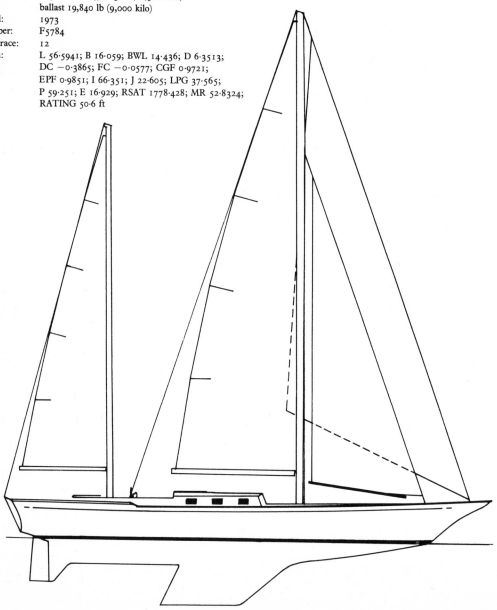

PETER VON DANZIG

Type:	One off
Builder:	Danziger Schiffswerft
Owner:	Akademischer Segler-Verein in Kiel
Nationality:	West German
Rig:	Yawl
Construction:	Steel
Dimensions:	Loa 59·00 ft (17·98 m) lwl 42·65 ft (13·00 m)
	beam 13·65 ft (4·16 m) draft 8·20 ft (2·50 m)
Launched:	1936
Sail number:	G77
Crew on race:	10 to 13
IOR Data:	L 47·075; B 13·484; BWL 12·844; D 7·1338;
	DC −0·1325; FC −0·0430; CGF 0·9680;
	EPF 1·000; I 58·825; J 19·619; LPG 24·015;
	P 61·942; E 27·230; MR 43·5162;
	RATING 42·1 ft

The oldest and most poorly equipped yacht in the race – much of her equipment was that fitted originally 34 years beforehand. But all her gear was well tried in ocean cruising so there was little chance of it failing unexpectedly.

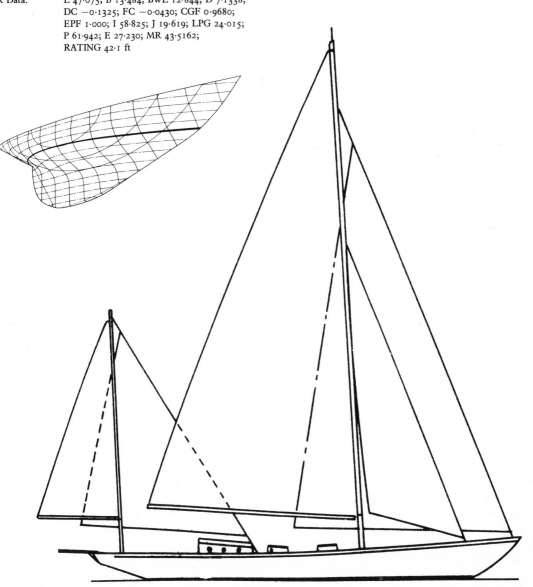

PEN DUICK VI

Type:	One off
Designer:	André Mauric
Builder:	l'arsenal de Brest, Brest, France
Owner:	Eric Tabarly
Nationality:	French
Rig:	Ketch
Construction:	Aluminium alloy
Dimensions:	Loa 73.00 ft (22.25 m) lwl 61.81 ft (18.84 m)
	beam 17.25 ft (5.26 m) draft 11.25 ft (3.43 m)
	displacement 70,547 lb (32,000 kilo)
	ballast 35,274 lb (16,000 kilo)
Launched:	1973
Sail number:	F5999
Crew on race:	14
IOR Data:	L 63.1971; B 17.264; BWL 13.658; D 6.5514;
	DC −0.0394; FC −0.0906; CGF 0.9893;
	EPF 0.9857; I 81.446; J 27.231; LPG 40.813;
	P 74.70; E 18.789; RSAT 2418.994;
	MR 63.4999; RATING 61.9 ft

An advanced design with many interesting features, built specially for the race and subsequent ocean racing for Tabarly by the French naval dockyard at Brest. Potential race winner but lack of development time after launching meant that structural defects came to light during the race rather than beforehand. She lost her main mast on the first leg when the mast step failed and again on the third leg due to a fitting failure, and retired from the last leg due to spreader failure.

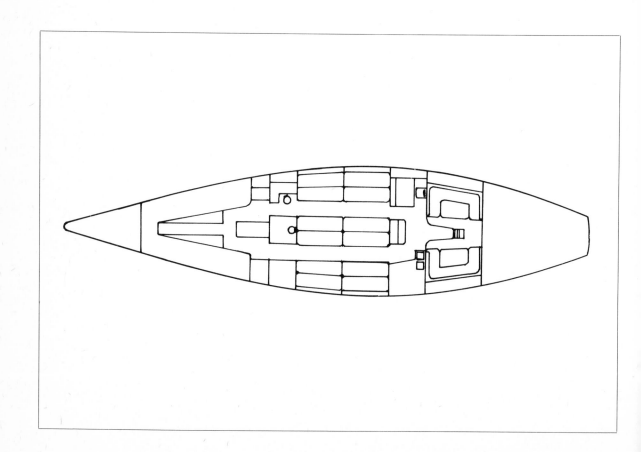

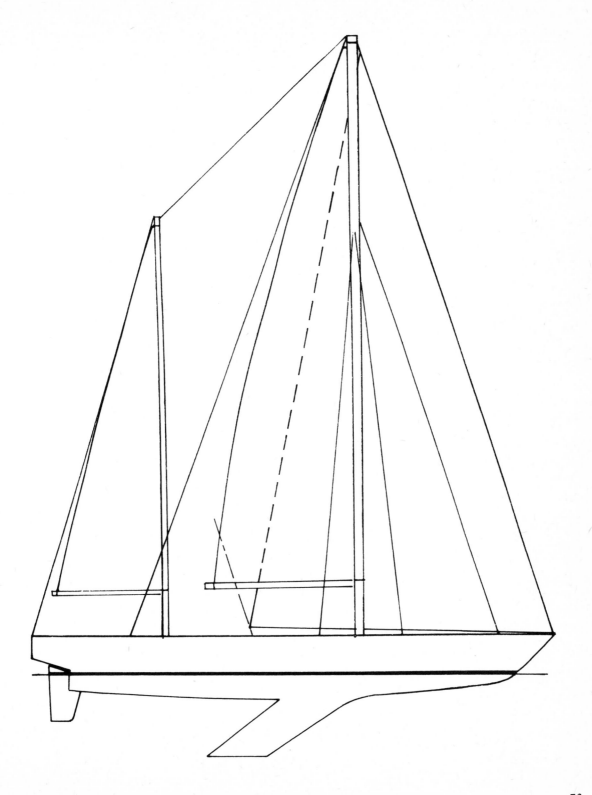

SAYULA II

Type:	Swan 65
Designer:	Sparkman and Stephens
Builder:	Nautor OY, PO Box 10, Pietarsaari, Finland
Owner:	Ramon Carlin
Nationality:	Mexican
Rig:	Ketch
Construction:	Glassfibre
Dimensions:	Loa 64·88 ft (19·79 m) lwl 47·00 ft (14·34 m)
	beam 16·33 ft (4·98 m) draft 9·13 ft (2·78 m)
	displacement: 56,371 lb (25,592 kilo)
	ballast: 25,000 lb (11,350 kilo)
Launched:	1973
Sail number:	MX7208
Crew on race:	12
IOR Data:	L 51·2894; B 16·260; BWL 14·849; D 7·1498;
	DC −0·0256; FC −0·1654; CGF 0·9804;
	EPF 0·9817; I 74·900; J 24·278; LPG 36·253;
	P 67·716; E 18·274; RSAT 2006·700;
	MR 49·2894; RATING 47·4 ft

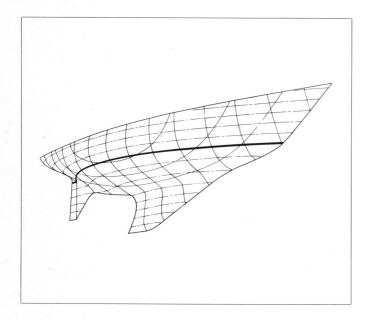

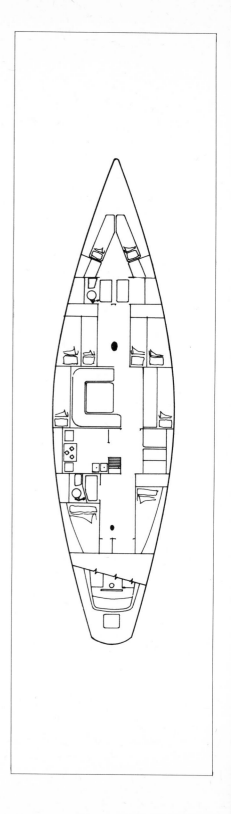

Sayula II is a Swan 65 – the largest of the Swan range of yachts designed by Sparkman and Stephens and built by Nautor in Finland. Apart from careful selection of the rigging and some of the fittings, she was a perfectly standard production boat built to a very high standard of finish. Although designed to the IOR, she was in no way a stripped-out racing machine but more a fast, comfortable cruising yacht. With an experienced offshore racing crew, these proved to be just the ingredients required to win the race.

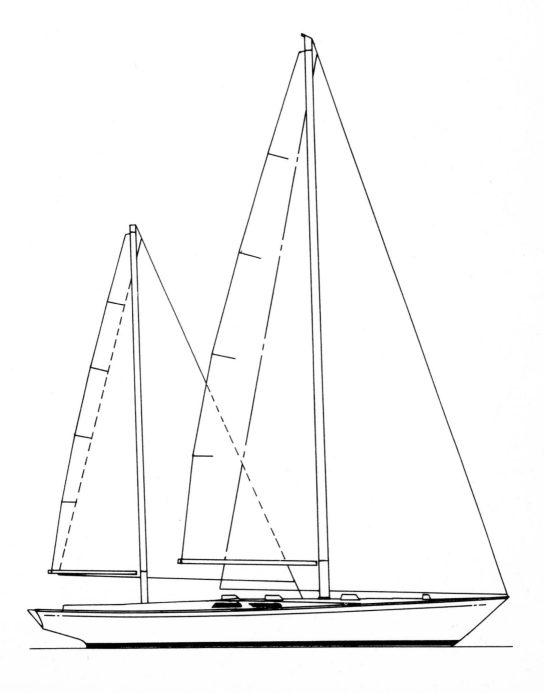

SECOND LIFE

Type:	Ocean 71
Designer:	E.G. van de Stadt
Builder:	Southern Ocean Shipyard Limited, New Quay Road, Poole, Dorset BH15 4 AB, England
Owner:	Brian Langmead (chartered to Roddie Ainslie)
Nationality:	British
Rig:	Ketch
Construction:	Glassfibre
Dimensions:	Loa 71·00 ft (21·65 m) lwl 55·75 ft (17·00 m) beam 17·39 ft (5·30 m) draft 8·07 ft (2·46 m) displacement 64,064 lb (29,085 kilo)
Launched:	1972
Sail number:	18
Crew on race:	12
IOR Data:	L 61·7033; B 16·460; BWL 14·430; D 6·6458; DC −0·7127; FC −0·1180; CGF 0·9739; EPF 0·9816; I 74·600; J 24·700; LPG 36·900; P 65·950; E 17·400; RSAT 2032·188; MR 58·1840; RATING 55·6 ft

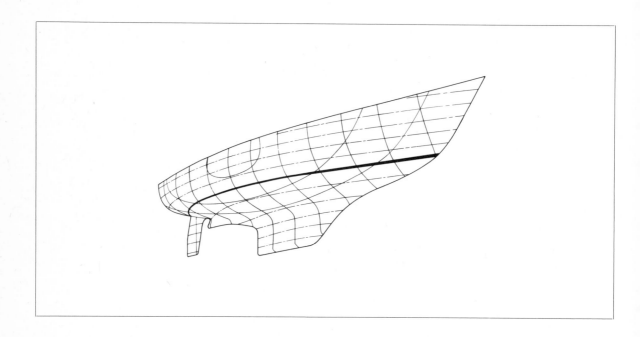

Second Life is one of the Ocean 71 class, the largest production glass-fibre yacht in the world. She was built initially for Dutchman Gerard Dijkstra for the 1972 Observer Singlehanded Transatlantic Race. She was chartered by Roddie Ainslie from Brian Langmead for the Round the World Race and the crew all shared the costs.

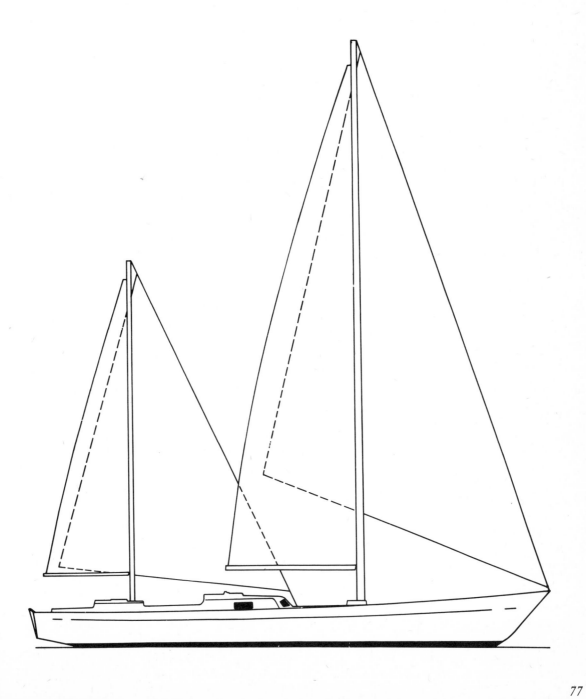

TAURANGA

Type:	Swan 55
Designer:	Sparkman and Stephens
Builder:	Nautor OY, PO Box 10, Pietarsaari, Finland.
Owner:	Gennaro de Flannineis
Nationality:	Italian
Rig:	Yawl
Construction:	Fibreglass
Dimensions:	Loa 55·33 ft (16·88 m) lwl 38·00 ft (11·59 m)
	beam 14·25 ft (4·35 m) draft 8·00 ft (2·44 m)
	displacement 37,220 lb (16,900 kilo)
	ballast 17,200 lb (7,890 kilo)
Launched:	1972
Sail number:	5551
Crew on race:	11
IOR Data:	L 41·6924; B 13·979; BWL 12·139; D 5·5062;
	DC 0·0328; FC −0·1837; CGF 0·9680;
	EPF 0·9778; I 61·039; J 20·161; LPG 30·741;
	P 55·528; E 19·029; RSAT 1407·361;
	MR 40·9838; RATING 39·1 ft

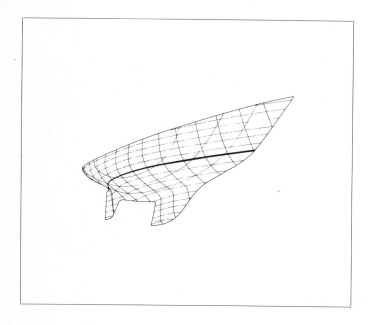

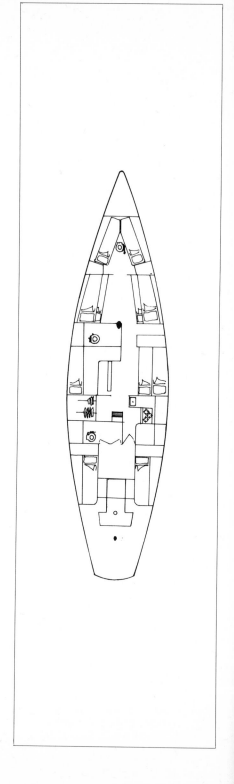

Like *Sayula, Tauranga* is one of the Swan range of yachts built by Nautor in Finland. A fast cruising and racing yacht designed to the IOR and built to the high standard of finish which is synonomous with all the Swan range.

33 EXPORT

Type:	One off
Designer:	André Mauric
Builder:	ACNAM
Owner:	O.R.P.I.F. (Office des relations publiques internationales flottantes)
Nationality:	French
Rig:	Ketch
Construction:	Aluminium
Dimensions:	Loa 60·00 ft (17·37 m) lwl 43·60 ft (13·29 m) beam 13·45 ft (4·10 m) draft 7·87 ft (2·40 m) displacement 30,660 lb (13,907 kilo) ballast 14,513 lb (6,583 kilo)
Launched:	1968
Sail number:	F4390
Crew on race:	7
IOR Data:	L 48·0316; B 12·605; BWL 10·984; D 5·1489; DC −0·2415; FC 0·0318; CGF 0·9885; EPF 0·9914; I 53·969; J 18·700; LPG 29·527; P 47·834; E 16·502; RSAT 1163·050; MR 45·0513; RATING 44·5 ft

33 Export was built for Alain Gliksman for the 1968 Singlehanded Transatlantic Race and had also been sailed in the Cape-Rio Race. She had been laid up at Deauville for some years before this race and was bought by a syndicate headed by Dominique Guillet and Jean-Pierre Millet, her co-skippers, who altered and prepared her.

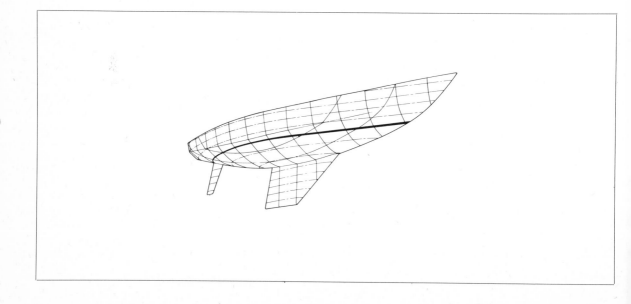

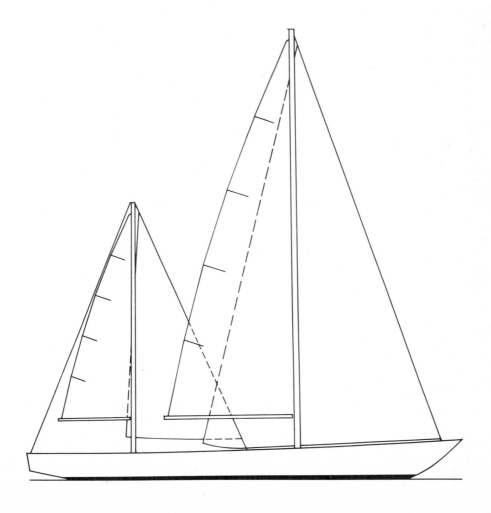

The Italian *Tauranga*, Eric Pascoli's Swan 55, at the start of the race on 8th September.

5
Leg One

It must have been anticipation, mixed with awe, that the crews of the 17 yachts experienced as they headed for the starting line off Southsea Castle on the morning of Saturday September 8th 1973. For them it was a voyage into the unknown; only Chay Blyth amongst them knew the real fury of the Southern Oceans, and for many it was with some trepidation that they had launched themselves into this race. Several have since admitted to being afraid, wondering how they had committed themselves to this enterprise. The feeling too of relief, now that the waiting was over, was ever present around Vernon Creek that morning as fond farewells were mixed with last minute efforts to obtain those very vital little things that always get forgotten.

Aboard *Burton Cutter* joiners and riggers rubbed shoulders with the crew busy stowing the $1\frac{1}{4}$ tons of liquid refreshment they carried in addition to the water in her tanks. The last few days must have seemed a nightmare to her two skippers, fighting to build the boat against impossible odds and a fast closing deadline. Eventually *Burton Cutter* was towed out to the start and hoisted her sails less than 30 minutes before the starting gun fired. For the first time Leslie Williams steered the 80 foot ketch, her hydraulic steering gear working without a moment's attention – the system not even bled, such was the rush to get this giant in action.

The sight that greeted the yachts must have emotionally affected even the hardest sailor in the crews. Over 3,000 boats had gathered in the eastern Solent to see these 17 yachts away on a 27,500 mile race of adventure. Carving her way amongst them was the three masted *Vendredi Treize*, the vast schooner of Claude Lelouche which Jean-Yves Terlain had sailed a year before in the Singlehanded Transatlantic Race, now proclaiming to all to listen to France Inter on 1,829 metres. There too was *Suhaili* with the bearded, friendly face of Robin Knox-Johnston, a mere sprat amongst the race entrants, but one which most competitors acknowledged with a wave. A fellow world girdling yacht, *Lively Lady* was amongst the spectator fleet, but her owner, Sir Alec Rose, was that day doing duty on the battery of Southsea Castle, firing the 100 years old cannon that boomed out the announcement of the start.

As noon approached the press of craft increased and it seemed that collisions were inevitable as dry mouthed crews shouted to surrounding boats to keep clear. To be damaged before the start would have been tragic. Miraculously, however, there were no crashes, but an eager fleet was not far from the line when the starting gun was fired. With $27\frac{1}{2}$

thousand miles to go no one would blame a poor start, but the efforts of *Adventure*'s skipper in putting her right on the line in pole position at gunfire displayed the Royal Navy crew's attitude to this race. They were determined to show their prowess here, just offshore from their home port.

Above, the sky was seemingly just as crowded. At one time there were 12 helicopters and nearly the same number of light aircraft above the racing fleet and the attendant spectator craft. For the 167 crew members of the racing yachts it would be the last crowds they would see for over six weeks. Few could have direct contact with more than their fellow crew members until Cape Town was reached. Some were new to ocean racing and very few had ever been cooped up in such confined surroundings for so long, let alone having to remain totally competitive for many hours on end. It marked a first in many ways, but it was generally acknowledged that this 6,600 mile leg would be a gentle shakedown and was ideally suited to preparing crews for the later rigours of the Southern Oceans.

The course was simple. Bembridge Ledge buoy to starboard and thence to Cape Town, read the instructions, but there can be little doubt that skippers, navigators and crews had been hard at work over the past months pondering the reliability of statistical information taken in conjunction with the acknowledged authority of *Ocean Passages for the World*. It must, of course, be remembered that the recommended courses given in this book are for square rigged vessels. Using them would mean the fastest downhill passage, but not necessarily the quickest way to Cape Town for a modern ocean racer. The ketch rigged boats, which are happier with sheets just started, mostly went to the west, *Sayula II* went 40 miles to the west of Trindade Island, whilst single masted boats like *Adventure* could afford to buck the SE Trades and take a more easterly course. *Sayula*'s course took her nearly a thousand miles more than the official handicap distance, but she had more wind than most of her rivals, averaging around 200 miles a day from Trindade to Cape Town. There was one other way and *CS e RB* chose to use it. A few years earlier Leslie Williams on his way to South Africa for the Cape Town-Rio Race had sailed close to the coast of Africa using thermal winds and avoid-

ed the ocean currents by staying well inshore. It had its dangers as there are myriads of shifting sandbanks that are uncharted particularly off the SW African coast. This time it did not pay for *CS e RB*, who on October 18th was reported in a position 20 miles inshore from Cape Frio!

From: *Ocean Passages for the World*

Channel to Arquipélago de Cabo Verde (Cape Verde Islands)

On leaving the English channel at once make westing, as the prevailing winds are from that direction. With a fair wind from the Lizard, steer a west-south-westerly course to gain an offing in long. 10° or 12° W.

If the wind should be from the westward keep on the tack which enables most westing to be made to get a good offing, and keep clear of the Bay of Biscay, even standing to the north-westward until well able to weather Cabo Finisterre on the starboard tack. By making a long board to the westward nothing is lost, as the wind will be generally found to veer, so that a change of wind will be favourable, and even permit a vessel to pursue a course with a free wind; whilst if embayed in the Bay of Biscay, any change of wind to the westward would necessitate beating to windward against the current. It must be borne in mind that the prevailing winds and currents have a tendency to set towards Ushant and into the Bay of Biscay when southward of it. To get well to the westward is therefore of the greatest importance. Ushant should, in no case, be sighted.

From long. 10° or 12° W, shape course to pass Madeira at any convenient distance, giving a wide berth to Cabo Finisterre, in passing it, as the current from the Atlantic usually sets right on shore there. In the winter months it is preferable to pass to the westward of Madeira, for the strong westerly gales which occur in November, December and January, produce eddy winds and heavy squalls eastward of the island.

From Madeira the best track is to pass to the westward and just in sight of Arquipélago de Cabo Verde (Cape Verde islands) as the winds are stronger and steadier to the westward than to the eastward of them.

Arquipélago de Cabo Verde to the Equator

In considering where to cross the equator it is necessary to bear in mind that if a vessel crosses far to the westward there will be a less interval of doldrum to cross, but it may be requisite to tack to weather the coast of South America, and these crossings vary during the year, as the direction of the SE Trade wind is more southerly when the sun is north of the equator than when south.

After passing the Arquipélago de C. Verde, stand to the southward between the meridians of 26° and 29° W, being nearer 26° W from May to October, and nearer 29° W from November to April. The equator should be crossed at points varying according to the season of the year as follows:

IN JULY, AUGUST AND SEPTEMBER, the southerly winds will be met with between 10° and 12° N. On meeting them steer on the starboard tack so as to cross lat. 5° N between 17° and 19° W. Go round then on the other tack, and cross the equator between 25° and 23° W.

IN OCTOBER, NOVEMBER AND DECEMBER, the southerly winds will be met with between lat. 8° and 6° N. On meeting them steer so as to cross lat. 5° N between 20° and 23° W, then take the tack which gives the most southing, and cross the equator between 29° and 24° W.

CAUTION: The South Equatorial current is not so strong in the northern winter as in the summer and autumn months; but the mariner must remember that the strength of the current increases as it advances towards the American coast.

Equator to Cape Town and Cape of Good Hope

Having crossed the equator as recommended, stand across the South-East Trade wind on the port tack, even should the vessel fall off to W. by S., for the wind will draw more to the eastward as the vessel advances, and finally to East at the southern limit of the trade. When in the vicinity of St Paul rocks, frequent astronomical observations should be made, the current watched and allowed for, and a good lookout kept, as these rocks are steep-to, and can only be seen on a clear day from a distance of 8 miles. The same precautions are necessary if passing westward of Arquipélago de Fernando de Noronha, when approaching the dangerous Atol das Rocas on

which a light was established in 1882. During the greater part of the year the South-East Trade fails on a line drawn from the Cape of Good Hope to Ilhas da Trindade and Martin Vaz. This limit varies from 3 degrees, according to the position of the sun.

When to the southward of the South-East Trade, fresh winds variable in direction will be met. Those from the north-east through north to north-west, if accompanied by cloudy weather, often shift suddenly to south-west or south, but sometimes the wind steadies between west and west-south-west. From Ilha da Trindade shape course to the south-eastward to cross the parallel of 30° S, in about long. 22° W, and the meridian of Greenwich in about lat. 35° to 37° S, whence to the Cape of Good Hope winds from the westward and southward usually prevail.

After passing the meridian of Greenwich, a strong northerly current will be frequently experienced; and on nearing the land, when bound to Table bay, great attention is required, as there it will be found almost constantly running strongly to the northward, and, if disregarded, a vessel may have difficulty and lose time in reaching the bay.

The attitude of the skippers before the start told much of their chances in the race. Tabarly moved like a mole, a wry smile on his well tanned face as all seemed in order on *Pen Duick VI*. In contrast the chaotic state of *Burton Cutter* seemed not to depress Les Williams. He was described in the French magazine *Voiles et Voiliers* as a 'devil of an optimist, always with a glass of whisky ready and his arm around a pretty girl.' Patrick Bryans carefully supervised the loading of stores on *Adventure* whilst on *Grand Louis* it appeared as if a family party was in progress. André Viant, her skipper, cheerfully acknowledged the shambles: 'The night before we go we will dismantle the boat and start stowing again', he said.

But these problems were behind and the regular watchkeeping routine begun. The early weather of the English Channel was its usual unpredictable self – thunderstorms at night, dying wind followed by fog – and made the crews realise that they were up against it for the next few months, even before they had got out of home waters.

Some failed to make it at all. George Faux could not obtain a navigation permit for the 52 foot ketch *Moksha*. The French authorities at St Malo and Deauville had both refused to grant him one and the head of the yard where her crew were trying to finish her, said 'hardly one leak was cured, there would be another one'. The creditors seized the yacht and Faux disappeared. *Voiles et Voiliers* hit hard at Faux: 'The sad story ended like we thought it would. This pretentious enterprise, pursued in grotesque fashion, would be a farce if suppliers had not trusted this adventurous cavalier, if firms had not helped him, if the crew had not believed the talk of a man whom our indulgence will qualify of cultivating lies.'

'It is the moral duty of the nautical authorities, federations, clubs and magazines to free yachting from the sort of person who is just ridiculous. Sponsorship has become necessary to the great nautical adventurer and the firms who have been had by the shifty ones could be disgusted for a little while. They would be wrong: sometimes the lies must be published so that the truth emerges.'

After *Adventure*'s initial advantage from the start line it was the turn of the two ketches of joint favourites Chay Blyth and Eric Tabarly to lead the fleet towards the Bembridge Ledge. The first blood went to *Great Britain II* with Len Price at the wheel, who had started to windward of the Frenchman. But with the sort of inevitability that the experts had predicted Tabarly's black hulled ketch once clear of land sailed away into what seemed an impregnable lead. With him were experienced yachtsmen, both offshore racers and small boat sailors, including the Olympic silver medallist crew Marc Pajot. There was one other Olympian in this race – Zygfryd Perlicki, who represented Poland at Kiel in the Soling class, and in this race he skippered *Copernicus*. The light weather that predominated throughout the 1973 British summer stayed with the fleet for a week, making the traditional Biscay gales a false legend. The winds after two days went westerly and boats went on the wind to stay clear of Ushant, but freed away off Vigo and gained direction south. The NE Trades provided a foretaste of long hauls in one direction with the only changes of sails to be in concert with the wind's strength. It

was downhill stuff and keeping an eye on relative velocity and gybing regularly to keep the best course made good were the skippers' major worries. It's interesting to consider in hindsight whether at this stage *Sayula II* was really racing hard on this leg. One report quotes a crew member as saying 'We delayed gybes until after dinner.' There was no such luxury on *Pen Duick VI* or *Adventure*.

The first strong headwinds found an unprepared *Burton Cutter* with Leslie Williams and Alan Smith finding out that their new vessel had sieve-like propensities. They were forced to heave to for the best part of two days to stop leaks in hatches, windows and deck fittings put on in haste. Ten days out in $31°30N$, $14°50W$ *Burton Cutter* reported that she had taken in a considerable amount of water through a stern gland and this had flooded her batteries. Behind them, on the same day, *Jakaranda*, the South African Admiral's Cupper, which joined for the first leg of this race in order to go home, signalled to the Portuguese ship *Angrade do Heroisme* by Aldis that her radio was out of order. *British Soldier* was also having problems, but her own peculiar brand. She reported the Japanese ship *Nile Maru* as not giving way some 15 miles west of Madeira, which caused her spinnaker to collapse. The problems were trifles.

Logs of the first three weeks record little that was startling. Flying fish added variety to menus and these did vary from boat to boat. Chay Blyth's men suffered a stiff regime. The diet consisted almost entirely of freeze dried foods – particularly curry; high protein items like sardines; cereals and biscuits. He was rigid over weight inside the boat and each man had only one spoon with which to eat. The water too was carefully calculated and when Blyth's estimated time for the leg was exceeded by five days, it meant two weeks of short rations. There was no beer to ease the problem and perhaps raise morale on *Great Britain II*.

In contrast the food on board *Sayula II* was all that anyone could wish. Ramon Carlin, her skipper, insisted that the 'inner man' was important. When men ate and drank what they liked, they were happier. Cocktail hour was observed as the crews came off watch. *Sayula*'s shortages became apparent only after they had crossed the line in Cape Town.

The tanker *Erskine Bridge* photographed from *Burton Cutter* as she passed close by at full chat in the Atlantic on leg 1. Despite attempts to attract her attention no one was seen on board and she passed so close that the wind was taken from *Burton Cutter*'s sails.

The wine and beer ran out on the way to the dock and there were only 24 jars of caviare left on board.

Food too figured high on the list of priorities aboard *Adventure*. Towards the end of the second week, her crew heard a report on the BBC World Service that on handicap she lay neck and neck with *Pen Duick VI*. It was sufficiently good news for skipper Patrick Bryans to call for a special meal. That night they sat down to soup, grouse, fruit and cheese washed down with a couple of bottles of Nuits St-Georges. The crew drank to their success and damnation to the Frenchman. They admit in hindsight that this was a little uncharitable, but it did seem to have the desired effect.

The third week saw the boats enter the Doldrums. The further west the less the distance that has to be sailed through this notorious windless zone. *Pen Duick VI* and *Sayula II* were out to the west, but further east *Adventure* found the doldrum belt relatively narrow and was through in three days. A

tremendous thunderstorm heralded the advent of the SE Trade for her and it brought all hands on deck with soap for showers and buckets for washing 'smalls'. *Sayula II* only once recorded losing steerage way, but had three calm areas to get through.

Once into the Trades the ketches, in the main, fell off to the west a little, gaining extra speed whilst sailing free. *Adventure* was designed to deal with these conditions and she prepared herself for a long port tack of some 2,000 miles or more on a rhumb line course to Cape Town. *Burton Cutter* took the same route, somewhat surprisingly for a ketch. The boats taking the freer course, although having to sail further, would pick up the westerlies and come into Cape Town with the wind behind them – it was a swings and roundabouts choice.

Crossing the Line (Equator) has an important significance for any sailor and on *Adventure* and *Burton Cutter* at least the traditional customs were observed. *Adventure* signalled Race Control 'Adven-

ture was boarded, greeted and granted free passage by King Neptune in 15°W at 1600 30th September. His Majesty was astonished at our rate of progress and indeed experienced some difficulty in boarding. He noted with pleasure that there was a crustacean in the crew and said he was delighted to see a naval vessel under sail after all these years.' The festivities on *Burton Cutter* had a fair amount of horse play in them before order was restored with a party courtesy of Pimms No. 1. *Kriter* too observed the rules with skipper Jack Grout in the role of Neptune and Philippe Bayle (with a beard) as Aphrodite.

The French ketch had organized watches into teams of five for four hours each with two-hour watches in the afternoon to effect rotation. The cook and navigator were outside the watches. They had some long periods of calm sitting 'on a lake for seven days'. Food on board *Kriter* was important. Each Sunday Ariane Grout cooked a special meal, but every day they ate well on cold meats, ham, sausages – and wine with each meal must have made it seem like home.

Pen Duick VI thundered along; the honour of France was at stake for her. She was excitingly revolutionary in her concept and from the start the experienced Tabarly had taken her to the front. At the Canaries the Frenchman was 24 hours ahead of his rival Chay Blyth and at one time he had achieved 17.8 knots under spinnaker in a Force 4 wind. The narrow boat with her spent uranium keel provided her skipper with the sort of mount he wanted. Then suddenly just after starting her leg into Cape Town from the west, the race for Tabarly was over. At midnight on October 3rd whilst sailing under number 3 jib, heavy genoa staysail and mainsail, *Pen Duick VI* was dismasted. She was 1,200 miles from Rio and 2,200 from Cape Town on a longitude 23°W.

Rio was the obvious place to go under the rig left. A jury bipod main mast was made from the two spinnaker booms and every bit of canvas utilized to help them along. but it was poor progress and *Pen Duick* did not make port until the night of 14th October. Tabarly had radioed to France on October 5th, 'Have dismasted – heading for Rio – arrange sending mast, boom, rigging – Yankee number 3 – heavy foresail – mainsail – six stanchions – 200 m

cord 24 mm – suggest raising spreaders 10 cm.

Albert Coeudevez at Yverdon in Switzerland at the Nirvana factory began work immediately and completed the work in six days. The Tonnerre sail loft in Lorient made the sails in short time and Sarma made the rigging and fittings, so that all could be shipped from Geneva aboard a military cargo plane on October 12th. But the mast would not fit and 1.6 metres had to be cut off the foot and welded back in Rio. A small army of workmen went with the gear and with them too went wheel steering to be fitted as the tiller had proved too much in heavy weather. Five days after he arrived in Rio, Tabarly was back at sea again pushing *Pen Duick VI* hard in an attempt to reach Cape Town in time for the start for Sydney. In the final seven days of the trip he covered 1,740 miles to make it with two days to spare.

Towards the end of the leg the fan began to close. On board *Adventure* careful interpretation of weather situations transmitted by morse gave the Navy's yacht an advantage. It was managed with a tape recorder. *Sayula II* also used these weather forecasts and both boats were criticized by their fellow competitors in Cape Town for using this perfectly legal aid to racing. No one planning a race of this nature should disregard any possible assistance they can gain from existing aids. From

A Chinese trawler encountered by *Burton Cutter* off the coast of West Africa on the first leg. An offer to go aboard for lunch was declined due to the race rules which forbade outside assistance.

Burton Cutter finishing at Cape Town to take line honours for the first leg of the race.

position reports it appeared to those on board *Adventure* that there was every possibility that they could be first across the line and with renewed vigour they urged every fraction of a knot from their yacht. At 0800 on October 15th, however, a twin masted yacht was sighted about four miles ahead. It subsequently proved to be *Burton Cutter*. Her hard windward course paid dividends. Four nights before, a sudden squall had hit *Great Britain II* and with the ketch heeling dangerously all hands were called to shorten sail. A spinnaker boom broke and knocked Bernie Hosking into the sea. A lifebuoy was thrown and its automatic light failed to function. The boat was brought round and Hosking's shouts were heard and he was spotted in the searchlight's beam. Seven minutes after going overboard he was recovered.

The winds played tricks as the Cape came closer and *Adventure* lay nearly becalmed with 250 miles to go. On the 17th she managed only 76 miles, but at least her crew knew that *Burton Cutter* was having the same problems. Then wind came from the south

west and the race was on again. *Great Britain II* was also in the offing and the competitive spirit in all three boats increased. *Burton Cutter* made it first early in the afternoon of Saturday 20th. *Adventure* was just over 24 hours behind, but she was assured of the handicap honours, the real prize for the leg. Three hours after *Adventure* had finished the scratch boat *Great Britain II* came home and another 24 hours elapsed before *Sayula II* crossed the line with *33 Export* following another day later. *Adventure*'s lead was a phenomenal 77 hours over *Sayula II* with *33 Export* five hours adrift in third place.

Cape Town's hospitality weighed heavy on the time of crews bent on preparing for the next leg. It was seemingly endless, but most welcome was the 40 Rand floating dry dock where essential underwater work was done. A notable absentee was *Sayula II* – her crew felt there was no need. They just had a scrub and claimed a psychological advantage. Socially all agreed that the Cape Town stop-over was an unqualified success.

At the end of the first leg the Royal Navy's entry *Adventure* had a slow drift down Table Bay to the finishing line.

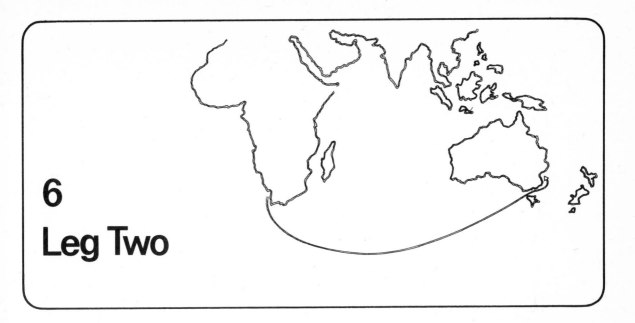

6
Leg Two

Every schoolgirl will tell you that to get from Cape Town to Sydney, you turn left out of Cape Town and follow the coast to the Cape of Good Hope, head in an easterly direction along the 40th parallel leaving Australia to port and once through the Bass Strait turn left up the coast to Port Jackson. At least that's how it looks on a large scale chart in Mercator's projection, but the world is not flat and the quickest way is by the great circle route. This however would take a yacht into the ice fields and put her in danger. *Ocean Passages for the World* has the most bearing on this essentially downwind leg.

From: *Ocean Passages for the World*

Route 1,091. Cape Town or Cape of Good Hope to ports in Australia and New Zealand

(1) MAIN ROUTE ACROSS THE INDIAN OCEAN (*a*) *and* (*b*) AND APPROACH TO BASS STRAIT (*c*) for Melbourne – all seasons, or for Sydney and New Zealand – winter months.

(*a*) *Rounding the Cape of Good Hope* – From Cape Town, vessels bound eastward are recommended to pick up the eastward track from Cabo de Hornos (Cape Horn) (Route 1,087) at the point where it is met by the track from the North Atlantic (Route

1,009) bound to the Indian ocean, namely at lat. about 40° S and long. 20° E. There is but little difficulty in passing eastward round the Cape of Good Hope at any time, though a greater proportion of gales will be met with from April to September, the winter season.

From October to April, easterly winds prevail as far south as the tail of the Agulhas bank (about 37° S), with variable but chiefly westerly winds beyond it. In May and September at the tail of the bank, easterly and westerly winds are in equal proportion, but between these months westerly winds prevail, extending sometimes close in to the coast. Should a south-easterly wind be blowing on leaving Table or Simons bays, stand boldly to the south-westward until the westerly winds are reached or the wind changes to a more favourable direction. In all cases when making for the 40th parallel southward of the Cape of Good Hope, steer nothing eastward of south, so as to avoid the area south-eastward of the tail of Agulhas bank, where gales are frequent, and heavy and dangerous breaking cross seas prevail.

(*b*) *Crossing the Indian ocean* – Having thus crossed to the southward of the (west going) Agulhas current, and picked up the westerly winds, the best latitude in which to cross the ocean must to some extent depend on circumstances.

Vessels bound to Australian ports would make the passage at about the parallel of 39° or 40° S, but those bound to Tasmania or New Zealand, would do so at between 42° or 43° S, especially from October to March, the summer months. Between 39° S and 43° S the winds generally blow from some western point, and seldom with more strength than will admit of carrying sail. In a higher latitude the weather is frequently more boisterous and stormy; sudden changes of wind with equally wet weather are almost constantly to be expected, especially in the winter season. Ile Amsterdam may be seen from a distance of 60 miles in clear weather.

In summer, many vessels take a more southern route, some going as far south as the parallel of 52° S latitude, but the steadiness and comparatively moderate strength of the winds, with the smoother seas and more genial climate north of 40° S, compensate by comfort and security for the time presumed to be saved by taking a shorter route. Tempestuous gales, sudden violent and fitful shifts of wind accompanied by hail or snow, and terrific and irregular seas are often encountered in the higher latitudes; moreover the islands in the higher latitudes are so frequently shrouded in fog that often the first sign of their vicinity is the sound of the surf beating against them.

South-eastward of the Cape of Good Hope, midway between Kerguelen island and the meridian of Cape Leeuwin, midway between New Zealand and Cabo de Hornos (Cape Horn), and north-eastward of Cabo de Hornos, icebergs are most numerous. The periods of maximum and minimum frequency vary greatly. It may happen that while ships are passing ice in lower latitudes, others, in higher latitudes, find the ocean free of ice.

The lengths of many of the Southern ocean icebergs are remarkable; bergs of 5 to 20 miles in length are frequently sighted south of the 40th parallel, and bergs of from 20 to 50 miles in length are far from uncommon.

It may be gathered from numerous observations that bergs may, in places, be fallen in with anywhere south of the 30th parallel, that as many as 4,500 bergs have been observed in a run of 2,000 miles, that estimated heights of 800 to 1,700 feet (243^m8 to 518^m1) are not uncommon, and that bergs of from 6 to 82 miles in length are numerous.

(c) Approach to Bass strait.

(i) North of King island (recommended). – In approaching Bass strait to make the land at Moonlight head or the light at Cape Otway, the currents must be carefully attended to, particularly during south-westerly or southerly winds; vessels have been wrecked on King island by not steering for Cape Otway. When approaching Bass strait in thick weather, or when uncertain of the vessel's position, do not reduce the soundings to less than 40 fathoms (73^m2). Soundings of 60 to 70 fathoms (109^m7 or 128^m0) will be found at 25 or 30 miles westward of King island. Outside this limit the soundings deepen rapidly to over 100 fathoms (182^m9).

The high bold promontory of Cape Otway is easily distinguished by the white lighthouse on it, and by the signal station, to which all passing vessels are recommended to show their number. It is desirable to round Cape Otway at a distance of not less than 3 or 4 miles.

Note – Directions for, and a description of, Bass strait will be found in Australia Pilot, Vol. II.

CAUTION. In approaching King island from the westward, especially during thick or hazy weather caution is required on account of the variable strength of the current, which sets to the south-east with a force varying from a half to $2\frac{1}{2}$ knots, according to the strength and duration of the westerly winds, and sounding is recommended.

(ii) South of King island (not recommended). – The entrance to Bass strait between King island and the Hunter group is not recommended, on account of Bell reef and Reid rocks which lie in it. If, from necessity or choice, entering Bass strait by this passage, keep to the southward of Reid rocks and Bell race, the latter being passed at the distance of $2\frac{1}{2}$ miles to the southward of it by steering for Black Pyramid on a bearing of 098°. With a commanding breeze the passage between King island and Reid rocks may be taken without danger by paying attention to the tidal streams, which set somewhat across the channel at times. From Black Pyramid pass about one mile north of Albatross islet, whence to Port Dalrymple, round the sunken danger Mermaid rock, off Three Hummock island, and then make a direct course.

(5) To SYDNEY – In all seasons first take passage

as in (1) (a) and (b). After reaching the longitude of Australia, there is a summer and a winter route as follows:

(a) Summer route – Leave the main route across the Indian ocean at about the 120th meridian E. and steer to pass round the south of Tasmania.

After rounding South cape, give a berth of 20 or 30 miles to Cape Pillar and the east coast of Tasmania, to escape the baffling winds and calms which frequently perplex vessels inshore, while a steady breeze is blowing in the offing. This is more desirable from December to March, when easterly winds prevail, and a current is said to be experienced off the south-east coast at 20 to 60 miles from the shore, running northward at the rate of three-quarters of a knot, while inshore it is running in the opposite direction, with nearly double that rate. From a position about 30 miles eastward of Cape Pillar, proceed on a course of about 012° for about 350 miles to a position 15 miles eastward of Cape Howe, whence continue as directly as possible to make Sydney, but keeping at first at a distance from the coast, in order to lessen the strength of the south-going Australian coast current, not closing the land till northward of South head, Port Jackson.

Some navigators prefer to stand eastward into long. 155° E, before turning northward for Port Jackson, and thus escape almost altogether the southerly set.

The start at Cape Town was colourful. The hospitality that the crews had enjoyed during their fortnight or so stay was coming to an end but their hosts were determined to see them on their way in true style. As it was a Wednesday the spectator fleet was small, but there were two South African Navy minesweepers with crowds of well wishers aboard. Most of the thank yous had been said, but a final farewell was displayed on a piece of Terylene sailcloth from the deck of *Sayula II*. It read 'Vanessa and Jill, we love you'. This sailcloth together with its caption were incorporated into the tallboy, when it blew out on the third leg.

The wind was light from the south when at half past one local time the 17 yachts set out. *Jakaranda* was missing from the first leg fleet, but the French yacht *Concorde* joined the race for the leg to Sydney. Four boats only escaped out into the stronger breezes offshore, whilst the rest remained becalmed off Sea Point in the lee of Table Mountain. *Great Britain II*, *Kriter*, *Pen Duick VI* and *Sayula II* made it whilst the rest lay windless until midnight. *Pen Duick*'s crew must have been tired. They had arrived only two days earlier after a record breaking run from Rio – only 15 days to do the 3,200 miles, at an average of 8·8 knots. Then they had sail repairs to complete before embarking on a tough leg across the southern Indian Ocean. Chay Blyth was now one short on board *Great Britain II*. Brian Daniels had to return to England for personal reasons and that left 11 men only to sail the big ketch – a fearsome prospect as her real sister ship, *Windward Passage*, normally races with a crew of 18. The smaller, slower boats had their own brand of problems. They had the shortest time to lick their wounds before the next start and the older and less well equipped yachts like *Otago* and *Peter von Danzig*, whilst with generally fewer maintenance problems than their more sophisticated rivals, were a necessary source of worry to their skippers.

Within hours of getting clear of Cape Town the southeasterly winds were blowing strongly on the competitors with the leaders heading south to get into the westerlies. Tactics were important in order to dodge the high pressure areas and the time to tack when the wind went southerly before the westerlies was all important. Blyth misjudged it and was caught almost windless in one of these highs for a time whilst the others skirted it.

The strong headwinds, however, took their toll. After two days of hard pounding to windward in heavy seas *Burton Cutter*'s crew became aware that she was trimmed well down by the bow, but the conditions were so bad they weren't able to open the forehatch and examine the forward watertight compartment for another day. What they then found was that the forward locker, up to the watertight bulkhead, was completely full of water with bags of sails floating on top. The boat had to bear away so that the seas were on the quarter and the motion more steady with less pounding on the bows. The flooded area was then pumped dry and the extent of the damage examined. Practically all the alloy stringers on the starboard side of the hull were adrift and about half of those on the port side as well. The alloy hull plates were panting in and out like a large bellows. It was quite frightening for all on board with loud booming noises and reverberations right through the boat as the plates went in and out. Clearly *Burton Cutter* had to get back to port to carry out repairs, and quickly at that. To carry on into the Southern Ocean would be suicide. The welding of the stringers had been incomplete and the penetration of the welding insufficient. There were gaps in the plate welding and continuing in the race would have led to the destruction of the hull and the total loss of the yacht together with her crew.

It was as well that *Burton Cutter*'s joinery was incomplete as there was plenty of spare timber on board and with that Les Williams and his crew began to shore up the forward end of the boat to reduce the panting of the plates. All the while the pumps were used to get the water out and where possible the leaks were partially stemmed. Once the repairs were completed, *Burton Cutter* headed north for Port Elizabeth where she was immediately slipped for more permanent repairs. It was then Williams' intention to rejoin the race, but the firm hired to re-weld the stringers and plates in Port Elizabeth was not sufficiently experienced and the two or three day stop became prolonged. The South African Bureau of Standards inspectors refused to accept the workmanship and eventually the whole job was done three times before *Burton Cutter* could go back into the water. Rejoining leg 2 was out of the question, but her owners and sponsor did investigate the possibility of shipping the yacht to Sydney so that she could race in the last two legs, but with the fuel crisis in full spate the chances of that diminished until the decision was made to sail to Buenos Aires for the BA-Rio Race and join leg 4 to get home. The two legs on which *Burton Cutter* might well have excelled were denied to her by her welding defects.

Once in the westerly airstream the winds remain remarkably constant at least in direction, whilst the strength varies from strong to hurricane force. The seas, undisturbed by land masses at the bottom of the world, build themselves into awesome precipices and cavernous valleys. Peaks of water tower over the men on watch on a tiny fragile yacht daring to make passage across the Southern Oceans. These are seas that have no equal and they are capable of tossing a 70 foot ocean racer wherever they should want. The sea knows no master and commands respect. To trifle with the sea is courting disaster.

Rigs varied from boat to boat and on the force of the wind. Spinnakers were risked and storm kites held out until blown to shreds on some occasions. Aboard *Pen Duick VI* they encountered one storm of tempest strength with more than 50 knots of wind whilst the small spinnaker was set. A literal translation from one of her crew's log reads 'One spinnaker (the little one) does not resist. One after another all the sails burst.' In a violent squall the French ketch is laid flat with her vents in the water, flooding the main cabin and again the storm spinnaker cannot take it, but in Force 9, with jib boomed out, *Pen Duick VI* continues to go at more than 12 knots through the snowstorms. The all-out effort to keep on course is demanding of the man on the wheel and whilst a top class racing helmsman can, if necessary, keep it up all day, straying only 10 degrees off a dead downwind course, the boat sailing most efficiently, the less skilled helmsmen find it difficult enough to keep to within the 30–40 degrees-off band and so their boats sail greater distances. Twin boomed jibs prove adequate rig for some and ideal for the single masted boats who dare to drop the mainsail entirely. It would seem silly to use a rig designed for going to windward when sailing with the wind dead aft for days on end, but there is always the fear that if a man goes overboard, a yacht with twin boomed headsails will take longer to return in an effort to recover him.

The fleet encountered a strong southwesterly gale on the 19th–20th November. Winds gusted well above 50 knots and blew for most of the time in excess of 40. This gale caused the first tragedy of the race. On board *Tauranga*, Paola Chamaz was at the wheel with Paul Waterhouse, a British Army corporal who had sailed the first leg on *British Soldier*, and another crew member on watch. The yacht was

Typical Southern Ocean view from the cockpit of *Second Life*.

running under twin headsails, one boomed out to windward and the other set free. She was surfing fast down the faces of the waves, and making full use of the wind. Paul Waterhouse went below for a minute to light a cigarette and as he came back up into the cockpit, *Tauranga* broached. The alteration of course put the loose footed jib aback and broke the spinnaker boom at the mast end, so that the alloy pole thrashed around on the clew of the sail. Waterhouse rushed forward to get the sails under control and retrieve what was left of the spinnaker boom before it could do any major damage. As he made his way along the deck the yacht returned to her original course and the loose footed jib filled with a bang. As the sheets went taut they were under Waterhouse and threw him high in the air, dumped him back on deck and then pitched him overboard with a second surge of power.

Tauranga's skipper got sail off and searched under power for Waterhouse for 3–4 hours, but with little hope of success. In those latitudes (*Tauranga*'s approximate position was 44° S, 55° E at the time of the accident) Waterhouse had little chance of survival

for more than an hour and with mountainous seas running it would have been a miracle if he had been spotted. He must have been badly hurt by his fall on to the deck and since he made no effort to grab a lifeline when he came down, it is highly likely that he was unconscious when he went overboard and would have drowned instantly. The following day the news was known at Race Control in Portsmouth via the radio of *British Soldier*, who had monitored the lower power transmitter of *Tauranga*, when she broke the awful story. The news spread fast among the other yachts and a greater awareness of position reporting for safety reasons became apparent in the fleet.

The same gale took its toll elsewhere in the fleet. On *Great Britain II* skipper Chay Blyth was facing heavy problems. His crew effectiveness had been reduced by one. Four days out from Cape Town, Eddie Hope broke an arm. From radio contact with Dr Robin Leach aboard *Second Life* Blyth got instruction on how to set the arm in a cast of glass-fibre. Unfortunately, by using too much catalyst to harden the resin the exothermic reaction burned the skin of Hope's already broken arm. He was in great pain, yet Blyth was aware of the danger of giving him too many pain killing pills and Hope had great reserves of strength. He helped with maintainance below whenever he could, but every jar on his arm was added agony. Then in the gale the problems increased for *Great Britain II* and her crew. Already on this leg a spinnaker boom had broken and a spinnaker blown away and on November 19th there was a loud bang and the mizzen mast fell forwards, broken just above the deck. It had surprised a lot of people that there was no standing mizzen backstay on *Great Britain II* when they saw her in Vernon Creek at Portsmouth. With the mizzen went the main radio aerial and Blyth ditched the broken spar into the sea. Later another spinnaker boom broke and Blyth later blamed it all on bad seamanship. A modest gesture, but perhaps more correct if termed lack of racing experience. The courage and tenacity of his crew of paratroopers was never in doubt, but several had not been to sea before the project and none had any knowledge of ocean racing. Only Chay himself knew what to expect in these oceans and on his own admission he was no racing man. But as the race went on so the hard gained experience of *Great Britain II*'s crew began to be reflected in their results. With only a sloop rig they pressed their craft hard on this leg, determined to beat Tabarly to Sydney.

Others too were having problems in the fierce conditions. *Concorde* had rigging troubles, the tangs on her mast were pulling down. *Tauranga* lost a spreader and *33 Export* had minor difficulties. A spinnaker halyard parted on *Peter von Danzig*.

The seas were mesmerizing, their perspective lost and out of focus they became great mobile mountains. Crews developed new techniques as they came to terms with them. The boats developed personalities as they picked their ways over the crests and charged headlong through the troughs. The fears of hulls collapsing disappeared and yachts were raced hard.

On November 23rd the hand of death struck again. Dominique Guillet disappeared at 1620 GMT at latitude 45°S and longitude 81°E in heavy seas and wind Force 9 to 10. At 1610, in view of the proportions which the storm was assuming, Guillet and Millet, the two skippers of *33*

Export, decided to take down the foresail to replace it by a smaller one. During this manoeuvre in which Daniel Millet and Tom Addeson also took part they were hit by a big breaking wave which pushed the boat over to starboard. As he was thrown on to the shrouds of the mizzen mast, Millet had the impression that one of the three others was hurled away by the wave. When the boat righted herself he noticed that Dominique was missing. Addeson threw an illuminated buoy which was aft into the sea. Daniel and Jean-Pierre Millet lowered the sail and replaced it by a smaller one in order to turn around and return to the rescue buoy. Another sail was hoisted aft to help in this manoeuvre. The engine was switched on as the wind was increasing steadily. After 20–30 minutes conditions deteriorated rapidly; Millet was forced to take the decision to abandon the search in order not to endanger the boat and her crew. By then the boat was about 2 miles from the accident, in a dark night about 350 miles west of the Kerguelen Islands, and to return to the scene of the accident, had it been possible, would have taken one hour of sailing.

The day before this Dominique Guillet had spoken to the Millet brothers' father over the radio and reported his great excitement and enthusiasm for the race. He admitted that at times he and the crew were scared but they had a good boat and he believed an even more splendid crew. The loss of the ebullient Guillet, loved by all the competitors, struck home even harder to the crews of all the yachts the dangers they were facing. Notices reminding them of the need for harnesses were posted by companionways of several boats even though it was believed that Guillet was wearing his and it broke. The warning should not have been necessary but in no time at all its value was proved.

Almost exactly half way between Cape Town and Sydney *Sayula II* capsized. After two days of 55 to 65 knot winds the seas had built up to such a size that eventually a freak wave reared up and turned her over. Butch Dalrymple-Smith, on board *Sayula II*, recorded his thoughts soon after the incident while still at sea and these appeared in the Australian magazine *Modern Boating*.

'It is not possible to adequately put into words

LEG 1
Portsmouth to Cape Town
Handicap Distance 6650 miles

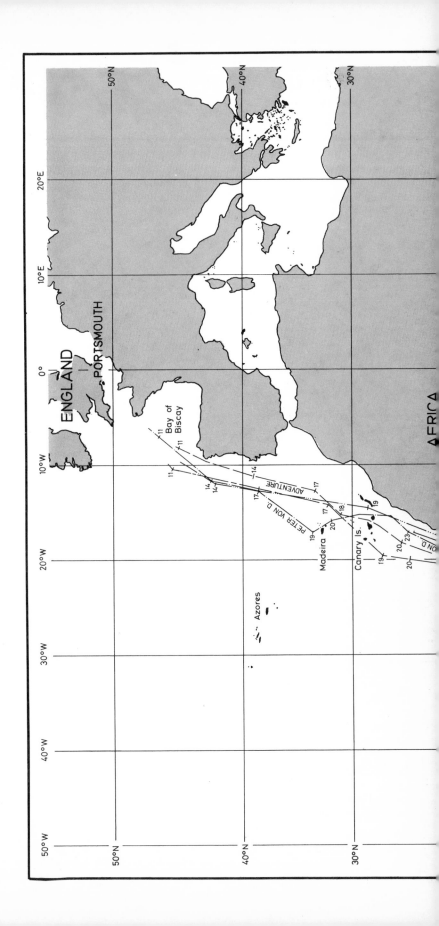

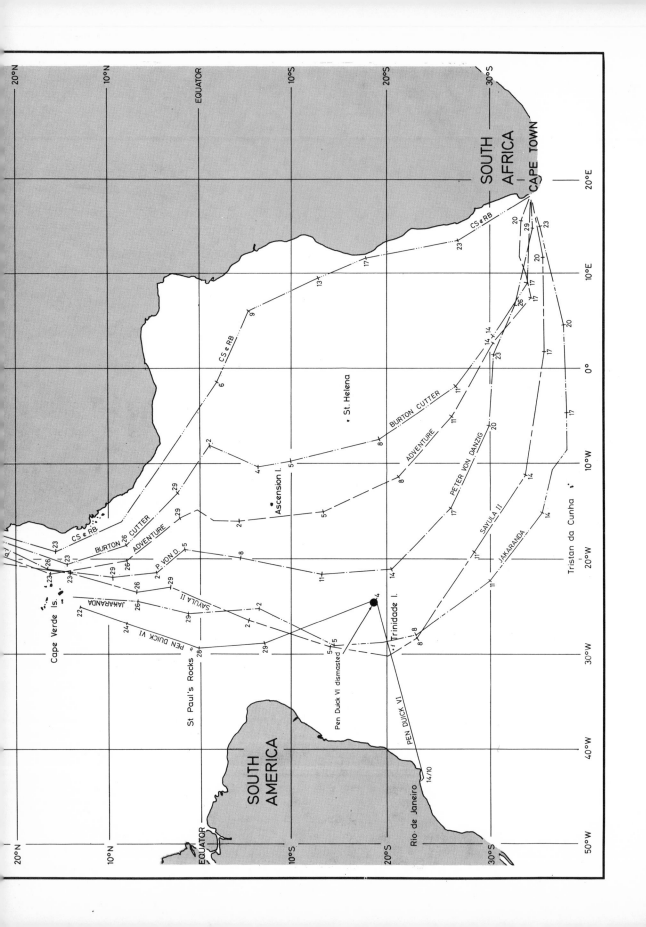

Well protected from the cold and spray, the helmsman of *Second Life* concentrates on keeping a steady course in strong winds somewhere in the Southern Ocean.

the feeling you get when your home and world turns from a comfortable microcosm of civilization into a wreck. In an instant the whole boat was in chaos. There was salad oil, jam and chicken noodle soup powder all over everything, four of five radios were put out of action and water flooded the bilges at a horrifying rate.

There's no bilge pump like a bucket in the hands of a frightened man. Even with an entire frightened crew it took four hours to get all the water out of the bilge and convince ourselves we weren't going to sink immediately.

When we took stock of the situation six of the crew were bashed around by the capsize enough to rule out watchkeeping in the immediate future, so the rest of us carried on cleaning up the shambles. It took us a day to get the boat in a state where we could sail again, but we weren't racing properly until a week later. For days after the crash, if the boat lurched on any sort of wave the crew went quiet and hung on tight for a moment, then slowly resumed conversation with sheepish glances all round.

At last we were sailing north again (north to Australia?). After being cold enough to believe we would never get truly warm again, one day we suddenly found heat in the sun and one by one the layers of clothes came off.'

A full description of *Sayula II*'s capsize with comments on the incident by Adlard Coles will be found in Chapter 10.

The gales persisted until nearly the end of the month and the batterings went on. *Grand Louis* lost spinnakers and so did her countryman *Pen Duick VI*. Personal logs reveal strange thoughts. From Alan Taphouse's, Tuesday November 20th on *Second Life*: 'I can drive a motor car again!' (his six month ban is up). 'Heard that Chay has broken his second spi pole – we are still catching him.' November 25th – 'Spent day repairing mainsail – a lot of stitching seems to be coming undone.' Meanwhile the boat log was noting 270 miles gone in a day. Tabarly's record run was 305 miles and bursts of 23 knots on the speedo!

Sayula's log is peppered with reminders to 'Wake Yvonne' and the salacious comment 'Conrady was seen on deck'. Cook and navigator were taking the butt of the crew's humour.

Guia went south of the Kerguelen Islands in an effort to stay closer to the great circle route and trim a few miles off the journey.

33 Export headed straight for Fremantle after Guillet's death. The shock to those on board was quite immeasurable. In the wake of the leaders the Polish boats *Copernicus* and *Otago* together with *Peter von Danzig* hung grimly on, nursed by their crews licking wounds in a couple of days of lightish winds.

The wind returned with added strength as the last month of 1973 began. The windspeed indicator went off the clock (maximum 60 knots) on *Second Life* and after pulling out a spinnaker halyard block and parting the halyard one day, *Adventure* discovered her steering failure on the next. She broached due to a lack of helm to hold her and her crew suspected that the stock was moving inside the rudder moulding. As the wind increased and returned to the west *Adventure* gave her helmsman a tricky time. To hold the 55 foot cutter on course the trim tab was used increasingly. Her problems were made more acute as this gale subsided, and whilst unreefing the main, the boom twisted and split into two. A total of 98 man hours went into its repair and two days later it was back in service; the same day that Tony Higham dived to inspect the rudder and discovered that he could move it for most of its travel without moving the stock. As the leaders approached Bass Strait the problems began again. *Pen Duick VI* was ahead but in the Strait was becalmed and then caught by two depressions with winds east and northeast, and as she crawled up the Australian east coast she was again becalmed. Averaging 4·5 knots was no use for *Pen Duick* whilst the middle-markers of the fleet were romping along in westerlies towards Bass Strait and good results on handicap. *Pen Duick VI* lacked sails and for several of the final days of this leg Patrick Phelipon was constantly at the sewing machine and Tabarly himself was working on them by hand in an effort to get more canvas on his spars.

Butch Dalrymple-Smith celebrated his birthday in the Bass Strait and in reply to a crew's query as to what he would like in the way of a present he unselfishly asked for a southerly for *Sayula II* to the finishing line. At the time she was screaming through the Strait that two years earlier one of her crewmen, Dave Bowen, had become the first to row. As she gybed off Gabo Island the southerly materialized and she carried her spinnaker to the finish and an overall win.

Tabarly was first across the line at Sydney Heads on December 7th and 10 hours later *Great Britain II* followed the Frenchman home. *Second Life* had her best passage and was third to finish. *Tauranga* had more problems before she finished. Short of the Bass Strait she had steering troubles and was forced to run off under reduced canvas whilst repairs were made. The effect was that she had to go south of Tasmania.

In Sydney it was pre-Christmas and holiday time, and things were slow to move. Customs and health clearance took a long time and as crews waited in the harbour, they drank and many a crew put his first foot on Australian soil not totally sober. *Great Britain II*'s crew threatened to get their own back for the way their 'Sail Para' had been altered in Cape Town to 'Sail Paralytic' by having car window stickers made saying 'Drink Navy and Fly Through the Heads'. There is no doubt that *Adventure*'s crew had earned their champagne when they arrived and for 48 hours few had had much sleep as they battled with light head winds and calms towards the finishing line. Only in the last 18 hours did they get some real wind to speed them on their way and in it they covered a creditable 150 miles passing *CS e RB* just before the finish.

The RANSA in Sydney extended its jetties with pontoons and opened its doors in welcome. Slipping too was made available, although everywhere was overloaded with the Southern Cross and Sydney-Hobart fleets in Rushcutters Bay at the nearby Cruising Yacht Club of Australia. *Second Life*'s party will remain in most memories as a highlight of the social scene and the generosity of Australians who took crews into their homes for Christmas was sincere and unforgettable.

Great Britain II photographed from the helicopter from HMS *Endurance* as she rounds the Horn.

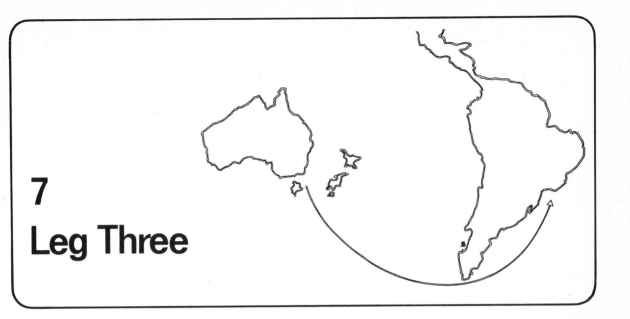

7
Leg Three

Long before they started in this race, it was the thought of Cape Horn that was the most daunting in the minds of the competitors. There was more than 4,000 miles of South Pacific Ocean to be crossed before it was reached, and if they were to be anything like the Roaring Forties of the previous leg there was every chance that this would be the telling leg. Even then there was a long way to go to the finish at Rio, but most would be happy to be in the South Atlantic tucked behind the thin finger of South America and away from the persistent gales of the Southern Oceans. Cape Horn has always been charismatic to seafaring men: its storms are fabulous. From the clipper ship days it has been held in awe. The single-handed circumnavigators have each had their say about it and the islands around it. Slocum in *Sailing Alone Around the World* wrote, 'Any landsman seeing the Milky Way [the rocks off Tierra del Fuego, northwest of Cape Horn] would have nightmares for a week.' About approaching it Chichester in *Gypsy Moth Circles the World* says 'I was as excited as a schoolboy at the end of term, waiting for the time to leave school.' He goes on to refer to it as 'the old Ogre'. Alec Rose in *My Lively Lady* writes 'I stood and stared at that great lump of land. This was it. This was the moment I had dreamed about and planned for. I thought of all the others who had

passed this way. Lone sailors as well as those in the great square riggers. I was just another one, looking with awed respect at this most feared of Capes.' After breaking out Aunt Aileen's fruit cake and splicing the mainbrace Robin Knox-Johnston wrote 'YIPEE' in his log shortly after rounding Cape Horn.

The great circle route goes deep inside the mean limits of the icebergs; Sydney and the Horn are on nearly opposite sides of the world. The pilot books make their recommendations but the favoured route seems to run south of the South Island of New Zealand and make for latitude 60° S at about 130° W and hold this latitude to 80°W to come up for the Horn. The passage to Rio is full of chance.

From Ocean Passages for the World

Route 1,260. Sydney to Cabo de Hornos (Cape Horn).

At all seasons and from whatever quarter the wind may blow, it is advisable on leaving Port Jackson to proceed to the southward rather than to the northward of New Zealand. Advantage therefore should be taken of the most favourable winds for either reaching the position in about lat. 48° 30′ S., between the Snares and Auckland isles, to join

Route 1,251 (a) or, if baffled by southerly winds and favoured by fine weather, the passage through Cook Strait may be taken with advantage, especially from October to February, joining Route 1,270 (2) from Wellington off that port.

See also Route 1,251 (b) for an alternative route passing southward of New Zealand.

Route 1,270. New Zealand to Cabo de Hornos (Cape Horn).

(2) From WELLINGTON OR COOK STRAIT – Join the Main route in long. 170° W.

(3) From PORT CHALMERS – Join the Main route at about the 180th meridian.

Route 1,251. Main Route across the Southern Ocean from South Africa to Cabo de Hornos (Cape Horn).

(a) *Usual route* – All seasons – Pass round the south end of New Zealand in about lat. 48° 30′ S, clear of The Snares (*Lat. 48° 01′ S, Long. 166° 36′ E*). From this point steer to the eastward between Bounty islands (*Lat. 47° 41′ S, Long. 179° 03′ E*) and Antipodes islands (*Lat. 49° 40′ S, Long. 178° 50′ E*), whence, inclining slightly to the southward, the route assumes, as a mean track, the parallel of 51° S from the meridian of 150° W, across the ocean to long. 120° W.; keeping at about 60 miles northward of this parallel from December to February (so as to be more clear of ice), and at 60 miles to the southward of it from June to August; but in this case, also, dependent on ice conditions. (*See* Note under (b), below.) From the meridian of 115° W, incline gradually to the southward, to round Islas Diego Ramirez and Cabo de Hornos (Cape Horn) (*see* Routes 1,375, 1,401 and 1,083 to 1,087, inclusive).

(b) *Alternative route* – Summer only – Some navigators take, during the summer months (December to February) a more southerly route from the position southward of Tasmania, so as to pass between Auckland islands and Campbell island in about lat. 52° S, and make the passage across the Pacific ocean in between lat. 54° and 55° S.

This course would, with a sea clear of ice, and favourable weather, doubtless ensure the quickest passage, as being the shorter distance, but experience has proved that at nearly all seasons of the year so much time is lost at night and in thick weather, and even serious danger incurred on account of the great

quantities of ice met with in these higher latitudes, that a parallel even as far north as 47 degrees has been adopted with advantage. Between this latter parallel and that of 50 degrees, it is believed the mariner will experience steadier winds, smoother water, absence of ice, and will probably make as short a passage, and certainly one in a more genial climate, and with more security, than in a higher latitude.

Note – The seaman in navigating this wide expanse of ocean, and also for rounding Cabo de Hornos, should be provided with the Ice chart of the Southern Hemisphere, No. 5032, published by the Admiralty, wherein he will find much useful information.

Route 1,083. Cabo de Hornos (Cape Horn) to the Channel.

(1) FROM THE PACIFIC TO THE ATLANTIC ROUND CABO DE HORNOS – Rounding the Horn from West to East is a comparatively easy matter, for the prevailing winds are favourable and the current sets strongly to the eastward as Cabo de Hornos itself is approached. The passage is usually made between lats. 56° and 57° S. to the northward of the route from the Atlantic ocean to the Pacific ocean (*see* Route 1,007 (8)); the current does not run strongly at 50 miles southward from Cabo de Hornos. December and January are the most favourable months; June and July, when easterly winds are not unusual, are the least favourable. August and September are months in which heavy westerly gales may be expected, with snow and hail.

Route 1,085. Cabo de Hornos (Cape Horn) to South American (East coast) ports.

At all times of the year, after rounding Cabo de Hornos, stand northward with the Falkland current between the Falkland islands and Tierra del Fuego, and carry it up the coast, with the prevailing westerly winds, to Bahia Blanca or Rio de La Plata.

From Rio de La Plata onwards to the northward, to Cabo Frio or Rio de Janeiro – see Route 1078.

Some frantic working by the crews during the holiday period in Sydney saw 15 boats get to the starting line inside the Harbour at 1800 local time, on Saturday December 29th. The re-start had twice been postponed. Originally, it had been intended to go soon after the Sydney–Hobart fleet on Boxing Day, but the race officers were advised against this and the extra three days gave a better chance for the crews of *Copernicus*, *Otago* and *Peter von Danzig* to complete their repairs and re-stock their boats with food and fuel. *Kriter* too had problems. The crack her crew had heard when she fell down a wave on the second leg was diagnosed when she went up on the slip in Rushcutters Bay. The skeg was split and it meant some round the clock working to put it in shape for the next leg. Four thick plates of stainless steel were bolted firmly across the split and the whole area glassfibred over for strength. *Peter von Danzig* made minor repairs to her wooden mast and the rigging attachment points. There were more serious mast repairs for *Otago*'s crew. She had been knocked down on December 6th and heeled over at 90–100 degrees. The mizzen mast was broken six feet above the deck, but they kept the top piece and in Sydney this was sleeved and welded after two feet had been cut out of it. The existing rigging was shortened to suit. All *Sayula II*'s minor damage was patched up. *Great Britain II* had a new mizzen and there was a host of new sails in lockers throughout the fleet. The sailmakers of Sydney had been kept busy with repairs and many of the crews had worked on their own in a hall that they hired. From the line-up at the second leg start, *33 Export* was missing. She arrived at Fremantle on December 7th and left again for Sydney eleven days later. There had been conflicting reports about her: some must have confused her for some reason with *Burton Cutter*. It was said at one time she would not do the third leg but go straight to Buenos Aires to do the BA-Rio Race and then join in again for the final leg. How she was to get to BA in time was never stated, but it would have been impossible under her own sails. She finally arrived in Sydney on January 2nd and left again on the 3rd.

The start was in light winds from the southeast and *Pen Duick VI* was first outside the Heads, but then came a period of flat calm. *Second Life* recorded nine miles only in the first six hours. There was a huge spectator fleet – the Sydneysiders are boating mad and only three days earlier they had filled the largest natural harbour in the world with small craft to see the Hobart fleet away. Now in their holiday period they turned out again to see this fleet begin its 8,370 mile race to Rio de Janeiro.

The majority headed south to round the South Island of New Zealand with only *Second Life* opting to chance the passage through Cook Strait, and for a couple of days it appeared that Roddie Ainslie's gamble might pay. Then the wind fell right away as they were forced to sail through a high pressure zone. Crewman Alan Taphouse recorded in his log of January 2nd 'We were becalmed all day – we seem to have made a monumental course error – the other boats are sailing fast in westerlies. Noon to noon distance 76 miles.' On January 5th, 'Becalmed again. We will be lucky to catch up our loss by Cape Horn. Noon to noon distance 40 miles.'

Second Life's problems after the start of the third leg were nothing compared with *Pen Duick VI*'s. Two hundred miles out of Sydney, her main mast crashed down yet again. For Tabarly it was a moment he must have dreaded for with that mast went his hopes of any further glory in the race. There would be no freighter aircraft winging its way to Sydney with a third mast inside, together with new rigging and sails, on this occasion. Now he was really up against it and his chances of making Rio in time for the start of the final leg depended on how fast he could mobilize the Sydney firms to get him under way again. Freddy Thomas and Graham Shields of Alspar, the Sydney metal mast makers, were in Hobart celebrating the success of their spars in the Sydney-Hobart when they heard of Tabarly's plight and caught the next available aircraft home to help.

There is no doubt that Tabarly was pressing *Pen Duick VI* hard when the mast came down, but the failure was due not solely to that. A stainless steel fitting holding the reaching stay failed and the compression of the spinnaker boom bent the mast back and broke it. Once again they were forced to cut everything and lose rigging, sails and fittings together with the spar. The metal of the fitting had failed. Perhaps another case of insufficient testing and sea trials before the race, but Tabarly's yacht left the builder's yard only a month before the start. Sailcloth and rigging were flown out from France, but sails had to be made up in Sydney and the crew went out to work to earn their keep for what became

The sight looking astern from *Peter von Danzig* as she rolled along in the Fifties in the southern Pacific Ocean on leg 3.

a more prolonged stay than they would have liked. The extra work in holiday time put an excessive load on the production in Alspar's factory. All the rigging terminals and mast construction had to be designed from scratch and there were alterations to be made to the boat itself. The Alspar mast was to be stepped on the keel and not on the deck like the two that had failed. Graham Shields argued that the gain in strength would more than compensate for the slightly smaller section that Alspar had immediately available. It wasn't until 1100 local time on Friday 5th that *Pen Duick VI* sailed from Sydney to rejoin the race. Tabarly's chances of making the re-start for leg 4 were slim, unless he could achieve a record breaking run and for that he needed luck and wind.

On board *Peter von Danzig* the pawls of a sheet winch slipped and the handle crashed against the foot of crewman Aki Müller-Deile. Several bones were broken and with no hesitation Reinhard Laucht, the skipper, set course for Bluff Harbour, New Zealand to put the injured man ashore. Whilst

there, the crew again repaired the lower jumper stay attachment points by tying them down with straps further down the mast.

The leaders were heading across the Tasman Sea when they met with a meteorological phenomenon of this area – a Southerly Buster. They were reaching with spinnakers and their only warning of the abrupt change of wind direction and the violent increase in strength along the front was a rapid drop in barometric pressure. It caught *Great Britain II* totally unawares and she lost both main and mizzen spinnakers as a result. *Sayula II* as well suffered damage to her sails when she encountered the full force of the Buster. She was carrying poled out Number 2 headsail, main, mizzen and the tallboy when the wind hit from ahead. By the time *Sayula II* had turned tail and fled, the headsail was a colander and 16 feet had blown out of the middle of the tallboy and disappeared into the sea 50 yards to leeward. It took two days to repair the number 2 and it contained 77 patches. The tallboy was repaired later, but had to be shortened because of

Peter von Danzig, with new spokes in her steering wheel after repairs in Sydney, in the Forties on leg 3.

lack of cloth. It contained the panel that bore the legend from Cape Town, 'Vanessa and Jill, we love you'. Tragedy was again to strike and this time it was on board *Great Britain II*. After they had weathered the early effects of the Southerly Buster, her crew had had a tough time, but had tried to make up for lost sleep. On January 7th at 0900 Blyth went on deck and decided that in the Force 5–6 winds they could cram on some more sail and called all hands. As the off watch crew went below Bernie Hosking was in the pulpit tidying up. He pulled at a sail tier caught in the forestay and it gave way suddenly. Hosking overbalanced and fell into the sea. John Rist, at the wheel, called 'man overboard' and the dan buoy was dropped overboard. There was a biggish sea running and getting the 72 foot ketch around to pick up a man was no easy business. Blyth and his crew made two triangular searches and during 2¼ hours only saw the dan buoy twice. They had no further sight of Hosking. In water temperature of 39°F. his chances of survival beyond one hour were slight; beyond two, nil. Hosking had been

overboard before, on the first leg, but then he was miraculously recovered at night. Now he was gone and his personal belongings were packed away by Alec Honey. Of the incident Chay Blyth wrote in his log 'Other yachts would have taken this harder or more emotionally. The reason it's not affecting us so much is that once again the training of the Paras comes out. You're steeled towards death. All of us in the yacht have seen active service, so have seen death before. This is more personal, but we keep our thoughts to ourselves. He will very rarely be mentioned now, more out of respect than anything else. Bernie was one of us. He wouldn't want it any other way.'

The next night and day Blyth described as 'fabulous sailing'. His men had rescheduled their watch routine to cover for their loss and were intent on being first in Rio. Their reason now was heightened: to do it as a tribute to their lost companion.

This long leg tested the crews more than any other psychologically, because of both its duration and the presence of the most feared landfall for

Peter von Danzig climbs up a sea under trysail as she battles her way towards the Horn.

sailors. In Rio stories were rampant of arguments, fights and even mutinies. It was said that one skipper ran amok with a gun and had to be tied up for a day. The truth of the stories can only be verified by the men who sailed and they disclosed nothing in being questioned; their loyalty to their shipmates came before all else. The cold in the high latitudes was an additional burden. One man wrote, 'it is monotonous and boring', another 'when it is cold, social life is dormant or dead. One comes in from the cockpit, little is said, one eats, one sleeps, one goes one degree only further than animal existence.' One of these who suffered disappointment wrote even more depressingly 'It [the race] is all about vanity, money and glory. I do not see what there is to gain from psychologically polluting such beautiful oceans.'

Psychologically polluted or not the South Pacific was kind. In the southern summer of 1974 it exacted no further toll of men. True the seas were big and the winds strong, but both lacked the fierce intensity that they had shown in the southern Indian Ocean.

The whales too were friendly: at least they were not antagonistic. Much thought before the race had gone into the way to deal with the problem of these giant aquatic mammals, such as what colour to paint the bottoms of the yachts and whether the echo sounder pulses would scare them off; whether or not guns should be carried or even hand grenades. On January 13th Captain George Vallings and the crew of *Adventure* sighted three which they 'identified' somewhat uncertainly as killer whales. Later the graffiti on the heads door finally laid any suspicion to rest. 'If the skipper says they were killer whales, then they Bloody well were killer whales.'

At this time they and most of the others were on the fringes of the ice field. The air and sea temperatures were constantly between 1 and 2° C. The icebergs varied in size from those 500 feet high and a mile across to small chips small enough to be described by the crew of *Grand Louis* as 'fit for a whisky glass'. The small dangerous 'growlers', which if hit by a yacht might surely have holed the hull, were always found to leeward of the large

First yacht round Cape Horn was Chay Blyth's *Great Britain II* on January 23rd, 26 days out from Sydney. She is photographed here with HMS *Endurance* from the Antarctic patrol ship's helicopter.

bergs and reasonably close to them. By staying upwind of the big icebergs the yachts were able to stay out of trouble. Even in the dark of the short Antarctic summer nights the big bergs were readily visible. But this was only because the weather remained fine whilst the fleet was in this area. Had it worsened the yachts would have had to head to the north away from the ice and give themselves further to sail.

The weather pattern in the South Pacific around the 60th parallel is of predominantly westerly winds, but these are affected by a series of depressions which pass below this parallel from west to east. The strong westerlies are above the depressions whilst below runs the full gamut of northeasterly, easterly and southeasterly gales. In January these depressions were further north than usual and brought comments of despair from crewmen who considered it unfair to monkey with God's holy ordinance in this way. They had all been reliably informed that this was a downwind passage, and whilst they had had plenty of that on the last leg,

they felt robbed of another terrifying downhill slide on waterborne toboggans.

Adventure followed close to the 60th parallel for 12 days and during that time her log shows that the wind was aft of the beam for 26 hours only. It was during this time that she had more steering trouble and was forced to use the emergency tiller on two occasions while new pins were put in the upper bevel box – the first one sheared.

Alain Colas in the 75 foot trimaran *Manureva*, sailing singlehanded around the world close to this racing fleet, had on board a facsimile machine for recording weather charts and the information from this he was radioing to the yachts in the race. First it went to the French who translated it and relayed the vital information to the others. The unified spirit that had begun with the deaths on the second leg and the agreed need to let everyone know one's own position in case of emergency, had now developed further. At the start of this race the idea of releasing details of a yacht's position and the weather it was enjoying had been totally foreign to all the skippers.

Kriter rounding Cape Horn on 26th January 1974.

The Royal Navy's ice patrol ship HMS *Endurance* was off Cape Horn in readiness for the fleet, keeping a watchful eye and relaying messages to and from the crews. She gave each yacht a suitable reception and her presence eased the minds of many. Some, however, felt cheated. They felt let down that at this milestone of their yachting life, they should be wet-nursed. It was only a temporary thought, because they all realized the efforts that were being made on their behalf.

After being becalmed for two days just out from the Horn, *Great Britain II* was the first to round. Majestically running with her red, white and blue spinnaker and mainsail set the big ketch gave *Endurance* a tough time steaming full out to catch her. Chay's maroon hulled boat was exceeding 10 knots as he passed Cape Horn for the second time in his life. He recorded then that one each way was enough for a life time and concluded 'That's my lot.' It was January 23rd – 26 days' sailing from Sydney.

Three days later *Sayula II* appeared at the Horn in sunshine, and to the accompaniment of 'La Cucuracha' and the 'Mexican Hat Dance' from *Endurance*, sped on her way to the South Atlantic. Her crew responded to the music by dancing a tango on the cabin top. Three hours later came *Kriter*. She too was flying along at 10 knots under a Number 3 genoa, sometimes peaking 15 knots. The crew tried to hoist a storm spinnaker, but the Force 9 gusts were too much so they boomed out the genoa instead. Alain Gliksman, her skipper, navigator and tactician, took her within 600 yards of the Cape, happy that he was some 28 hours ahead of his great rival André Viant in *Grand Louis*.

Disaster very nearly overtook the French schooner as she closed Cape Horn. In bad weather she had been well to the south and had only sighted the rock-bound island of Diego Ramirez when it was two miles away and straight in front of her.

Close behind came *Adventure* and when she was seen by HMS *Endurance* she was 'driving along under heavily reefed main, a small staysail and spitfire jib, shearing wildly in the confused water on the crests of waves and sometimes catching a bursting top, sending sheets of spray as high as the masthead'. The next morning she was 15 miles east of Cape Horn, rocking gently in calm water and 2 knots of breeze after rounding at dawn on January 28th. From *Endurance* came a seven gun salute; the wadding of the sixth blasting a hole in *Adventure*'s Number 1 jib topsail.

Within sight of Cape Horn at 0200 on January 30th *Second Life* was knocked flat by a 60 knot gust. The clew of the Number 2 genoa parted and the boat came upright. For her the wind was very variable, light then gusty. The next day she was becalmed and Alan Taphouse comments 'This is billed as the roughest piece of water in the world?!' Then came *Tauranga* and *British Soldier* and a day later *Guia*. The Italian sloop was short of water and headed straight for Port Stanley in the Falkland Islands to pick up this and other stores. Whilst there her skipper bought a whole sheep for three dollars. They lost 12 hours in this manoevre, having to stand off in bad weather before entering the harbour.

Peter von Danzig was next, the 1936 yawl rolling heavily in a lumpy swell under mainsail and jib. She was laid flat in one series of squalls. *CS e RB* rounded later in the day with only the two Polish boats, *Otago* and *Copernicus*, behind.

The rest of the leg to Rio was relatively incident free. *Great Britain II* gained line honours for the first time on February 7th. On the previous evening the denizens of the mizzen cabin of *Second Life* invited the rest of the crew for a cocktail party in their cabin. A written invitation was posted and the crew dressed for the party. Wendy Hinds put on make-up for the first time since Sydney and was escorted to the party leaving a special dinner in the oven. It started at 1830 and went on till 2200 except for a break at 1900 to hand the starcut spinnaker. Despite the hilarity, *Second Life* recorded the fastest passage from Cape Horn to Rio de Janeiro of any yacht in the race. Her skipper must regret his decision to go through Cook Strait.

Sayula II spent six hours covering the last mile to the finishing line at Rio. It proved her undoing in the leg since she was beaten for first place on corrected time by *Adventure* by $5\frac{1}{2}$ hours. The longest leg provided the closest finish.

The luxury of the Iate Clube do Rio nearly proved some crews' undoing. They spoke of Rio as a place that rots ships and men. Hot weather, cold beer, attractive señoritas and the Mardi Gras contributed to make the stop-over almost as energetic as the leg itself. Some crews had minor scrapes with authority, but nothing that a well slipped backhander couldn't sort out. Even the four 'skinny dippers' who took their air hostess girl friends swimming late at night from Ipanema beach got themselves out of goal with a few cruzeiros.

The repairs to boats and sails took time. Keith Lorence set up trade as a sailmaker on the Yacht Club's ballroom floor, as there were no sailmakers in Rio capable of dealing with the problems. His work didn't stop only on *Sayula II*'s sails, but he also worked on those of *Great Britain II* and *33 Export*. Blyth's yacht had a lot of necessary repairs. One of her coffee-grinder winches had packed up, the deck had sunk in two places and down below there were bulkheads shattered by compression loads. In the last fortnight of the leg she leaked 20 gallons an hour. The crew worked hard to put it right before the re-start.

Kriter fitted her 'Gliksman flap' designed by Alain in conjunction with Brenneur to lengthen the boat aft by 30 cm to increase the hull speed and alter the effect of the stern wave, without increasing the yacht's rating. *Grand Louis*' rating was reduced from 44·5 to 43·4 because of a wrong original interpretation of the recovery surface between the two masts – 50% instead of 35%.

As the yachts prepared for the staggered restart Tabarly and *Pen Duick VI* were still at sea and there seemed no hope of them getting to Rio in time to join the final leg. And so it proved. Before he had arrived Tabarly knew the meaning of Rio's most popular word – *mañana*.

Guia, owned by Italian Giorgio Falck, flying a spinnaker acquired from *Ginkgo*, which Falck bought at the end of the 1973 Admiral's Cup Series, as she approaches the finish.

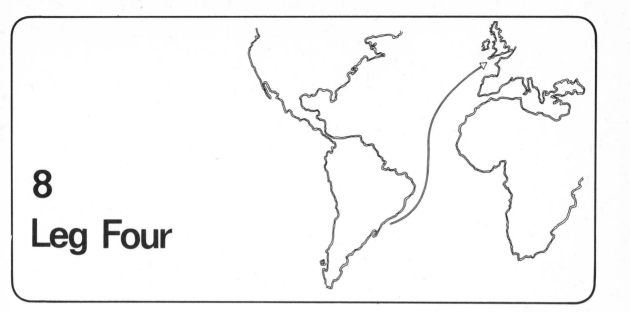

8
Leg Four

Fiesta time in Rio at the end of the longest leg of the race and one which included the rounding of the dreaded Cape Horn may well have been one of the things the crews looked forward to before the event began, and its memory will linger long in their minds whenever they think back to the race, but by the time of the re-start all were more than ready to leave. Most had altered during the past six months and they were more than ever aware of being competitors in a race rather than pleasure sailors on a cruise. The waiting they disliked, and whilst every effort was made to make them welcome ashore in the Iate Clube and in private homes, the need to go again was evident everywhere.

From: *Ocean Passages for the World*
Route 1,076. Rio de Janeiro to Europe or North America

Make first a stretch to the south-eastward to about long. 35°W, and then stand northward, in the SE Trade, crossing the Equator between 27° and 32°W; and after passing through the Doldrums, steer direct for American ports, or to the north-westward, and westward of the Arquipélago dos Açôres (Azores), if bound to European ports.

The re-start was planned in four groups spaced over six days. It was a decision that was not popular with the competitors who argued that it could easily lead to some yachts getting different weather patterns which would make nonsense of the handicaps. *Sayula II*'s crew were happy when they thought they were starting at the same time as *Adventure*, but horrified when they learned that they were to start two days after their principal rival. They felt that if they started together, with the time they had in hand, they had only to stay near *Adventure* to win, but if the Royal Navy's cutter picked up some breeze in the first week of the leg while *Sayula II* lay perhaps becalmed off Rio, then all the hard earned advantage they had accrued would be spread across the water and the race would take the form of a lottery. The reason for the staggered re-start was simple. The Race Committee were attempting to eliminate the lengthy time lapse between the arrival of the leaders in Portsmouth and the finish of the smaller, slower yachts. Part of this reason must have been so that the publicity value of the race did not deteriorate. It did provide two great climaxes with the separate arrivals of the first boat home and the overall winner. Pressure from the skippers of the bigger boats did however reduce their leeway by one day and *Great Britain II*, *Pen Duick VI* and

The Royal Navy's Nicholson 55 *Adventure* leaving Rio. Prior to the start of the last leg she put in six or eight hours training each day.

Burton Cutter were scheduled to start only one day after *Sayula II*, *Second Life* and *Kriter*, which left Rio on March 10th. The biggest group containing *Adventure, British Soldier, 33 Export, Tauranga, Guia, Pen Duick III* (which had joined the fleet for this leg only), *CS e RB* and *Grand Louis* left Rio on March 8th and the 'babies', *Peter von Danzig, Copernicus* and *Otago*, two days before them. The pilot book is terse and written for square riggers, but much of what it says makes sense except for the early stretch to the southeastward. The boats expected light headwinds to start this leg and got them. With an adverse current they were kept pinned inshore, and it was a long beat so progress was slow. *Second Life*'s first five days' progress from her log read 74, 96, 114, 90 and 80 miles. She had done that much in two days on the second leg in the southern Indian Ocean regularly. Few can have suspected how long the work to windward would persist; once clear of the Azores and its associated area of high pressure the southwesterly winds should have prevailed, but that was not to be.

Up the Brazilian coastline *Adventure* enjoyed the windward work. Her cutter rig was designed for it and her skipper Roy Mullender had been happy to see the two-masted boats sagging off to leeward after the start, where *Adventure* had made the best showing. In Mullender's own words 'There didn't seem to be any other dinghy racers on the start line so we came out of that well.' But it wasn't regular, consistent winds that the skippers had to deal with: they varied in strength with sharp squalls whipping the sea into white foam and causing crews to reef the yachts heavily, down to periods of near calm where every mile gained was more than usually earned by constant concentration and trimming sheets in much the same way as crews would on an afternoon race around the buoys. Whichever way it was hard. Downwind sailing at least keeps yachts relatively level, but with 20 degrees of heel and a pitching, slamming motion, life on board becomes unpleasant. Keep it up for days on end and the unpleasantness turns to irritation and this coupled with boredom can break down crew morale fast. Racing crews how-

LEG 4
Rio de Janeiro to Portsmouth

Handicap Distance 5500 miles

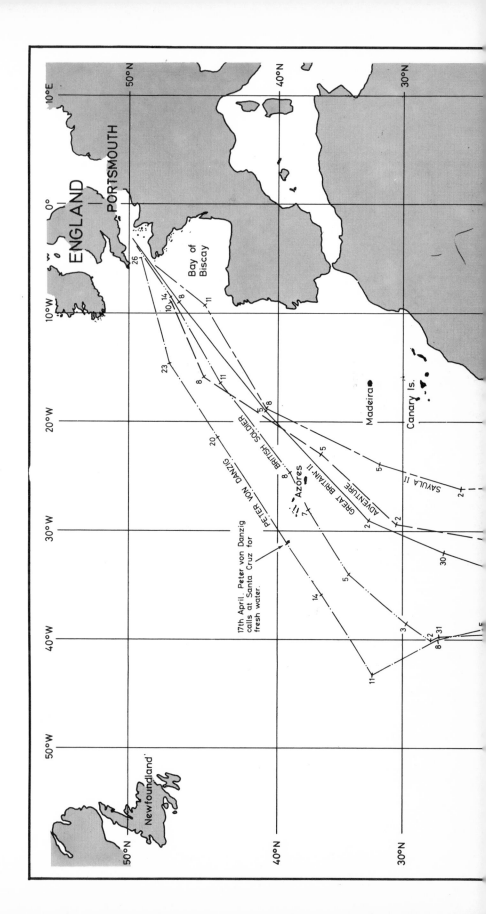

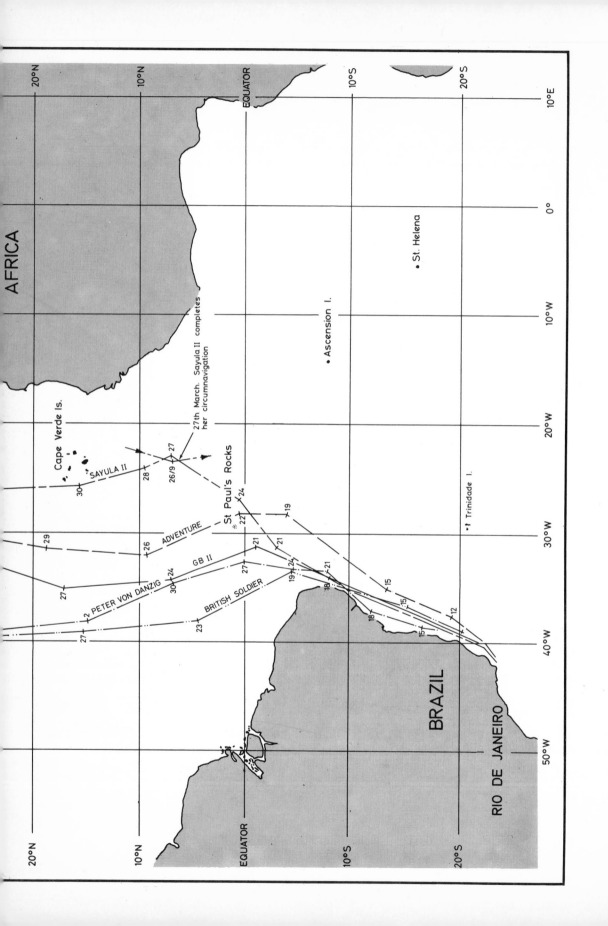

AFRICA

20°N

10°N

EQUATOR

10°S

20°S

10°E

0°

10°W

20°W

30°W

40°W

50°W

Cape Verde Is.

SAYULA II

St. Helena

Ascension I.

Trinidade I.

St Paul's Rocks

ADVENTURE

GB II

PETER VON DANZIG

BRITISH SOLDIER

27th March. Sayula II completes
her circumnavigation

30
28
26/9 27
27

29
26
24 30
27
24

27
2
23

27
27
21
27
24
19
21
21

22 24
19
18 21
15
18
15
15
12

BRAZIL

RIO DE JANEIRO

20°N

10°N

EQUATOR

10°S

20°S

20°W

10°W

0°

10°E

Part of the vast armada at the start. *GB II* has got the weather berth on *Pen Duick VI*.   *Paris Match-Garwood*

Burton Cutter–destined to complete only the first and last legs.   *Aquapics-Fisher*

(Top) A well worn Oliver Stern Veyrin ashore when *Trente Trois Export* finished
(Bottom) – and the scenes around her with welcoming friends.   *Aquapics-Fisher*

Chay Blyth and his crew relaxed on deck as *GB II* 'homes' up the Solent. *Aquapics-Fisher*

Adventure displays her efficient cutter rig as she slips to windward.

Only a few more yards to home for *British Soldier*.   *Aquapics-Fisher*

Sayula II's 'navigatorium'.   *Aquapics-Lorence*

Butch Dalrymple-Smith comes back along *Sayula II*'s foredeck after a routine check.   *Aquapics-Lorence*

Guia after 27,500 miles and still her crew are nursing every fraction of a knot.   *Aquapics-Fisher*

(Top) *Sayula II* in the Solent under short canvas. Note the doubled-up forestay.   *Aquapics-Fisher*

(Bottom) *Kriter* with the end in sight – FIN on the stern with its last leg extension.   *Aquapics-Fisher*

Sayula II – on watch in the South Pacific Ocean. *Aquapics-Lorence*

(Top) The 'Cowboys' of *Second Life* in Sydney.   *Aquapics-Fisher*

(Bottom) *Peter Von Danzig* drying out after the second leg.   *Aquapics-Fisher*

Second Life hard on the wind on the way home. *Robin Leach*

(Top) The Southern Oceans on *Sayula II*. On deck with a white bow wave.
(Bottom) Down below–stereo headphones and a letter home. *Aquapics-Fisher*

When the wind heads, the spinnaker has to come down. *Aquapics-Lorence*

A happy Ramon Carlin and a much relieved wife, Paquita, now the race is over.   *Aquapics-Fisher*

After days of light winds at the beginning of leg 4 the boats finally picked up the Northeast Trades. Here *Peter von Danzig* drives to windward under trysail in a Force 7–8.

ever revelled in the windward work of the Trade Wind belts where 180 miles a day was commonplace, but getting to them proved problematic.

Working north from Rio up the coastline was a case of taking the most favourable tack and holding it, keeping within 50 miles of the shore and making for Cape Frio. James Myatt, skipper of *British Soldier*, elected to work the counter-current close inshore and this tactic paid him quite handsomely. It was risky as the winds there are far less reliable than they are offshore and even there they flick around frequently.

The ocean does have its hazards and one of them fell in the path of the race. The Arg dos Abrolhus is a patch of shallows 400 miles from Rio and some 40 miles offshore. For many of the fleet its light was the last contact with land until the English coastline and from then on knowledge of their whereabouts depended entirely on astro-navigation. The SE Trades didn't really materialize and so progress was slow. Earlier the winds at least were predictable. On March 15th, seven days out from Rio, *British Soldier* signalled Race Control that 'Every day the weather is about the same – the wind changes direction at

1000 and 2300 and it gets very strong around 1800.'

To win the race *Adventure* had to beat *Sayula II* home by 3½ days, and the Mexican yacht had nearly all the advantages, starting two days behind the Royal Navy's boat. She had only to follow *Adventure*'s track in order to get much the same weather and both Roy Mullender and Ramon Carlin were aware of this. The position reports were now twice weekly and there had been a move to make the yachts report daily. This would certainly have handed the tactical advantage to *Sayula II* and made life easy for her crew. As it was *Sayula II* scorned the easy way out and sailed her own race taking the most easterly track of them all. *Grand Louis* went to the east as well but not as far as *Sayula II* whose navigator, Ray Conrady, was using the morse weather information in an attempt to skirt the Azores high and avoid the calm associated with it.

The NE Trades north of the Equator were steady and progress in them was good for everyone. The two biggest boats, *Great Britain II* and *Burton Cutter*, seemed set for a ding-dong tussle on this leg. Blyth and his paratroopers were beginning to get the maximum performance from the Gurney designed ketch. On each leg they had improved although the boat had begun to leak and they were short handed. They weren't giving away a thing and had they had the boat earlier and got some experience of driving it to its limit before the race began, the outcome might well have been different. Blyth's aim was to be first home. For him this race was another adventure challenge and to pay for it he had to get the publicity. And whilst the public as a whole would be aware that he hadn't won the race even if he did get to Portsmouth before all the others, the publicity would be as good as if he had. It must have been a great stimulus to Blyth.

The race for Leslie Williams had been a disappointment. *Burton Cutter* had let him down after his line honours victory on the first leg. She wasn't strong enough, but Williams wanted to do battle with his old rival Blyth and rejoining the race for the final leg gave him the chance. He too had a publicity problem. The £10,000 provided by Burton Menswear provided Williams with a moral obligation to do well. To get back to England first would provide crew and sponsors with a sop to cover the

disappointment of not completing the whole course.

Burton Cutter's challenge petered out in two separate days of flat calm, neither of which her rival had to endure. This was early in the leg and put *Burton Cutter* 300 miles astern of *Great Britain II*, a position from which *Burton Cutter* had little chance of recovery. Williams had other handicaps. The bow plating was still suspect and he was not able to drive the ketch hard into head seas without the risk of further damage. He planned because of this and the rig configuration to sail the boat free making the best speed with a mizzen staysail set. On a leg which became mostly closehauled the course forced on Williams gave him little chance.

Great Britain II, for once, was getting her fair share of luck. She still had her leaking problems however and pumping her was a regular watch change occurrence. The strains on the big ketch were more than her builders had allowed for. It was the first monohull of this size they had handled and even the architect Alan Gurney may have had his doubts about her construction in foam sandwich where tying in bulkheads and stringers is more difficult than with normal glassfibre construction. Her working was allowing water in around the keel bolts and the extra effort of pumping her dry was strength sapping for Blyth and his short-handed crew. Perhaps only men with the fitness and determination of the paratroopers could have managed to keep up the pressure. Blyth's statement before the start 'I'm only concerned about line honours. If we're first across that line in Portsmouth, in the shortest real time, that will be my kind of victory' was the goad and now the breaks were beginning to go the way of the deep-red hulled boat. Just for once the area of high pressure which normally remains constant over the Azores was forced northwestwards almost to Newfoundland. *Great Britain II*'s path would have taken her through the 'high' and its associated calm weather, but Blyth had luck on his side. It enabled him to stay well out to the west at the Equator, crossing it around longitude 34° W, in order to take advantage of the southwesterly winds of the North Atlantic and romp home with sheets eased.

Sayula II was meantime well to the east, a course that would have stood her well in the northeasterly

The handicap winner, *Sayula II* sailing close-hauled through the Solent as she approaches the finish on Easter Sunday.

winds associated on that side of the Azores high and she lost out when the high pressure area migrated. Roy Mullender on *Adventure* was faced with a problem of race tactics. His aim had been to cross the Equator to the east of St Paul's Rocks (01° 00′N, 29°25′W). On March 15th *Adventure*'s position report, known to the entire fleet, put her on the usual route past Salvador (around 13°S 35°W). Roy needed to go east but not to let the others know just what he was about. No one was likely to let *Adventure* get away with anything on this leg. They had seen what had happened on the first leg and there was going to be no repeat of that. *Sayula II* and *Grand Louis* would never let *Adventure* run loose again. Three days later when *Adventure* next reported her position she had made a lot of easting despite running into the light variable winds, mostly from the north, of the Doldrums. Her move brought comment from *Grand Louis* on the radio hook-up. '*Adventure*, you are doing something very strange.... I think you are being clever perhaps.' These two sentences put the rest of the competitors on their mettle as to Mullender's tac-

tics and his principal rivals were quick to exploit the idea. Around this time Blyth was having trouble with the radio receiver on *Great Britain II* and whilst calling for someone to 'come in please' did not disclose his position 'blind' as other yachts had done when their receivers had failed. It caused him to be dubbed 'Shy Blyth' by the crew of *Adventure*.

When the positions of March 22nd came through, *Grand Louis* had done something to cover the easterly progress of *Adventure*. She was only 30 miles northwest of *Adventure* and also east of St Paul's Rocks. The report from *Sayula II* put her in the wake of these two, about 150 miles astern, but subsequently it was proved that she was quite a bit further east, and once north of the Equator she went the furthest east of the entire fleet. The winds were fickle. The same hour's run on two consecutive days could be $\frac{1}{2}$ mile and 10 miles. The NE Trades were anything but steady although they showed less variability than the southeasterlies on the south side of the Equator. Skippers spent their time ensuring that they were on the most favourable tack in their northerly passage to the Azores. *33 Export* was leading the fleet although she had stayed up to the west at the Equator on the same track that *Great Britain II* and *Burton Cutter* were to take behind her.

Back at Rio, Eric Tabarly arrived with *Pen Duick VI* after a 39 day passage from Sydney on the night of March 16th and the next day he told representatives of Associated Press that he was retiring from the race. He never did in fact complete his declaration form for the third leg. *Pen Duick VI* put to sea however in pursuit of the fleet on March 21st, but it was a disappointed Tabarly in charge. The pressure on the Frenchman to go on was great, yet his subsequent withdrawal into Brest, caused by 'mast troubles', showed that his heart was no longer in the race. He had already begun to formulate his plan of attack for the one-stop round the world race in 1975 and he was entering *Pen Duick VI* in the Newport-Bermuda Race in June.

It had always been difficult for Zygfryd Perlicki on *Copernicus* to relay his yacht's position. The Polish skipper had problems with his Marconi Falcon II set which was identical to that on *Otago*, whose skipper, Zdzislaw Pienkawa, also found problems in communication. Condensation caused failure, generally intermittent, but sufficient to keep their reports out of the lists on most occasions. When on March 20th there had been nothing heard of *Copernicus* since she had left Rio, a request went into Lloyds for shipping to keep a special look out and report any sighting. It wasn't until April 7th that she was sighted. Then the P & O ship *Paiko* reported her 28°23'N 29°20'W with yacht and crew in excellent condition.

For her 34 days of this leg *Sayula II* spent all but two closehauled. Further to the east, she passed close to the Cape Verdes, tactics which did not seem to pay as well as *Adventure*'s who passed close to the east of the Azores. She at least had her spinnaker up at times. On April 4th with about 1600 miles to go to the finish *Adventure* was becalmed for six hours but then began to make progress in the right direction using the working spinnaker set shy. After 12 hours and 100 miles of travel she had to hand it for a star-cut used as a storm spinnaker and was surfing at over 9 knots. At this time Keith Richardson went up the mast in a bosun's chair to retrieve a halyard tail

and came down claiming that for thrills his trip had any funfair machine licked. The rolling of the boat and the surges in the surfing conditions must have made his masthead excursion more than thrilling. From the Azores to Ushant paths began to converge. *Sayula II* was hampered by rigging problems and kept her secret from her rivals. A routine examination of her masthead gear revealed that two strands of her 1 × 19 stainless forestay had fractured close to the terminal and so her rigger, Butch Dalrymple-Smith, fitted a doubler. The only wire at his disposal was a spare main halyard and so he used this doubled to take the shock loads off the forestay in an attempt to prevent any more strands parting. The jibs were still hanked to the 1 × 19 wire stay. It did the trick, but only just. By the time she finished 5 of the 19 strands had gone and others were going in the backstay and runners.

It was a symptom not unknown elsewhere. *Tauranga* and *Second Life* had similar problems. The work hardening of the metal strands forced their skippers to ease up on the last lap. Like them, *Sayula II* had to pace her race. In fair winds the tension and shock loads on the forestay would be lighter but in headwinds of any strength use of the big headsails would be precluded. And for her the wind came from ahead nearly all the time. Her crew worked hard to get the most from her in the lighter winds and nursed her through the strong ones as they prayed the rig would hold together. It needed all their seamanship and anticipating the line squalls was of paramount importance. If they had been caught by one similar to that encountered in the Tasman Sea shortly after the start of the third leg, their race could have been prematurely ended with the prize almost in their grasp.

Kriter, despite the alterations to her stern, never seemed to get in touch with the others on the final leg. She lost out in the early lighter winds off the Brazilian coast and never managed to get back in the hunt. She followed a mid-fleet course but caught all the bad luck. Once it begins to go against a boat it follows a cyclic pattern and getting to the right side of wind shifts in any race once one bad one has made its mark is a hazard with which every racing skipper will be familiar. Similarly those who get

The French *33 Export* fighting through choppy seas a few miles from the finishing line.

the first one right seem to be rewarded throughout the race. Luck goes hand in hand with the skill in this sport, but even the best have to suffer on occasion.

Once north of Ushant the competitors considered themselves in home waters but for the leaders there were light northeasterly winds to face – right on the nose for the last leg to the line. But the humour began to improve and the enquiries into Race Control began to escalate as the days went by. There was one from Buckingham Palace to ask for an ETA for *Great Britain II*, a family interest no doubt in the yacht which Princess Anne had launched and from which a cable on her wedding day went out requesting Mark Philips as a substitute helmsman. On the same day, far out at sea from the boat in which Blyth completed his solo circumnavigation, came another cable to Sir Samuel Whitbread. It combined gratitude, pathos and patriotism. 'From *British Soldier* – regret your super beer finished at 34°N 34°W. Thank you for it and a splendid race. Rule Britannia.' At the time *British Soldier* was slogging into a NNE gale and had blown out her

Number 3 genoa. The day before she had reported a northerly wind of 10 knots with a calm sea and no swell. For all it varied every day.

Spotter aircraft began to fly on April 8th. As an excercise, finding a tiny yacht in the middle of the ocean must be a superb test. The RAF at St Mawgan put up a Nimrod reconnaisance plane to find Chay Blyth's *Great Britain II* in the morning and by 1400 radioed that under 8/10ths cloud at 900 feet with visibility down to one mile they had found *Great Britain II* sailing a course of 110° at a speed of 6·5 knots at 47° 44N, 09° 19W, into a northeasterly wind closehauled. On shore the pundits calculated her arrival and felt certain that nothing could stop Blyth's main objective of carrying off line honours.

The Navy's eyes were peeled for *Adventure*. Around HMS Vernon members of her crew from other legs began to gather to welcome her home and her daily reports began to tell her story of being hard on the wind in variable northeasterlies – the same sort of winds which Blyth was getting. Right down the Western Approaches the unusual weather seemed set for days.

By April 9th *Great Britain II* was down to 3 knots only on a course of 020° but she hadn't far to go. Two days later at 0900 she was only 40 miles from the finish. She was approaching the eastern Solent in light easterlies with her red, white and blue spinnaker just drawing. The press of spectator boats around her grew visibly as she headed for the finishing line. There were shouted interviews from news hungry pressmen and waves from wives and sweethearts of the crew. Paradoxically by coming home on Maundy Thursday, Blyth did himself a minor disservice. Publicity was one of his principal aims and Good Friday is one of the three days a year that newspapers are not printed. But he would get the lion's share and there can be no doubting the sincerity of the welcome that he received when he crossed the line at 1330. An open day at HMS Vernon allowed the public in to cheer the crew into their berth. The dispassionate air of the paratroopers in what must have been an awe-inspiring hour as they docked and cleared the authorities, was a tribute to their training. For them it was another job done and done well. The reward for Blyth came fast. Jack Hayward who had financed the major part of the project for *Great Britain II* promptly made a present of the yacht to her skipper. A hundred and forty-four days at sea put *Great Britain II*'s performance close to the record runs of the old clipper ships, and while it is unfair to compare the two, it goes to show perhaps just how good the seamen of a hundred years ago or more were in getting their craft to sail. They had no efficient way of going to windward but had to chase the favourable winds all over the oceans when headwinds threatened.

The second place in the race for home proved to be a close affair when later on the day that Blyth finished, *33 Export* signalled that she was 30 miles from the Lizard with 200 left to go and had just passed *Adventure*, two miles away. On board the Navy's yacht they had heard of Blyth's arrival and knew that they could beat him on handicap for the leg and had begun to feel elated. Then they spotted *33 Export* with a spinnaker up like themselves, but couldn't identify her at the range. Suddenly both yachts were headed by the breeze and with the speed that the spinnaker came down on the white ketch, the *Adventure* crew knew she was no cruising boat. When they closed a little, Roy Mullender, through binoculars, knew from her slab-sided hull exactly which boat he was up against and the race was on all over again. *Adventure* chose a starboard tack which took her straight for Anvil Point. *33 Export* opted to go offshore on port.

The sighting had put new life into *Adventure*'s crew. They knew that their rival for the principal honours in this race, *Sayula II*, was 160 miles astern and barring accidents was set to take the Whitbread Trophy. They now knew however that she was suffering from severe rigging problems and they were in with just a tiny hope although none of them would have wanted to win that way. Roy Mullender expressed it well later when he said that with five strands of *Sayula*'s forestay gone, *Adventure* was within fourteen nineteenths of winning the race.

Adventure's moment of glory came in the early hours of the morning. Her tactics had paid off. The knowledge of the Solent area and the back of the Isle of Wight and the tides were all contributory factors to her success. Off St Alban's Head she had a hard time nearly becalmed in a foul tide on Good Friday afternoon. She anchored with only 37 miles to go in this 27,500 mile race. But then she got some wind to go south of the Wight in darkness. And with full sail she romped past Bembridge Ledge, the first mark of the course, which she had passed nearly eight months previously, under full cutter rig bound for home. Under parachute flares she crossed the line and headed into Vernon Creek for a welcome from her supporters. Her crew had thought that finishing at 0218 would have seen a small crowd to greet her but as she came into the dock the intensity of the lights of the television crews was almost blinding and the cheers for the boat with a double homecoming almost deafening. Across at Gosport was the yard in which she was built and in Vernon Creek a heros' welcome. Wives, girlfriends and fellow crews were easily outnumbered by her supporters in the Service and a party was a certainty for the crew. Maybe she should have flown a paying-off pennant in the tradition of the Navy, but *Adventure* wasn't built just for this race. Her working life for adventure training in the Navy was about to continue. Her crew's steak dinner in Vernon was a welcome

Adventure securing in Vernon Creek in the middle of the night after finishing the race.

respite from the regular sea meals, and the party continued well into the daylight hours.

Not much later that morning the hapless *33 Export* finished. The French had brought their own support party and she was greeted with every bit of Gallic exuberance. The yacht *Wild Rocket* was the base for every Frenchman in Portsmouth and at 0825 they gave their welcome to her skipper Jean Millet, doubtless with thoughts of Dominique Guillet who had perished in the race.

But it seemed that the finish was an anticlimax. There was nowhere else to go. And for *Burton Cutter* on that Saturday when she crossed the line just after 1630 the anticlimax must have been greater than ever. Her crew and sponsors had big disappointments to bear, yet they would have been hard to detect. Her welcome was bathed in champagne and she was fêted as if she had won. The party spirit continued.

No one more than André Viant with his schooner *Grand Louis* could get the atmosphere enhanced. Some days earlier his friends had organised a celebration for André on the Sunday night at a Ports-

mouth hotel. It was up to the skipper to make it and he came in late on Saturday to ensure a success ashore. His performance with a boat written off by most was overshadowed for a time by the hospitality of 'The *Grand Louis* Party'.

It was overshadowed too by the arrival of the race winner on Easter Day. *Sayula II* with all her rigging problems arrived to be greeted by the priest who had blessed her, shortly after 0500 on the Sunday. She sailed up the Solent and as she did collected an ever increasing fleet of spectator boats. She first appeared with mainsail and staysail only but with nothing to lose (and incidentally nothing but glory to gain) and four miles to go hoisted a jib top and put at least 2 knots more on to her speed. She tacked for the line and the sail handling was expert, a true example of the drive of her crew. Ramon Carlin was at the wheel; although he tried not to be, it was his crew's insistence that the honour should be his. He is a modest man and one who did this race for personal enjoyment. He took with him some of his close family and some of the world's top ocean racing sailors – his formula for success was

Crew members on board *Great Britain II* after the race celebrate with beer and champagne.

good. As *Sayula* nudged the dock in Vernon the scene was almost unbelievable. Sombreros kissed cameras and bottles of champagne exploded. Yet one crew member when asked just what he wanted most said 'fresh milk' and caused a temporary hold up in the celebrations.

It was the first time that a Mexican yacht had ever won a major race and nowhere do they build races more major than this one. *Sayula II*'s success was the result of thinking and planning, and the good organisation of a top class crew, the sort of thing that can win any yacht race.

Sayula's crew arrived in time for the *Grand Louis* party and distinguished themselves with modesty and individual success, but then there will never be another first race around the world to win; and there will never again be piano playing like Tjerk Romke de Vries'.

What followed became part of yachting's history. There is no second, as Queen Victoria was told of a race in 1851, but the praise to all who took part remains. Yachtsmen acknowledge the skill of the losers, for only a decade before the whole idea of

such a race would have been laughed out of court. But the race was now over. No one could beat *Sayula* and the press began their homeward way.

Sayula had two days in which to preen herself before another finisher. Then came *Guia* and *Kriter*. They were teased by light winds and both finished in most testing of conditions – fickle winds and foul tides. Less than an hour separated them.

The fleet fell in from day to day. *Second Life* managed, against all odds, to do it with a party to match their Sydney effort. But Roddie Ainslie had a baby to meet. The one which stopped his wife Sue from going on the race. The tail enders, *Otago*, *Peter von Danzig* and *Copernicus*, whose friendships had hardened in their adversity, brought to Portsmouth their own brand of stolid humour, and a resolve to get amongst ocean racers with craft more suited to competitive racing. Their corinthian attitude must be admired for it certainly closed political and ethnographic breaches between Poles and Germans. They left Portsmouth later for a cruise home in company bound for a German Baltic port.

9
Performance of Boats and Gear

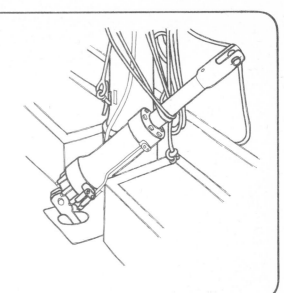

When the sixteen yachts met in Vernon Creek in September 1973 intending to race around the world, all the crews were hopeful of winning. However, only a few could have really felt that the boat and gear they had was ideal for the race.

There were many limitations. The most common one was money, or rather lack of it. Some yachts, for instance, were desperately short and in many instances they were prepared to patronize firms offering a special deal, without regard for the quality or suitability of the product.

Second Life was in a difficult position, having to make do with the gear available, and weighing up the priorities carefully before spending the limited resources available. One cannot help thinking that if the money is limited, it is better to follow the example of Giorgio Falck who chose the 45 foot *Guia*, and others who went for smaller boats with better equipment.

Great Britain II's biggest limitation with respect to the hardware was that it had to be designed and manufactured exclusively in the United Kingdom. This was very restricting since it is only in the United States that stock equipment capable of withstanding the strains of sailing a boat of 70 ft or 80 ft overall can be obtained. Not only is it available in the States but it has been tested on a number

of large yachts built to the IOR limit such as *Windward Passage*, *Ondine* and *Kia Loa*.

Some of the contestants, particularly *Grand Louis*, *Sayula* and *Burton Cutter*, although being specially built for the race, had to compromise with their other role of cruising or chartering when the race was over. In many respects, particularly in deck layout, winch selection and rig, the two roles are at variance, but in retrospect the added comfort and below-deck facilities helped the crew's morale and fitness, and hence boat performance, a great deal.

Both *British Soldier* (ex *British Steel*) and *33 Export* (ex *Raph*) were proven boats and represented their skippers' ideas of the perfect boat for the race. Both having been designed and equipped for single-handed sailing, it only required conversion of the accomodation to make them suitable for this race. Subsequently it was decided to put a new mast into *British Soldier*, and spinnaker gear had to be found for both boats.

Otago and *Peter von Danzig*, although crewed by cheerful and spirited young men, could hardly have held much hope of winning the race outright. Their success in completing the circumnavigation is a tribute to their enthusiasm. That the gear held together was helped by two things – everything

Guia's articulated rudder, dropped from the hull for inspection after the race at Camper and Nicholsons' yard at Gosport. A similar rudder was used on *Southern Cross*, the Australian America's Cup challenger in 1974. *Guia*'s gave no problem during the whole race.

breakable on board had been broken long ago and the boats were not driven as hard as most of the others.

Apart from *Peter von Danzig*, the only boat with any appreciable record of ocean racing was *Guia*. Her layout and equipment are typical of an ocean racer of her vintage (1970), except for her very bendy main boom and her double articulated rudder. In a race which was extremely hard on spars and steering systems, despite all the shaking heads and words of warning in Portsmouth it all stayed in one piece, and probably the extra control of the rudder counteracted the notorious difficulties of similar designs downwind.

As *Copernicus* had been built in Poland, her crew had the enormous problem of equipping a modern racing yacht in a country with so little previous experience in the sport.

Of all the teams in the Whitbread Race, the most logical and determined approach was by the Royal Navy entry *Adventure*. They systematically worked out the requirements for the race of boat, gear and crew, and worked hard to achieve them. By opting for a smaller boat, the Nicholson 55, they were able to equip her very well.

They had a further unique advantage. The British Services were planning to purchase several of the Nicholson 55 class for adventure training. By buying the sails and rigging for a subsequent sistership in advance, the RN was able to have a spare set to call upon if necessary. At each stop, the sails were returned to England for repair while the boat continued on the next leg with the spare set. By the time *Adventure* reached the next stop, the repaired sails were waiting on the dockside.

In the course of her work-up, *Adventure* sailed 15,000 miles in all conditions, with the crews who would take her round the world. These work-up cruises showed up any defects in equipment and enabled many ideas from the crews to be put into practice and tested well before the start of the race.

The boat which caused the most envy among the competitors was Eric Tabarly's *Pen Duick VI*. A strong, purposeful hull, a very sophisticated rig with winches and deck gear to handle it. Her maiden voyage, following the fleet round the Fastnet Race, had proved that she had plenty of speed, coupled with a low rating. There were no apparent compromises to cost or comfort on deck or below.

Looking around an offshore racing fleet today, sloops would be found to the virtual exclusion of everything else. Boats with two masts are a rarity, and even cutter rig is favoured only on the western side of the Atlantic. However, the fleet in the Whitbread Race included eleven ketches, two yawls (*Tauranga* and *Peter von Danzig*), one schooner (*Grand Louis*), and only one cutter (*Adventure*) and one sloop (*Guia*). It is interesting that the majority of contestants feel that if they were doing the race again, they would prefer a single masted rig. The reasons are clear when one looks at the *apparent* advantages of the ketch rig in the context of this race:

1. Except on a dead run or when hard on the wind ketch rig is efficient, and on a reach a ketch can

The ill-fated *Pen Duick VI* seen here at the start of the race. Although she finished the first leg she was delayed in Rio whilst a replacement mast was flown out from France and fitted.

set an impressive amount of extra sail. Unfortunately for the ketches, about half of the race was dead down wind or dead against it.

2. It is said to be safer to have two masts than one. This is a myth, because if the main mast falls, as Eric Tabarly found with *Pen Duick VI*, you need more than a mizzen up before you can get anywhere or even steer. Any ketch with a triatic stay also has the risk of losing both masts if the main mast is lost. If the mizzen alone falls, as happened to both *Otago* and *Great Britain II*, very little performance is lost as the boat sails on as a sloop.

3. The boat will be well balanced at all times. This is due to being able to stack the sail area well forward when there is plenty of wind, avoiding weather helm, while being able to avoid the lee helm associated with light weather by setting the mizzen and bringing the centre of effort of the sail plan aft. Most crews felt, however, that the advantage is minimal, and the best compromise would be to use a single mast set slightly further forward than normal in a sloop to help control in the vital running legs.

4. The sizes of the individual sails of a ketch are smaller, so they are easier to handle. True, but unfortunately, there are also many more sail changes to be made.

On any long distance race, the record books show that the two most common causes of retirement are loss of steering and dismasting. It was evident before the start that all competitors had taken special precautions in both these areas. However, many of them had problems.

Worst hit was Eric Tabarly, when his boat was dismasted only twenty-six days after the start. Many theories have been expressed on why *Pen Duick VI* lost her mast, but the best evidence, the mast itself, lies inaccessible, three miles down on the Atlantic floor. The mast was deck-stepped, the compression being taken by an alloy crosspiece mounted on top of an aluminium tube, transmitting the load directly down to the keel. The crosspiece was built of two plates, 10 cm high by 8 mm thick, firmly welded to a 7 mm thick alloy plate on top of the tube. When the lining was taken out of the boat in Rio, it was seen that this crosspiece was badly distorted and the support was compressed by about 20 mm.

Why did this vital component fail? The original calculations of designer André Mauric predicted a mast step compression of 27 tonnes maximum. Throughout construction a safety factor of two had been allowed for, thus the part was expected to sustain a load of 54 tonnes before failure. Tests were done on a laboratory press which showed that a mock-up of the same part could withstand a load of 60 tonnes without distortion. At the moment of failure, other forces must have been at work; maybe the shock load of the boat pounding into a wave, and the resulting inertia, applied a load onto the step which the support could not withstand. When the rigging snatched tight again, the compression in the mast was too much, and the whole rig collapsed.

Pen Duick's second dismasting, in the Tasman Sea, is less mysterious. A faulty stainless steel shackle at the foot of the inner forestay, a sudden squall with a shy spinnaker, the casting breaks and there is nothing to resist the compression of the pole. Without the support at deck level, the mast buckles and collapses. It was all over for the luckless Eric Tabarly.

Although the most spectacular and the most discouraging, *Pen Duick*'s was not the only dismasting of the race. Both *Great Britain II* and *Otago* lost mizzen masts on the second leg and sailed into Sydney dressed as sloops. Chay Blyth is the first to admit that he was carrying too much sail, but many observers who had noticed the lack of mizzen backstay (relying on runners to brace the mast back) were saying smugly 'I told you so'.

No such criticism could be levelled against the seamanship of *Otago*'s crew. The mizzen was furled at the time, when a wave crashed over the boat laying her flat and the force of water was enough to break the aluminium spar six feet above the deck. Several other boats only narrowly avoided dismasting.

British Soldier broke a strand in both aft lower shrouds.

Grand Louis twice had to replace her forestay.

Second Life finished the race in Portsmouth with one strand broken in her forestay, but afterwards on inspection found the tangs on the mast holding other stays on the point of breaking.

33 Export also narrowly escaped dismasting. Her masthead fitting fell apart when the crew were overhauling the boat immediately after the race.

Adventure avoided trouble by having all her standing rigging replaced in Sydney. She was the only boat with rod rigging.

The most dramatic near miss must have been *Sayula*'s. While leading the race on the last leg two strands of her 19 strand forestay were found to be broken, with still 2,500 miles to go and no spare. To quit was unthinkable, but at the finish, it was found that five strands were broken in the forestay. Strands had also broken in the runners, standing backstay and inner forestay.

The top of *Sayula*'s forestay showing the parted strands of the 1 × 19 stainless steel wire siezed with insulating tape.

'Belt and braces' on *Second Life*. Note the wire strop doubling up on the rigging screw for the main shroud as a precaution in case the rigging screw should fail.

Main booms and spinnaker poles also succumbed. *Adventure*'s crew on the second leg managed one of the more ingenious repairs by converting the bottom of a pressure cooker into a new plate for the main boom end fitting.

Great Britain II must have established a new record by breaking three spinnaker poles on one leg of the course. They went on to break several times more, and with every repair the poles got heavier until they became quite difficult to handle.

All the boats in the race had wheel steering except for *Pen Duick VI* whose laminated wood tiller looked incongruous on such a powerful 65 foot fin keel ketch. It proved a little too optimistic in practice. It was calculated that it required a force of 113 kg at the end of the tiller to turn the rudder at full speed. Not surprisingly, Tabarly had a steering wheel fitted early on. It was prefabricated in France and flown out to Rio de Janeiro with the new mast.

The most serious form of steering failure is when something goes wrong with the rudder itself. It was this that happened to *Adventure* in the second leg, when the colossal pressures of driving a boat hard downwind in gale force winds caused the rudder stock to come loose inside the glassfibre structure of the rudder. Fortunately there was still some friction between stock and rudder so the boat retained a measure of control, particularly when the steering wheel was coupled to the small trimming rudder on the back of the keel.

On the same leg *Tauranga* had problems when the topmost bearing of the rudder stock broke away from the underside of the cockpit floor. Fortunately the crew were able to brace it with wire lashings so the effect on her performance was marginal, but she had to bear away and pass south of Tasmania whilst repairs were carried out.

The Offshore Rating Council's safety regulations stipulate that any yacht racing with a steering wheel must be able to use a jury tiller in the event of the steering mechanism failing. Three of the competitors had to resort to this.

The Polish yacht *Otago* lacked modern fittings and refinements. This picture show the lower end of a shroud with shackles used to make up for short length.

33 Export twice had a steering wire break between the wheel and the rudder quadrant. Spares were carried and it was not difficult to thread new ones. *Grand Louis* also had to resort to tiller steering, once due to a broken wire and once due to a sheave breaking.

But it was *Adventure* which had the worst luck with her steering. After fitting a complete new rudder and stock in Sydney, which had been flown out specially from England, the steering failed twice on the third leg of the race. On these occasions it was not so serious, merely the fracture of a shear pin in the upper bevel box on the steering pedestal. The pin was replaced while continuing to steer with the tiller.

Before the start no one really knew what stresses would be applied to the yachts' hulls in the Southern Ocean. One thing was certain, it would be worse than any racing yacht had ever experienced before. No one underestimated the need for a strong hull, but there were several solutions to the problem. Of the purpose-built boats, Jack Grout's *Kriter*

In the latter stages particularly on legs 3 and 4, *Great Britain II* suffered from leaks. Here repairs have been carried out at the aft end of the root of the skeg when she was refitted after the race.

Kriter at the end of the race showing the 'Gliksman flap' – an extension to the hull aft of the transom to improve water flow. This addition did not alter her rating.

was strongly constructed of cold moulded timber. The workmanship was excellent, but still the skeg in front of the rudder cracked suddenly in the Indian Ocean. It was reinforced in Sydney by bolting a stainless steel plate on each side. The force of water was even enough to rip off the inch wide rubbing strake each side of the bow.

Grand Louis was of foam/glassfibre sandwich construction as was *Great Britain II*. The French boat had no major problems but the paratroopers in *Great Britain II* were forced to pump almost continuously when the keel worked loose and water started leaking in around the bolts holding it on. Bulkheads were smashed as well under the severe pounding of the last leg.

Metal is a favourite form of construction as it bends before it will leak. *33 Export*, *Burton Cutter*, and *Pen Duick VI* had hulls of aluminium alloy, and *British Soldier*, *Otago* and *Peter von Danzig* were steel. The steel boats had no problems, but both *33 Export* and *Burton Cutter* cracked welds in the

The oldest yacht in the race, *Peter von Danzig*, was built in steel in 1936. Her battered topsides give away her age as she lies in Vernon Creek after the race.

bow plating on the first leg. For Leslie Williams it was a recurring problem. He was forced to heave to for two days to minimize the damage, and then have more frames fitted forward in Cape Town. It was not enough, for two days out on the second leg, he was in trouble again and had to put back to Port Elizabeth. He was forced to abandon the two middle legs and rejoin the race in Rio where, five months later, the boat was rebuilt for the third time with the help of the Brazilian Navy.

Four of the boats were stock glassfibre production models. *Second Life* is an Ocean 71, *Tauranga* a Swan 55 and *Adventure* is a Nicholson 55, completed to the Service's specifications for adventure training yachts and fitted with a strengthened mast. *Sayula II* is a standard Swan 65. A newspaper paid tribute to her Finnish builders, Nautor OY by describing her at the finish as looking as good as if she had only just left the factory.

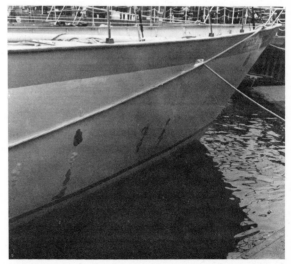

The starboard bow of *Burton Cutter* seen after the race. Note the marks on the topsides and paint blisters caused by repairs to the aluminium construction from inside which were carried out in South Africa after she had retired from the second leg, with serious structural failures.

The 'knitting' at the foot of *Second Life*'s main mast. Internal halyards are led to winches grouped round the mast.

An old-pattern, windlass-type sheet winch on the aft deck of the Polish yacht *Otago*.

In view of the amount of sail changing and sheet trimming involved, it is surprising how well the running rigging stood up to sailing the equivalent of seven years' normal racing. If one considers it normal to replace halyards and sheets every second year, it is remarkable that many of the boats finished using the same gear that they started with.

Snap shackles caused many problems. Basically designed for smaller boats, they were not up to the strains imposed by large heavy boats in strong winds. After having repeated failures, *Grand Louis* went back to old fashioned D-shackles with a screw pin. It might have taken a fraction longer to change sails, but the reliability more than made up for that.

On spinnaker guys, where it is vital to be able to release the sail under load, some of the bigger boats used a rope seizing which could be cut and replaced each time the spinnaker was dropped.

There were also problems with winches. *Great Britain II*'s coffee grinders broke chains and the winches on *Burton Cutter* seized up when the grease got washed out with spray. The crew of *Second Life* wound teeth off sprockets in their sheet winches. The root of the problem was that skippers, realizing that fast sheet trimming was not vital on this style of race, specified smaller winches than normal for the loads entailed.

The whole race was a marathon test for every piece of gear on the boat. Blocks burst, battens split and jib hanks bent. Equipment which lasts for years of normal sailing failed despite careful use. Spinnakers popped like balloons and other sails tore under the onslaught of wind, water and chafe. Some boats carried sewing machines. They were seldom idle.

Many boats arrived at the stops with their sails in tatters, and submerged the local sailmakers in a deluge of work. Keith Lorence of *Sayula II* used the boat's electric machine to do some repairs for *Pen Duick VI* in Cape Town, and for *Great Britain II* and *33 Export* when he opened for business on the dance floor of the Iate Clube do Rio de Janeiro.

When the race finished at Portsmouth, technical staff from a wide selection of manufacturers descended upon the yachts and examined in detail their own equipment; in some cases going to the extent of stripping their fittings from the yacht and taking them back to their factory for close examination. Some firms even sent their representatives to the stop-over ports to examine and service the gear

Toe rail attachment point on *Great Britain II* shows the extent to which a shackle pin elongated the hole.

between legs. So one thing is certain: that the experience gained in testing — in many cases to destruction — a vast selection of stock modern yacht hardware will enable manufacturers to introduce many improvements years before they would otherwise have done so. And this will be to the advantage of all yachtsmen, whatever size of boat they sail.

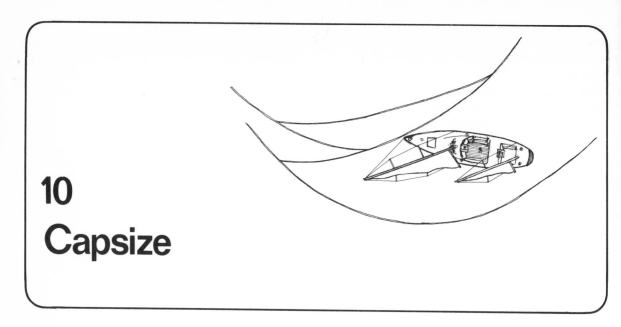

10
Capsize

The greatest fear of any yachtsman setting off into the vaste open wastes of the oceans of the world is that of a capsize. Yachts have been known to disappear without trace – and not only yachts but big ships too – and the most probable explanation of their loss is that they have been capsized by freak waves.

Freak waves can occur almost anywhere during heavy gales and arise from the synchronization of different wave trains, especially when a shift of wind sets up new wave trains crossing the existing ones obliquely. It is in the Roaring Forties and Fifties of the Southern Oceans that they are likely to be most dangerous as the prevailing strong westerly winds have unlimited fetch with no land to check them or to change their path, so the waves can build up to their maximum height. Here may be found the rogue sea on a gigantic scale that erupts suddenly and that yachtsmen fear most.

On this race a number of yachts were knocked down or fell over to more than 90°. Although each incident was slightly different and, naturally, had its own peculiarities, the pattern was almost always the same. The yacht is running before the sea and probably surfing down the face of the waves. Suddenly a wall of water erupts astern of the yacht, she surfs rapidly down the face of the wave, the bow digs in and she broaches. The subsequent chain of events depends upon the characteristics of the wave. The yacht may just be thrown on her beam ends (!) with the mast and sails flat on the water and recover when the wave passes. Or, if the wave is really large and steep, the yacht drops down its vertical face and falls into the trough, usually suffering considerable damage. This is when windows can be broken, cabin tops smashed and hatches ripped off. If sufficient water finds its way below, the yacht sinks.

Otago was knocked over on the 2nd leg and broke her mizzen mast despite the fact that there was no sail set on it at the time. *Kriter* received a number of knockdown blows during one of which an ominous crack was heard which subsequently proved to be the skeg cracking away from the hull.

At 48° 20 S, 90° 37 E on November 24th *Sayula II* capsized. Butch Dalrymple-Smith graphically described what happened to the 65 foot ketch and the way the crew restored the yacht they first believed was sinking.

I was sitting on the dinette facing across the boat. I had just put a new tape in the eight-track – Led Zeppelin 'Houses of the Holy'. I can't hear that again without getting a little bit nervous. The boat was sailing along smoothly and normally and then there was zero gravity – no up, no down. Then there was the most almighty crash and the side of the hull leapt towards me. I landed feet first on the cupboard which houses the eight-track, and fell in the corner between the deckhead and the cupboard.

An enormous pile of mattresses, floor boards and everything imaginable grew on the side of the saloon. And there was this regular, interminable rain of cans, water and bedding from the upper side; most of the tins bouncing off the deckhead on the way down to the pile. I did not feel upside down. It was rather like an hallucination. It is impossible to believe that your whole world has suddenly been turned upside down. But looking at all these things falling across the boat, you know that obviously something is amiss.

Keith Lorence was under the pile. How could he survive? I started heaving floorboards and stuff off him, but I think it all fell back down on him.

When *Sayula II* capsized on the second leg, these steaming lights and their mounting brackets on the fore side of the mast were badly bent and twisted.

Water was gushing in through a broken window in the cabin top. I followed him to the hatch, grabbing a foul weather top on the way. I felt the mast was bound to be over the side 'Is it still up', I said, and it was.

'Let's get the sails off' he said.

We moved out on to the foredeck, slipping and sliding on salad oil and noodles that had mysteriously found their way on deck. We waited for help, 15 seconds or so, and then by ourselves dropped the small staysail and tiny storm jib, the only sails we had been carrying. The two men on deck, Bob Martin and Roberto Cubas, had hauled themselves back on board by the time we reached the deck and Bob was getting the boat on course again. We didn't realize at the time the difficulty he was having just physically turning the wheel because of all the broken gear, sheets and halyards draped across it.

The more immediate problems were inside the boat and we returned below. What a shambles there was. Ramon had already started bailing into the garbage bucket while someone else was pumping on the internal bilge pump. Ray was trying to transmit a PAN call, someone else was trying to get into the aft cabin. Another crewman was anxiously trying to hand the full garbage bucket out of the main hatch which was occupied by a party trying to get a crewman with a suspected broken leg below... All this in an area not much bigger than a telephone box.

Eventually, a semblance of order was restored. The injured crewman, Roberto Cubas, was laid out in the aft cabin and treated, two more bilge pumps were brought into operation and a bucket chain got going. However, amidst this hive of activity, three of four of the crew, dazed and shocked, were meandering around vaguely, not knowing what to do. Bilge water was pouring out from between the two starboard fuel tanks to the extent that I, for one, reckoned there must be a leak up there somewhere. And I was scared. We were about 49° south, just over half way from Cape Town to Sydney with the water temperature 2° centigrade. And I was sure we were sinking.

I thought the fuel tanks, which are very heavy, had punched a hole in the side of the hull when we fell off the wave because of all this water gushing

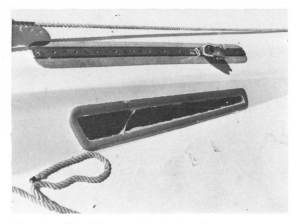

The cracked window which occurred when *Sayula* capsized on the second leg.

down from underneath the fuel tanks. I realized much later that when we tipped right over, we took a lot of water which sat in the locker compartments up the side of the boat and it was this water rushing down, plus fresh water from two of the water tanks which broke their connections. We lost 140 gallons of fresh water this way. But after two hours of frantic effort, it became clear that we were not going to sink quite yet as we freed the bilge of most of its water. No bilge pump worked more than 50% of the time as there was so much muck in the bilge.

Cleaning up, where do you start? The floorboards were all over the place. Chicken noodle soup and salad oil everywhere made even standing hazardous. About five hours of back-breaking work followed and then, thanks to Yvonne, a hot supper. Cantis Orinday and Dave Bowen did the vital job of repairing the cabin window. The ship was safe and suddenly we began to feel cold. Then followed the coldest night in the world. The only four dry bunks were occupied by the wounded. All the mattresses in the main saloon were soaking. The six of us left to keep watch slept, or tried to sleep, in full oilskins on the bare floorboards. It was as cold and wet below as it was on deck.

The six exhausted watchkeepers spent two hours on and one hour off for the rest of the night. Although the wind was down to 30 knots, no one could work up enough enthusiasm to put up more than the Number 5 storm jib and storm staysail. That night, we were in no mood to enjoy the most fantastic

celestial light show in southern sky . . . the southern Aurora in full blast. At first light, we had boiled eggs and then set the Number 3 jib poled out with full main on 10 knots of wind from astern. Drying out began. With the deck looking like a Chinese laundry, we set the 1·5 ounce spinnaker.

We knew it was all over at about 1100 (zone time) when Cantis and Ramon managed to start the engine on the first push of the button. Everything electrical and mechanical had been wiped dry and sprayed with WD40.

With the noise of the engine and the warmth of the sun, the wounded realized they were still alive and ventured forth. The six of us thankfully retired into the dry bunks, 24 hours after the capsize. Later, the opportunity came to compare experiences, to reflect, and piece together what really happened to *Sayula II* in the capsize. The boat herself was well prepared to survive the capsize.

The boat carries 400 gallons of fresh water in the standard tanks and about the same amount of diesel fuel. The hull itself is extremely strong and so are the masts. When Ramon suggested to Nautor they build an extra strong mast they just laughed at him because they reckoned the mast was over-strong already. And they were right. The capsize came on the morning of November 24th at about 1000 local time. The timing was fortunate for it gave us a lot of daylight for recovering. The wind, north of west, had been blowing at 50–55 knots for two and a half days. It did not give us any problems but it raised this appalling, unpredictable sea. I always visualized the Southern Ocean as endless lines of long rollers. It is not like that at all; the waves come at you in all directions. The waves are certainly big. I remember looking at one I believed was about as high as the boat is long.

But the ones to worry about are not the waves that look very fierce as they roll down on you from astern, but the ones that start off small and suddenly peak absolutely underneath you. They don't necessarily come from the stern, but often from the quarter. You cannot see this wave forming until a moment before it strikes the boat and then it is too late. It was this sort of wave that rolled *Sayula II*. Two men were on deck. Bob Martin, one of the best helmsmen we had, was steering and the other was

A cockpit shot of *Sayula II* taken in Sydney. Note the missing main compass from the top of the pedestal and missing starboard coaming compass, both of which were ripped off in the capsize. The port coaming compass can be seen in place.

Roberto Cubas. Both were clipped on. We had only a storm jib up, tiny sails, there mainly to make it easier for the helmsman to keep the head away.

Sayula II was on the face of the wave when the falling crest caught the stern first, forcing it down the wave faster than the bow. With the bow gripping the water and the stern in the falling water, the boat slewed around almost broadside on to the wave. And then the wave broke. The boat literally fell – no one knows how far. It was impossible to tell from below and the people on deck were up to their eyes in water so they could not see.

So the boat just dropped, and when it hit it was further over than horizontal because we broke the cabin window which meant we had hit partly on the deck. Everything fell out of its stowage. A peanut butter jar broke on the main skylight. The tools in the workshop made nasty marks on the deckhead. From the trajectory these fallen articles must have taken, the angle was conservatively 155 degrees. In the after cabin, the marks caused by vodka bottles and other things that were stowed below the cabin sole would indicate the boat went over still further, to 170 degrees, which is near as dammit to upside down. But this may have been a slight distortion because of the flipping action of the stern as it fell. The Avon dinghy, which was stowed in one of the cockpit lockers, smashed through the seat above it and would have gone over the side had it not been caught by the mizzen boom. The broken Brookes and Gatehouse masthead unit and bent steaming light confirmed that the mast went well and truly under.

About two and a half pounds of dark plum preserve landed in the radio. And there were more mysterious happenings. Why was the broken top of the peanut butter jar under the starboard pilot berth sheet when the sheet had been tucked in both sides? Why was the mustard in the sewing machine locker? How did the salad oil and chicken noodle soup end up over the deck?

While both men in the cockpit were thrown off, both were hanging on to something belonging to the boat as well as being secured by their lifelines.

Roberto was holding on to a stanchion down to leeward that was in fact dragging him under water. The mizzen boom dropped on his leg and he thought for a while it was broken. When he finally dragged himself back on board, the stainless steel cliphook of his safety harness was so badly distorted, it would not close. From then on, people on deck had at least two lifelines on and possibly more in similar circumstances.

Bob Martin was hanging on to the mizzen backstay and when the boat recovered was able to climb back aboard without much difficulty. There was so much water everywhere there was not much difference in being on board and over the side. He was able to resume course before we dropped the sails.

While we had a spinnaker up again within 24 hours of the accident, we were not really racing properly until a week later. The psychological effect of it made people lose interest in pushing the boat. And it was noticeable that afterwards sitting down to a meal, when the boat just lurched a little, all would stop talking and start hanging on. The casualties were: two out with broken ribs, one torn shoulder, one concussed, one aggravation of an old back injury and Roberto's injured leg. The damage to the boat was: starboard mizzen lower shroud broken, binnacle and starboard compasses lost; cover of port cockpit seat broken; stern pulpit twisted; lights on the mainmast twisted, wind gauge vane broken off; window in main cabin broken; deckhead in after cabin and workroom torn; four out of five radios out; depth finder out, sheet winch handles and shackles lost; mizzen spinnaker and Number 2 mizzen staysail lost; horseshoe life ring and man-overboard pole and light lost; mizzen staysail halyard broken, dodger frame bent and dodger torn; steering wheel buckled, numerous other pieces of gear and food written off.

Adlard Coles is probably the leading authority in the world on the behaviour of yachts in heavy weather. He has a lifetime of experience cruising and racing offshore and has made a close study of the subject; his book *Heavy Weather Sailing* is the standard work on the subject. After reading Butch's account of *Sayula*'s capsize and discussing the incident with him, Adlard made the following comments.

The amazing thing about this incident is that *Sayula II* was not dismasted. Nevertheless a considerable amount of water was shipped. A great deal of damage was done to the boat but, apart from the broken deck window through which the sea poured, none of it was structural or disabling which is certainly a credit to her builders, Nautor OY of Finland.

This near disaster follows the well established pattern of the freak wave. At one moment all is well despite the very heavy weather and high seas. The crew, although tired, is confident and everything is under control. Then totally unexpectedly the wave arrives and in a matter of seconds disaster may follow. *Sayula II* was running fast and as she was racing in a great international event she had no alternative such as streaming warps, nor is it certain that she would have suffered less had she done so. I have often wondered what happens if a yacht finds herself perched on the edge of a precipice of water, or indeed falls into a hole.

It is interesting to note that the freak wave which caused the capsize struck *Sayula II* towards the end of the storm, apparently after a front had gone through, with a veer in the wind which created dangerous cross seas over swell built up over the previous two days. At least, this is my assumption, as there was no second freak wave and the weather improved rapidly, the wind falling to 10 knots within a few hours of the mishap.

Although meals may not matter much in modern fast ocean racers in 200 mile races taking 30 hours, I remain convinced that substantial and regular meals pay racing dividends in long events, where results depend on morale and endurance especially in heavy weather.

It must be recognized that *Sayula II* was a new boat of very strong construction and rigging, with a strong and experienced crew, far superior in every way to most of the smaller and sometimes elderly boats which voyage the oceans.

11
Life on Board

Where did they come from, the 300 men and a few girls who made up the nineteen crews on this, the most gear-, boat- and crew-breaking race in the world? They came from everywhere. Doctors, bums, retired men and university students, they went for fun, because they like the sea, sailing, racing. And they wanted to be able to say that they had done it.

Then there were the professionals. Men doing the race for personal prestige, photographers and journalists after the picture or the story of a lifetime. It was later that the regrets came out. Men couldn't stand the crowding, the squalor, the frustration of the first leg or the cold and terror of the second. Fights developed on board. Little niggles flared up into blazing rows. It is hard to find out the details afterwards; crews stick together, revealing nothing, and one or two leave for 'personal' reasons.

For some it was comfort and compatability all the way. The family boats, *Grand Louis* and *Sayula II*, found no problems. The head of the family becomes head of the boat; although others may select sails and drive, he becomes the chairman of the board and guides the overall effort. There was an advantage in having a gradient of age and experience as *Otago* found out and *Peter von Danzig* missed. Fewer arguments, more smiles throughout. The Service crews had the advantage of background. Not so much the Service discipline act, for with enlisted men sometimes in charge of officers it hardly applies, but a group of men who have spent the last few years doing what they are told are more likely to obey when ordered out on to a wet, icy foredeck when all they want to do is to get warm and dry and go to sleep.

Selection and screening of the crews varied from boat to boat. For some, it was a problem of sorting out the few sheep from a multitude of goats. For others it was all they could do to find the twelve animals, sheep or goats, and persuade them to set out on this, the most uncomfortable and time consuming of sporting pursuits.

The men behind *Adventure* had a clear idea of the type of person they were after. A notice circulated throughout the Navy produced a response of over three hundred applicants. Those not eliminated by conflicting job requirements were tried out in training cruises, often spending three or four days away from port. Afterwards the assessments included such revealing questions as 'Can he cook?', 'Is he good natured, does he easily take offence?' and 'Would you trust him steering the boat downwind at night?'.

Helpful sign for Chay Blyth's paratroop crew aboard *Great Britain II* – only one or two of them had ever sailed before they were selected.

Great Britain II had a different selection procedure. Chay Blyth and his Parachute Brigade liaison officer, Captain John Williams, were more concerned about keenness, fitness and compatability than sailing ability. Their original number of 300 applicants was soon reduced to a more manageable number by holding crew meetings at short notice in Scotland, six hundred miles away from the barracks. They met in a cottage where they read up the theory of sailing and navigation or went on strenuous runs through the deserted highlands. Only the fit, the keen and the good natured survived.

Other selections were more casual. Leslie Williams used the contacts he had made over many years ocean racing in different parts of the world. He ended up with a cosmopolitan mixture of French, Italian, English and New Zealanders. *Sayula*'s crew were just as varied. To back up six of his family from Mexico, Ramon Carlin had three Americans, a Dutchman, an Australian and an Englishman. Before the race was over South Africa and Canada were represented on board as well. It is fitting that for a race which en-

circled the world, there should be international co-operation on an individual level like this.

Jean-Pierre Millet was hoping to have a representative on the crew of *33 Export* from each of the countries they were to visit. It was tragic that the young Brazilian Dominique Rulhe was killed when the aircraft bringing him to Europe crashed.

Peter von Danzig was crewed by German students. They all belonged to the Akademischer Segler-Verein, one of whose interests was sailing the boat on long cruises into the North Atlantic or racing in the Baltic. The only selection procedure on *Second Life* was that each crew member had to raise the £3,000 crewing fee, which covered the expenses of this totally unsponsored entry. The skipper's wife, Sue Ainsley, was originally planning to go with them, but found she was pregnant just before the start. She stayed behind and gave birth to a daughter while her husband was bringing *Second Life* up Channel to the finish.

It was a financial sacrifice for everyone. Some gave up their jobs, hoping to get another when it was all over. Doctors and dentists had to find replacements. Others had understanding wives who could run their businesses while they were away. Those who were doing one leg only tried to get special leave from their jobs. Then there were the young ones, sometimes the sons of wealthy parents, proud that their sons could achieve what they had only dreamed of.

The race to Cape Town was only a break-in period. Those pleasant days of calm and sunshine gave way to the sterner conditions of the southern legs. This is where they found out what it was all about. As it gets colder the niceties of life are forgotten. Social life is dormant or dead. One comes in from the cockpit, little is said, one eats, one sleeps, one goes one degree closer to the animal existence. There is the tiredness. One cannot sleep enough. One hour outside in the cold and you are all in. And then there is the fear – irrational, confused fear.

It all combines to produce a level of stress seldom seen outside the Services on active duty. Different people show different symptoms. Some simply refuse to go on deck, but more turn passive, wandering around vacantly, only pulling, winding, moving or clipping on when told to so; becoming machines,

Crossing the Line ceremony on board *Burton Cutter* during the first leg. Here crewman Chris Edwards is being initiated.

A welcome, cool dip in the South Atlantic for the crew of *Peter von Danzig*. Note the dinghy astern ready to pick up any stragglers.

incapable of self starting. Others develop badly defined illnesses, an aching shoulder, a pain in the back. The aches are real enough but the cause is all in the mind. For the watch captains it becomes impossible to take quick decisions. Even trivial problems require long deliberation. There is always the worry. What if someone falls overboard? How long will the spinnaker hold together? Is the rudder creaking more than normal? It is conditions like these which show the value of the race for adventure training of Service personnel.

Morale, that indefinable something that keeps a crew working, smiling and healthy long after fitter, more experienced, better fancied crews give up. The spirit that keeps men living when others are only existing. One can almost plot a graph of it throughout the day, peaking at the inter-ship radio schedule (children's hour!) and at meal times, falling to an all time low when hands are called to drop the spinnaker at two o'clock in the morning.

Different things help. Keeping everyone busy enough to avoid boredom but not exhausted; good food; pleasant surroundings; a plentiful supply of

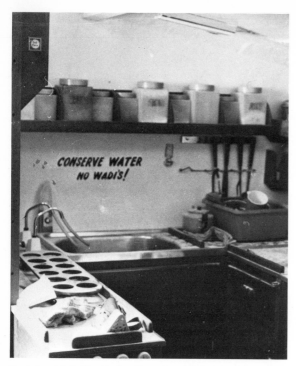

Reminder on the bulkhead in the galley on *Great Britain II* that fresh water is in short supply on long ocean passages.

Loading stores aboard *Tauranga* in Vernon Creek before the start of the race – packets holding 432 tins of Coca-Cola and 88 loaves of sliced bread are on deck – just a small sample of the pile of stores that had to be stowed.

good books; music (on the tape player) and even the occasional party.

Few were as fortunate as the crew of *Sayula II*. With a well ventilated, fully lined, centrally heated boat, condensation and interior dampness were seldom problems. The eight track stereo with nearly 100 tapes was equipped with two pairs of headphones in case one man's favourite was another's annoyance. It helped having private cabins. Anyone could find privacy when all he wanted was to get away from it all. And every day there was cocktail hour at the end of a six hour watch. Perhaps this was their secret.

Food is a problem, from the first planning stage to the washing up. And it is so important. *Kriter* was typical:

Number of crew multiplied by three multiplied by the number of days at sea. With a crew of twelve this meant a total of 9,180 meals. As many hors d'oeuvres, main dishes, desserts, rations of bread or biscuits, not forgetting beer, wine, fruit juice and of course water. Mineral water for drinking, bulk water in the tanks for the cooking.

You must think of what will be available at the stops. One is surprised not to find worms in the brackish liquid distributed by the water board in Rio. The simple explanation is that they could not stay alive in it!

Kriter's provisions were planned by Maurice Dreux, who listed the following: 120 kg of bread specially treated per leg, plus fresh bread at each stop; 250 kg ham; 25 kg preserved sausages; 200 kg tinned butter; 250 boxes of cheese portions; 400 tins of sweetened milk, 100 unsweetened; 500 tins of crème caramel; 100 tins of peas, beans, spinach to be added at each stop; potato and powder on top of that. A certain amount of braised beef in jars, boeuf bourguignon, osso bucco, etc.; 100 kg sugar, 200 kg pasta, 200 kg rice, 3,000 plastic bottles of mineral water, 250 litres of wine per leg, 800 to 1,000 tins of beer, 300 bottles of Evian and fruit juice. Plus a lot of little things, things to nibble, chocolate, dried fruit; few spirits but 50 magnums of Kriter champagne, to toast the capes and for receptions in port.

The crew of *Peter von Danzig* in party spirit in the Roaring Forties on the second leg.

Reinhard Laucht, skipper of *Peter von Danzig*, holds up a couple of barracuda caught off the coast of Australia.

A few boats had the luxury of a deep freeze. On *Sayula* they were enjoying fresh steaks, chicken and chops right up till the last three days of each leg.

The preparation of food was just as important as the supplies. Some boats had a full time cook, often a girl, but it was more common for the whole crew to take turns in the galley. On *Grand Louis* the crew vied with each other to produce the best dishes from the limited food available. Eventually they each developed their own speciality, a soufflé, a roast or crêpes suzette.

The British Services' boats were conducting sea trials of a new bread mix recently developed by the Royal Navy victualling laboratories at Botley. You only have to add sea water, mix and bake. With this, any cook could achieve some results, but those chefs with the right knack of kneading it and getting the oven temperature correct produced delightfully light and tasty loaves.

As well as the formal meals there were always hot drinks, sweets, chocolates, dried fruit and chewing gum for those on watch. All necessary to replace the

139

As the wind increases somewhere in the Southern Ocean, sail is reduced and two of the crew of *Second Life* secure the reefed mainsail to the boom.

energy expended in driving the boat and surviving in the sub zero temperatures.

Gas stoves were most common, usually with an oven. Even *Pen Duick VI* changed over to gas in Cape Town when it was found that an alcohol stove did not give enough heat. There were inevitable problems getting cylinders refilled in strange ports with strange gas fittings. *Peter von Danzig* had no such trouble finding paraffin for her two burner primus stove and the main saloon light taken from the old clipper *Passad*.

An unusual problem was that cylinders of butane, normally stowed outside the saloon to minimize fire risk from leakage, sometimes got cold enough to make the fuel reluctant to boil. (Boiling point butane -0.5 to $-11.7°$C.)

The wise ones stowed dry gear in plastic bags, for even in the most leakproof boats the interior is perpetually damp with condensation. It was common practice to take wet clothes to bed to dry them out with body heat. After being cold enough to believe they would never get truly warm again, as crews

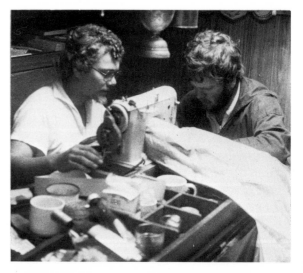

Sail repairs on the saloon table of *Peter von Danzig* during the race.

The crew of *Great Britain II* (without skipper Chay Blyth) in Vernon Creek after the finish.

sailed north into the Atlantic they suddenly found warmth in the sun, and one by one the layers came off. Oilskins, neck towel, sweater, shirt, two pairs of trousers and thermal underwear. You notice things. When the socks come off you can see how much your toe nails have grown. For many it is the first time their bodies have seen the light of day since a day after Sydney.

At the conclusion of a television documentary on the race one crewman had the last word by saying he would never do the race again, not for a million dollars. A more enigmatic view was expressed by another who said 'I wouldn't want to do the race again, but then I wouldn't want to see another race go off without me.' It is the love-hate relationship that the aficionados have with ocean racing.

Many of the participants hope to do the race again, but this time differently – a better boat, a new crew. Most are hoping to be in charge of the boat next time.

Optimistically they believe that just to take part is the passport into a new world where sponsors queue up to provide expensive boats for embryo Magellans.

Except on *Grand Louis* and *Pen Duick VI* few crew came from among the familiar faces around the ocean races of the world. Only a couple were keen enough to take part in races of the Southern Cross Series in Sydney on the way through.

A yacht at sea can be the most remote spot in the world. Even an astronaut on the moon can expect help quicker than a yacht in the middle of the Southern Ocean. Many of the boats had a doctor in the crew. *Peter von Danzig* even had two, so a patient could ask for a second opinion! Some made do with that most dangerous of animals, the failed medical student. However, if it was working, there was always the radio, and Dr Robin Leach of *Second Life* extended his practice to cover other boats in the fleet who needed his advice.

12
Medical

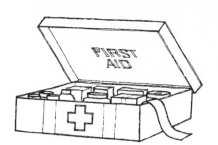

by Doctor Robin Leach

It was in the bar at St Thomas' Hospital that I first canvassed opinions as to the medical problems which might be encountered during this epic race. One colleague was most encouraging: 'It will be just like being in general practice,' he said, 'Except that . . .' He then unfolded a series of facts to underline the exceptional circumstances. Three hours later, and not entirely uninfluenced by our venue, he concluded by saying 'You'd be a fool not to go — you have no choice. I won't go!'

Of course he *was* correct in most that he said — if I remember clearly. It was like being in general practice although my experience of this field is limited. In port, relaxation and preparations for the ensuing legs often produced their casualties of one sort or another. Dyspepsia and photophobia were usually corrected by lunchtime but, alas, seemed a recurring problem. It was only after a certain time in each port that the crews became acclimatized to the local brews. The most vivid experience in the fleet general practice came from Rio de Janeiro. After nearly six months at sea the weary crews seemed to succumb much more easily to infections. Ear trouble, tonsillitis and local skin sepsis were common. Maybe it was the heat combined with the length of stay in Rio or perhaps it was just Rio.

Few if any of the crews spoke Portuguese and so it was my lot to try to interpret the various ailments. However, when sailing, excess niceties of language are often (if not de rigueur) absent. Those with limited English learnt a great deal — most not generally acceptable at a Buckingham Palace garden party. Their message was thus conveyed with consummate speed when they had a problem.

One of the niggly things that occurred on all the yachts was the splitting of finger tips. After days of immersion and drying in salt water the skin of the hands and fingers becomes sodden with fluid. As it dries out the skin tends to crack — especially at the nail edges. Vaseline helps quite a lot with the problem but a good remedy came from Dr Roger Tamlyn of *British Soldier* (third leg). He used lanoline to rub into the hands. Although I have not tried it myself it is said to clear the problem in a couple of days. Repeated applications are necessary to keep the skin supple.

On *Second Life* we were lucky that no major accident occured. Two narrow squeaks do come to mind. One crew member was lifted by a huge wave in the pulpit. Harnessed to the deck safety lines he crashed down on his knees. He was lucky to receive only deep bruising to his shins. Nevertheless a very painful situation which could have resulted in a fracture. The other occasion was more serious. After setting the starcut spinnaker another member of the crew caught a bight of the lazy sheet around his arm and was dragged to the length of his harness under a wire lifeline. The wind caught the sail and his arm was jammed between the sheet and the lifeline. He was swiftly cut free but not before he sustained a severe contusion which put his arm out of working order for ten days. He was not completely fit for nearly two months. The contusion was down to the bone and the resulting swelling was more spectacular than dangerous. The skin itself was intact and therefore gave good protection against infection in the retained fluid.

Other yachts had their problems. There were two doctors on the sturdy German yacht *Peter von Danzig*. They had to put into New Zealand when one of the crew broke a bone in his foot. It must have been reassuring for the patient to know that he could always ask for a second opinion – even in the Southern Ocean. However one of the doctors was an orthopaedic surgeon. After a brief and hospitable stay in New Zealand, the bone was sufficiently healed to allow the crew member to rejoin in Rio de Janeiro.

Not all of the yachts carried doctors and occasionally problems were presented from several hundred miles away over the radio telephone. A crew member from *Great Britain II* re-fractured an arm on the

The old pattern, top action sheet winch on *Peter von Danzig*. When the pawls slipped, the handle flew back breaking the foot of crewman Aki Müller-Deile when the yacht was 100 miles off New Zealand. He was put ashore at Bluff Harbour, received hospital treatment in New Zealand and hitch hiked to rejoin in Rio.

second leg and I was consulted about his management. As they were ahead of us at this time it was tempting to say heave to and we will come across and have a look – ethically not on. Having no plaster of Paris on board the only splintage they could arrange with any degree of permanancy was glass fibre. Swaddling the arm with old clothing the crew of *GB II* prepared to set the arm. They did run into some problems as the heat of reaction as the glass fibre set proved rather intense. Nevertheless the cast looked reasonable in Sydney and had immobilized the arm, which was its job.

The Sun and the Sea

Dehydration and salt deficiency seem to be things which one would not expect to meet when surrounded by vast areas of salt water. They can be extremely important especially with a super added illness. Physical work produces large amounts of sweat and is a sure way to lose salt, and with it water if not replaced. This fact was treated with some scepticism until one crew member fell ill with a mild attack of gastroenteritis. This produced even more fluid and salt loss. When the attack had cleared the crew member was left feeling mild aches and pains all over and extremely lethargic. I repeated my suggestion that fluids and salt tablets should be taken and this time it was accepted. Within a few hours he was feeling much better and in a day was back working. The rest of the crew followed his example and took regular salt tablets in the tropical parts of the race. Although a lot of the cooking was done in sea water their improvement generally after taking salt tablets suggests that cooking in sea water alone is not enough in tropical climes. Care must also be taken when there is a slight breeze blowing as sweating becomes much less obvious.

Another problem with the sun and sea was not experienced until the first part of the final leg. When on deck in extremely humid conditions, clothing is kept to a minimum (if any is worn at all). With the crew in swimming trunks and water splashing on to the decks one often became soaked several times in quick succession. Sweating and coating with salt produced a rash confined to the swimming trunk area. The lack of fresh water to cleanse the area was sadly missed. More itchy than sore, these rashes cleared after leaving the hot weather. This phenomenon was christened 'gunwale bum' by some of the crews.

The sun in the tropics is an ever present problem and for those who revelled in it too deeply and too soon, a danger. Common sense and experience proved to everyone that gradual exposure was the order of the day. Once a tan had been acquired very little trouble was encountered. We found that some members of the crew were particularly sensitive and had to wear a protective cream on their noses and shoulders to reflect or absorb the ultra violet light. A hat was helpful but sometimes impracticable. Uvistat cream was the one used in preference to others although yellow petroleum jelly absorbs some UV light. Uvistat is also useful for those cold sores which appear in response to UV light.

Post Port Syndromes

In general the atmosphere at sea is very healthy, probably because of the high salt content of the atmosphere. In cold climates very few bacteria can exist and the *Antarctic Pilot* mentions that very few of the bacteria found among the penguins are pathogenic to men.

Our main problems came after we had been in a port for one of the stops. Having had two weeks in Cape Town the crew of *Second Life* were stricken by a flu-like illness during the first week out. This was almost certainly viral in origin and presented as aches and pains, sore throats and fevers. Lasting only a few days it passed from one to another fortunately never attacking more than one or two crew members at a time. It was suggested that it might be due to a reaction to the port but this would not account for the fever. Symptoms were relieved by aspirin.

A similar experience followed stopping in Sydney when florid tonsillitis swept through the crew. This came from a known contact and was equally as severe as the flu epidemic. Undoubtedly a long period at sea lowers one's resistance to everyday infections merely because one is not exposed to them. Whereas they would often not be noticed in normal life, subclinical infections become obvious after lack of exposure.

The Cold

Working a four hour watch between four people sounds very reasonable. When the sea and air temperatures are both at 2° Centigrade problems inevitably arise. It no longer becomes possible to spend the whole hour of your share on the helm and we had to reduce helming to 20 minute stints. This allowed some time for warming up below decks before braving the elements again. In these temperatures and with seas that accompanied them decisions had to be made with great care. Aware that low temperatures slow one up mentally and physically we tried to be one step ahead all the time. The length of time taken to change a headsail in a moderate sea is significantly increased at low temperatures. Hands do not work properly. Fingers have no feeling and you actually move slower. Making decisions is also a difficult problem and undoubtedly time was lost by all yachts by slow sail changes be they up or down.

Dr Robin Leach in the cockpit of *Second Life*. Note the notice on the companion door reminding crew members to wear their safety harness.

Psychological Aspects

There has never been such a long, fully crewed yacht race. A proportion of the crews changed at the ports of call. Others did not change at all. We had a nucleus of eleven people on *Second Life* who did the whole race. Living together in a flat with three other people can be a test of tempers even under what may seem ideal circumstances. To put a group of people together for a 28,000 mile race in a 70 foot yacht would seem social suicide. Yet it was not.

The variables in such a situation are infinite and it is impossible to completely evaluate why crews did not actually have mutinies and come to blows. Yes, there were differences of opinion – what a sterile procedure it would have been if there had not. Nobody would have gained very much at all. Perhaps the fact that we were all talking to each other at the end of the race is the biggest achievement of all.

Those who tried to carry an argument too far soon learnt to shut up. This is an important point as half way between Sydney and Rio de Janeiro there is very little latitude to bear a grudge vociferously. It seems that to a certain extent a crew does need a whipping post on a long trip. One of three or four members of the crew would, quite unannounced, become the person to moan at for a few days. The issues were often trifling and that crew member had to take the abuse that was given to him until the needle pointed to another. Often the most inexperienced of the crew, they never complained but seemed to realize that this was a necessary imposition. In that respect we were lucky that no one did take offence.

What would seem trifling things now that the race is over, were blown up at sea. Somebody had a perpetual sniff. One seat was always occupied by the same person. Somebody starts reading a book before you have finished it. Late on watch again. The heads are blocked and no one admitted to being last to use them. Entertainments on board were confined to reading – vast amounts – sleeping and a cassette tape recorder. The daily chat to the other boats and the reports to Portishead were also highlights for which the crew crowded around.

It is possible to live together for long periods at sea – this has been known for hundreds of years. How a crew would react to racing a yacht which is comparatively small compared with the clippers was in doubt. The loneliness, the feeling that there are so many thousands of miles of ocean around does not exist. The horizon each day is no more than 15 to 20 miles away – usually much less. This is your environment. Only when reaching a port did slight restlessness occur. Sexual frustration was not encountered at sea.

Medical Precautions

It would have been very easy to take a dozen courses of every known tablet to cover oneself as a doctor on this race. This is obviously not feasible – but I did try. Antibiotics, analgesics, skin creams and lotions, laxatives, anti-diarrhoeals, drops for ears and eyes, antacids, were all in abundance. Material to stitch with, plaster of Paris, bandages and surgical and dental instruments. There is no doubt that we had too much on board medically speaking. However, one would have looked stupid if something had arisen which needed a drug which you had vetoed from the medical chest. It's not so bad if you haven't thought of it. The trouble is that if you do think of bringing something and don't you are bound to need it, and vice versa.

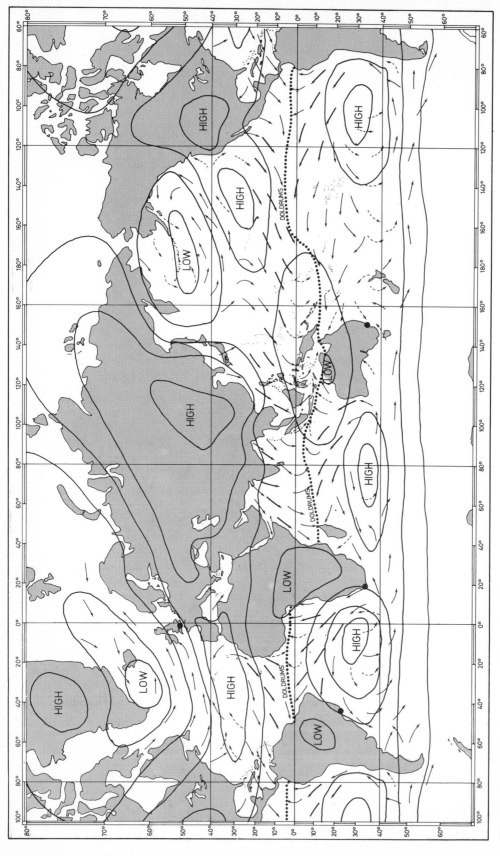

World Climatic Chart for Month of January

This chart depicts the average climatic conditions likely to be encountered in the month of January – the height of the northern winter and southern summer. The heavy lines surrounding the high and low pressure areas indicate lines of equal barometric pressure. The high pressure areas remain fairly constant whereas the travelling lows or depressions which move from west to east across the temperate zone are more variable.

The heavy arrows indicate the direction of the reliable Trade Winds which can be expected to blow in the direction shown for more than two-thirds of the time. The light arrows indicate less constant winds and where the arrows are broken or omitted the winds are variable.

The line of dots shows the area of Doldrums where the weather is changeable – light, variable winds alternating with squalls and thunderstorms.

13
Navigation

For the majority of yachtsmen, navigation is confined to short hops along the coast or passages of no more than a hundred miles or so from one point of land to the next. Very often there are buoys or light vessels to provide definite reference points along the route and, when out of sight of land, the prime means of navigation is usually by radio direction finding equipment. Navigation in these relatively confined waters is very often influenced by the state of the tide and local weather forecasts. By delaying sailing a few hours the wind may have moderated and the tide changed, thus producing completely different sea conditions – slipping past a headland in slack water before the tide turns can mean a difference of perhaps six hours in passage time; an error of a few hundred yards can mean the difference between a safe passage and shipwreck.

This is coastal navigation and pilotage, calling for frequent plotting of position and the ability to recognize when changing patterns of weather dictate an immediate change of tactics. Ocean navigation is very different. The overall plan is governed by ocean currents, which flow in the same direction for months on end and whose routes mainly fluctuate with the seasons of the year, and by the Trade Winds which blow more or less steadily in a given direction. But although the general weather pattern is

fairly predictable, the accuracy with which it can be predicted varies considerably from one region to another. Also, local weather systems can be superimposed on the general situation in an area and produce less predictable conditions.

In ocean navigation the position of the yacht is fixed, at the most, three times a day, and probably only once or twice, by taking sights of celestial bodies with a sextant – this is called astro navigation. By measuring the angle of a celestial body above the horizon (its altitude) and referring to navigation tables, it is possible to produce a position line. The position of the observer will be somewhere along this single position line. The line is plotted, that is drawn, on a chart or large scale plotting sheet and two or more other position lines obtained by measuring the altitude of other celestial bodies. If the measurements with the sextant have been taken accurately and the subsequent calculations have been carried out correctly, the lines will all intersect at the same point which will give the position of the yacht. In practice, however, in a yacht it is seldom possible to fix the position to an accuracy of less than a mile and so the position lines cross, producing what is called a 'cocked hat'; the position of the yacht is usually taken to be the middle of the cocked hat.

When conditions are good the navigator will try to take sights of morning and evening stars and a noon position from the sun. Bright stars or planets and the moon can be used at dawn and dusk provided they are visible and there is a well defined horizon. What can happen, however, is that the sky can be overcast at the time the navigator wishes to take his sights so the heavenly bodies are not visible, or poor visibility at sea level obliterates the horizon. Then there is nothing he can do but wait for next time and knowing the weather pattern in Northern Europe it would not be surprising if he had to wait for up to a week on occasion. But this did not prove to be the case during the race for seldom did more than a couple of days go by when it was not possible to obtain a sight.

The accuracy of a sight depends initially on the navigator measuring the altitude of the sun, star or planet accurately. If the yacht is being flung around all over the place his job is not easy and in rough conditions it is difficult to obtain a true horizon as the observer's eye is so near the water that a wave often intervenes between it and the horizon. But despite the difficulties, most of the navigators on the race reckoned that even in the worst conditions they were able to get a position which was accurate to within 10 miles. The larger the boat, the steadier the platform on which the navigator is standing and the easier it is to obtain an accurate sight. Thus the bigger yachts like *Sayula II*, *Pen Duick VI* and *Great Britain II* were able to obtain more accurate positions than the little 45 footers, *Copernicus* and *Guia*.

The Bible for any navigator planning an ocean passage is the Admiralty publication *Ocean Passages for the World* which was written originally at the end of the last century from information received from the captains of ships of the British Royal and Merchant Navies. It has been revised a number of times and the edition available to those taking part in the race was published in 1950. But the section dealing with sailing ship routes has probably remained largely unaltered since the turn of the century and certainly very little has been added to the information on the route round Cape Horn since the Panama Canal was opened in 1914. A similar publication to *Ocean Passages* was produced in Germany but when the skipper of *Peter von Danzig* looked at it he found that the sections on the Indian and Pacific Oceans had not been updated since the 1890s; he did use the Atlantic section, which was the third edition printed in 1910!

Provided with *Ocean Passages for the World* are charts giving details of the general surface current circulation, sailing ship routes and climatic conditions. *Ocean Passages* is an invaluable book for ocean passage planning but it has to be remembered that the recommended routes were made with square-riggers in mind and much of the information was originally compiled from reports supplied by the captains of such vessels. Square-rigged ships cannot sail to windward with any degree of efficiency so they chose downwind routes for their passages. Also available are Routeing Charts which give predictions of weather conditions and the strength and direction of winds for each month of the year in different areas.

In the initial stages of planning the race it was necessary for the organisers to decide the amount of time to allow for each leg so that arrangements could be made at the stop-over ports. The RNSA produced detailed predictions which ran to nine duplicated pages and took into consideration the times of the largest and smallest yachts, depending on the conditions likely to be experienced. Copies of these predictions were circulated to all the entries although the skippers and navigators of each yacht naturally made their own predictions. There is not room in this book to reproduce the RNSA's predictions for all four legs of the course, but those for the first leg are an interesting example of the exercise.

Prediction of Stage Duration for Round the World Race

A study has been made of the route for the 1973 Round the World Yacht Race to try and determine the probable duration of each stage of the race.

Calculations were based on information given in the Routeing Charts with occasional reference to *Ocean Passages for the World*.

In order to calculate times on each stage the following tables of speeds in different wind conditions were assumed.

Table 1.   Yacht rating 64 ft IOR. TCF 1.06. Maximum speed without planing or surfing 11.5 knots.

	Speeds		
Beaufort Wind Force	Close-hauled	Reaching	Running
2	4	4	4
3	6	6	7
4	7	8	9
5	8	10	12 ⎫
6	7	10	13 ⎬ Surfing
7	6	11	13 ⎭
8	5	10	11
9	3	7	9
10	Hove-to	3	5

Table 2.   Yacht rating 36 feet IOR. TCF 0.86 Maximum speed planing or surfing 8.5 knots.

	Speeds		
Beaufort Wind Force	Close-hauled	Reaching	Running
2	3	3	3
3	5	5	6
4	6	7	7
5	7	8	9 ⎫
6	6	8	10 ⎬ Surfing
7	5	8	10 ⎭
8	4	7	8
9	2	5	6
10	Hove-to	2	5

All estimated speeds have been rounded off to the nearest whole number for ease of working.

Stage 1. Portsmouth – Cape Town (Start 8th September 1973)

	Elapsed Times	
	Large Yacht	*Small Yacht*

A. Portsmouth to 50 miles west of Ushant. 260NM.

Winds variable, probably westerly 1–7. Speeds calculated for Force 4 westerlies 10% addition to distance for windward work. 3% added to elapsed times for calm.   1 day 18 hrs   2 days   1 hr

		Elapsed Time	
		Large Yacht	*Small Yacht*

B. 50 miles west of Ushant to 100 miles west of Cabo Villano. 390NM.

Winds variable. Force 0–7, probably westerly, Force 5 veering northwesterly towards southern part of leg.

Assume 50% distance in Force 5 westerly, 50% distance in Force 5 northwesterly. 5% addition to distance for windward work. 3% added to time for calms.

2 days 3 hrs 2 days 12 hrs

C. 100 miles west of Cabo Villano to southern limit of NE Trade (11°00′ N 32°30′ W). 2,250 miles. Portuguese Trade and NE Trade cover entire leg. Trades vary in strength Force 3–6, occasionally lighter and stronger.

Assume wind abaft the beam throughout the leg, distance run in wind strengths as follows:

25% Force 3
25% Force 4
25% Force 5
25% Force 6.

3% added to elapsed times for calms and light airs.

10 days 0 hrs 12 days 12 hrs

D. 11°00′N 32°30′W to 4°00′N 32°30′W. 420NM.

Through the Doldrums. Wind variable and mainly light. Assume yachts travel at minimum speed throughout leg. No allowance for calms as winds greater than Force 2 should be experienced for short periods.

4 days 9 hrs 5 days 20 hrs

E. 4°00′N 32°30′W to Cape Town. 3,700 miles. Mainly to windward through SE Trade and variables, with possibility of favourable winds in last 500–1,000 miles.

Assume wind strengths and points of sailing as follows:
10% Force 2 close-hauled
10% Force 3 close-hauled
20% Force 4 close-hauled
20% Force 5 close-hauled
10% Force 6 close-hauled
10% Force 4 reaching
10% Force 5 reaching
10% Force 4 running

15% added to distance for extra ground to be made to windward.

24 days 16 hrs 29 days 21 hrs

Total elapsed times		42 days 22 hrs	53 days 20 hrs
Total distance		7.090 NM	
Mean day's run		163 NM	131 NM
Corrected times		1068·48 hrs	1093·92 hrs

Possibility of a large spread of finishing times

In a race of this length it is obviously possible for different competitors to experience different weather patterns. If all competitors followed the same route it is estimated that the possible delays due to unfavourable weather patterns compared with other competitors would be of the following order:

a. Start to NE Trade   2 days
b. NE Trade   1 day
c. Doldrums   1 day
d. SE Trade   1 day
e. SE Trade – Finish   3 days

Total   8 days   (unlikely to be cumulative)

Probability of competitors following different routes

In forecasting elapsed times it has been assumed that competitors will follow the orthodox route. It would be possible to make this passage by a course which followed the rhumb line more closely and although it would be shorter, any advantage gained by sailing a shorter distance would probably be lost in entering the Doldrums in a more northerly latitude, and by light headwinds which would be encountered in the Gulf of Guinea.

Summary of the whole race

The main difficulties in making the study were:

a. Deciding upon the likely performance of the yachts under difficult conditions.
b. Calculating elapsed times in the areas of variable winds.

It is hoped that these two difficulties have been resolved in a satisfactory manner; but if not, sufficient information has been given to allow the Committee to formulate different conclusions.

A number of possible problem areas have not been considered. One of these which may be of relevance is the difference in stores to displacement ratio for large and small yachts. It is quite possible that on the long legs of the race a small yacht will be significantly handicapped by the weight of the stores on board. For *Belmore*'s passage from Rio de Janeiro to Portsmouth in 1962, the stores embarked sunk her six inches below her designed waterline, and her performance was adversely affected for the first four weeks of the voyage. This problem will obviously be more acute in the small yachts than the larger ones.

The question of the downwind fliers has not been considered in any detail. No doubt a boat with a very high downwind potential could make very fast times on parts of several stages of the race. The price of very fast speeds downwind is the risk of broaching violently, and while this risk is acceptable when racing in the Solent or English Channel it is considerably less acceptable in the Southern Ocean. For this reason it is considered unlikely that a boat of this type could be driven hard enough on the downwind legs to realize her full potential. A lack of knowledge of the performance characteristics of boats of this type has precluded its inclusion in detail as a third class of yacht in this study.

NOTE   THE COMMITTEE DO NOT NECESSARILY AGREE WITH ALL ROUTES AND RECOMMENDATIONS CONTAINED IN THE ABOVE. THEIR CALCULATIONS OF THE HANDICAP DISTANCE WILL TAKE INTO ACCOUNT THE COURSES THAT A PRUDENT NAVIGATOR WOULD TAKE BETWEEN PORTS AND WILL BE BASED ON SIMILAR SOURCE MATERIAL.

These predictions proved to be reasonably accurate, for on the first leg the first yacht to finish, *Burton Cutter*, took 42 days 7 hours and the last yacht, *Peter von Danzig*, 52 days 12 hours.

To the landsman, or even the sailor whose experience of navigation is limited to coastal passages, the prospect of having to determine one's position in the middle of a vast area of ocean, many miles from the nearest land, is daunting to say the least. However, once one has mastered the use of the sextant and become familiar with the subsequent calculations, it is a relatively simple operation. With the benefit of the information available on ocean currents, winds and weather patterns, the ocean navigator has a reasonably straightforward task when planning the overall route to take. The difficulty is that seldom is it possible to adhere rigidly to a pre-determined plan – for either winds from the least expected direction force the yacht to sail away from the preferred course or the prospect of weather which is likely to be encountered results in altering course to get the right side of an approaching depression.

Wilhelm Grütter, one of the crew of *Jakaranda* on the first leg, wrote, 'Navigation was done by the skipper and Bill Damerell and occasionally by Yvonne van der Byl, and I just watched the white man's magic with open-mouthed admiration as the crosses connected to each other in a line not dissimilar to the classic clipper route (which is what the skipper had said he was going to do). His best feat came one evening in the cockpit when we had gathered for the customary ceremony of tossing messages in bottles over the side. (To do this, you first had to dispose of the contents of the bottle!) John stood up, pointed something like four points off the starboard bow and said "Martin Vaz should be somewhere over there", and it was. Our last sight of land had been a rather hazy impression, early in the morning, of Ilha Boa Vista on the 15th day. John "discovered" Vaz on the 29th day.

'The weather did, to my naïve eye, more or less what the charts said it would do. Of course, when one wanted a five knot westerly, it was invariably easterly, but it had the fullest right to be there according to the weather chart averages. We had our best day's run on the tenth day when *Jakaranda* did

227 miles from her previous noon position and at the end of the day, the skipper's six-hour watch had clocked 53 miles. (This was between Madeira and the Canaries.)'

Roy Mullender, skipper of *Adventure* on the last leg, commented: 'The NE Trades are the most reliable winds in the world but if when you get there you find that the wind is blowing from the north it is probable that you are there during one of the five days a year that it is doing so.'

Around the world there are a number of almost permanent high pressure zones and a corresponding number of low pressure zones, the positions of which may fluctuate from season to season but which, nevertheless, remain in fairly predictable areas. In the northern hemisphere, winds circulate round high pressure areas in a clockwise direction and around low pressure areas in an anti-clockwise direction. In the southern hemisphere the opposite applies – anti-clockwise around highs and clockwise around lows. In the North Atlantic, for instance, the predominant climatic feature is the Azores High which produces westerly winds in latitudes north of $35°$ to $40°\,N$, northerly winds down the east coasts of the Iberian Peninsular and North Africa (the Portuguese Northerlies), and Northeasterly Trade Winds across from the Cape Verde Islands to the West Indies. There is a similar high pressure area in the South Atlantic producing an anti-clockwise pattern. The Trade Winds on the Equator side of these systems are more regular in force and more reliable in direction than the westerlies encountered in more temperate zones where depressions moving from west to east provide constant fluctuations. Thus, although the prediction on a Routeing Chart for a particular point may indicate a prevailing Force 4 southwesterly wind for 60% of the time, you may arrive there on one of the days of the month when the wind is Force 1 easterly.

Near the Equator, right round the world, lies an area of Doldrums where there can be light, variable winds punctuated by violent thunder storms and strong winds, and it is in this area that the progress of a sailing yacht becomes most unpredictable. If you are lucky you keep moving and slip through without being becalmed – but you may wallow around for a week with little wind.

Second Life creams along on a reach under reefed mainsail whilst her navigator tries to find the sun for his noon sight.

There is a large high pressure area in the southern Indian Ocean and another in the South Pacific off the western coast of South America. Funnelling between these high pressure areas and the Antarctic region is a series of depressions moving from west to east. These occur right across the Southern Ocean on the routes from Cape Town to Sydney and Sydney to Cape Horn.

When sailing from Portsmouth to Cape Town the aim is first to get clear of the English Channel and shape a course to the south and west as quickly as possible to pick up the Portugese Northerlies. This is easier in a modern, close-winded yacht than it was for those sailing in square-riggers who were advised, 'Ushant should in no case be sighted' and to gain an offing 10° or 12° west to avoid being carried by currents into the Bay of Biscay.

On the first leg of the race most of the yachts followed the same course down as far as the Canary Islands and on to the Cape Verdes. The winds were mainly southwesterly until a latitude of about 35° N – level with the southern end of Spain – and then became light, northerly increasing to Force 4 to 5

in the Trades. The band of Doldrums just north of the Equator is wider to the east and narrower to the west, but a yacht which can keep going and cross to the east is to windward of a yacht which crosses more to the west, when she finally picks up the Southeasterly Trades.

In the South Atlantic section of the course, the choices open were to sail the longest distance, going first west of south and then approaching Cape Town for the last 1000 miles on an easterly course, the route taken by *Sayula II* and *Jakaranda*; to take a mean course, initially slightly to the west, then veering towards Cape Town, the route followed by *Adventure* and the line honours boat, *Burton Cutter*; or to work close inshore along the coast of Africa in an attempt to pick up onshore breezes and sailing inside the north-going current, the route taken by *CS e RB* which did not pay.

Sayula II sailed 1,000 miles extra by taking the westerly route but kept going with a good wind most of the time. This course was chosen because, being a ketch, she was not so close-winded as the sloops and cutters and was, therefore, going to do better fol-

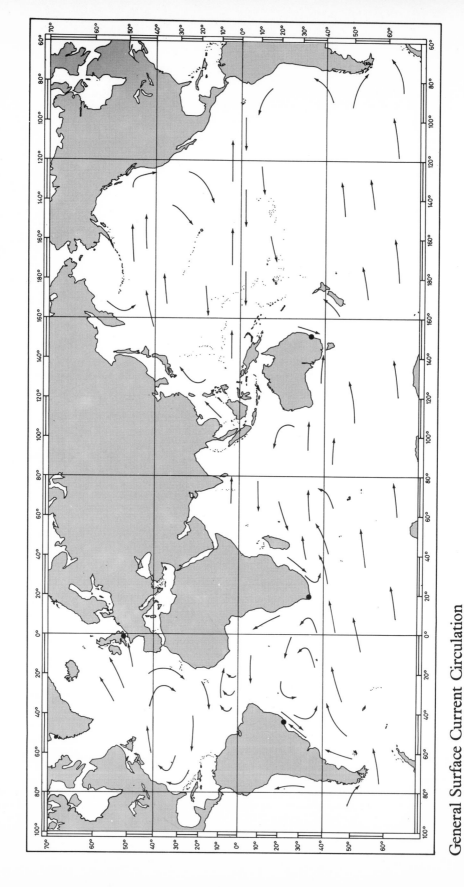

General Surface Current Circulation
The arrows indicate the general direction of the surface currents likely to be encountered round the world.

lowing a route with a freer wind where she could use her reaching speed potential to the full. In fact she went a long way west and sighted Trinidade Island, about 30° W and 20° S – further west than had originally been planned due to working to the west to keep in the most favourable winds. Although *Sayula* sailed the greatest distance on this leg, her navigator Ray Conrady reckoned it to have been worthwhile as she maintained two knots higher speed when reaching than when close-hauled and this compensated for the extra distance sailed.

On the second leg, the great circle route from Cape Town to the Bass Strait – between Tasmania and the Australian mainland – goes well south into the ice and over the solid ground of Antarctica. The biggest decision facing the navigators on this and the third leg was how far south to go. The further one went, the shorter the distance but the greater the possibility of encountering ice and meeting head winds on the wrong side of depressions. *Copernicus* took the most northerly course – most southerly point 44° S – whilst the Italian yachts *CS e RB* and *Guia* went furthest south – *Guia* to 52° 10′. The rest of the fleet spread out between 45° and 50° S.

On the third leg, from Sydney to Rio, the recommended route passes south of South Island, New Zealand and all the yachts except *Second Life* took this course. *Second Life* passed through Cook Strait between North and South Island but this did not pay because she ran into light winds whilst the rest of the fleet were battling with strong winds for a few days after passing the southern tip of South Island. The great circle route for the third leg goes further south than for the second leg but there was no point in going too far due to the risk of ice. About half the fleet sighted ice during the third leg but only two yachts went below the 60° S parallel – *CS e RB*, which took the most southerly route of all going as far as 61° 40′ S and spending over a week below the 60th parallel, and *Adventure* which took the most southerly route of the fleet immediately after clearing South Island and then stayed around the 59th parallel for ten days.

After rounding Cape Horn the yachts were faced with northerly winds, and, as they approached Rio, the Brazil Current which sets in a southwesterly direction down the coast. The paying thing to do was

to pass between the Falkland Islands and the mainland with the north-going Falkland Current and then to keep well offshore. Those yachts which closed the coast too early definitely lost out against those which kept off until the final run in to Rio.

Captain George Vallings, *Adventure*'s skipper for this leg, gave the following account of the approach to the Horn and passage into the South Atlantic:

'We started to edge north from the 60° S parallel towards the Horn on January 25th. We had been on or near the parallel since January 13th and during these 12 days the log shows that the wind was aft of the beam for 26 hours only and we had logged over 2,000 miles. No wonder the downwind flyers had not been able to get away from us.

'As we approached land we at last got the westerlies we expected and *Endurance* joined us at 1600 on the 27th when we were about 100 miles short of the Horn. It was a great moment as she appeared out of the gloom – at the time we were running in quite a big sea with a wind speed of some 35 knots. We were far from sure of our position at the time but *Endurance* rightly could not help. So in a falling wind and good visibility we pressed on with spinnaker flying, hopefully into the night. Our landfall at 0200 next morning indicated that we were in fact, by good fortune, only five miles north of track. However, navigation had not been easy, with few opportunities for stars between New Zealand and South America and even the sun often not visible for several days running. The only radio aid, the air beacon on Tierra del Fuego, is screened by mountains and unreliable. On top of this our main compass had got worse and worse, developing unpredictable heading errors. The work on the bevel box on which it is mounted did not improve it. Throughout the voyage the hand bearer remained the only reliable compass, whilst thankfully the log and the echo sounder were excellent.

'We rounded Cape Horn at dawn on January 28th. The wind was variable two knots and as the sun rose we sat in the cockpit drinking tea. Hardly the romantic image, but good for photography. Later that day *Endurance* bade farewell. She did a great job for all the yachts in the race and her Radio Supervisor must have the patience of Job – he was a real friend to us all. It became *Endurance*'s custom, as she left to go back round the Horn to meet the next yacht, to put on a special show appropriate to the country of the yacht concerned. For us there were pirates, songs and a seven gun salute. There was so much enthusiasm over this and the ship was so close that the blast from the sixth gun made a hole in our Number 1 topsail — we soon repaired it.

'I cannot pass on from the Southern Ocean without mentioning the birds which were with us all the time except, funnily enough, when we were in the ice area. I cannot explain this unless they were very susceptible to temperature. The albatross is well known as a most beautiful bird — the white version found nearer South America. Several times we disturbed a sleeping albatross and, although they are so elegant in flight, they are most ungainly trying to get airborne under the bows of a yacht. Enough of the albatross though because it was the petrel in many different forms that gave us most joy. Heaven only knows where they came from — at one time we were 2,000 miles from the nearest land — but they were always there cavorting energetically up and down the waves. These birds and our daily chats with *Grand Louis* on the wireless made the ocean a much less lonely place than it would otherwise have been.

'Our plan from Cape Horn was to pass west of the Falkland Islands and thence to a position 300 miles south of Rio. That track takes advantage of the north-going Falkland Current and avoids the strong contrary Brazil Current inshore further north. It is usually a bad mistake to attempt to close-fetch inshore against the prevailing northeast wind and southwest set. The plan, which was corroborated by Argentine naval friends, paid off.

'However, the first two days after rounding the Horn were most frustrating as we made slow progress through the strong tides in the Le Maire Straits and off the Falkland Islands. It was like going down Channel in light airs and missing tides at Portland, the Start and the Lizard. We only just weathered the Falklands. It was dark when we approached the westernmost island, Jason West Cay, which is described in the Pilot as low-lying. We were on the lookout for it but without the echo sounder we might still be there. The island is only about 20 feet high and we did not see it until we were very close. The helmsmen first remarked on the

strong smell of fish. I wrote $\frac{1}{2}$ mile in the log but someone crossed this out and indicated he thought it was much closer. To have tacked, say, 10 miles to the east, would have lost two hours we could ill afford — we relied on the echo sounder and on our sense of smell.'

Olivier Stern-Veyrin navigated *33 Export* on the third leg and studied the weather charts for December in the South Pacific which were obtained from the Meteorological Bureau in Sydney. These showed that the lows tended to travel from the west to the east around 55°S. So *33 Export* remained north of this latitude for much of the time — the furthest south she went was 56° 31′S — and from 140°W to 80°W experienced winds of from Force 4 to 6 from between southwest and northwest. In fact only on one day during this period, from January 29th to February 8th, did the wind swing north of northwest, and then only to north. *Grand Louis*, on the other hand, shaped a course about 58°S to 60°S and experienced winds from northwest to southeast, although of course she sailed a shorter distance. Stern-Veyrin believed that following the recommended clipper ship route, as they did in *33 Export*, was best because it ensured fair winds, little or no risk of ice and warmer temperatures — from 8°C to 12°C during the period as opposed to the 2°C to 5°C recorded on board *Grand Louis*. Exactly which route was best is difficult to determine because yachts sailed at different speeds and experienced their weather at different times. Probably the more southerly route was better for a close-winded yacht like *Adventure* but not so good for *Grand Louis*, a schooner and therefore not at her best to windward.

On the last leg the problem facing the navigators was almost the mirror image of that facing them on the first leg. They had to work north up the coast of Brazil against the contrary Brazil Current and head winds to pick up the SE Trades before crossing the Doldrums near the Equator and finding the NE Trades. It was then a case of deciding whether to face the possibility of having to work to windward virtually through the middle of the Azores High following fairly closely the great circle route or to sail close reaching on starboard tack skirting round to the west of the Azores High to pick up the predominently westerly winds which could be expected when making a more northerly approach to the English Channel.

In the event, *Sayula II* having gone furthest west on the first leg, proceeded to go furthest east on this leg. In fact she completed her circumnavigation of the world in just about six months on March 27th at about 07°N, 23°W, whereas most of the others did not do so until they entered the English Channel.

British Soldier did the other thing and went west of north until she hit the westerlies. Once she got through the Doldrums and picked up the NE Trades she clocked up from 170 to 200 miles a day on a close starboard reach, with a best day's run of 220 miles. When about 27°N and 40°W, she ran out of the Trade Winds and experienced a couple of days of light, variable winds from the east before picking up winds from the west which gradually increased in strength from 5 knots to over 30 knots and lasted for four or five days until the Azores were sighted. It was then mainly close-hauled work, with some tacking when the wind went northeasterly, all the way home. The only yacht to go further west than *British Soldier* was *Peter von Danzig* which was about ten days behind her and had to stand on about 300 miles further than *British Soldier* before she picked up the westerlies, which is a good indication of how the weather pattern can vary in quite a short period of time.

On balance the more easterly route seemed to pay on this occasion, for *Sayula II* had some very good runs off the Canaries in strong southerly winds and had a free wind for most of the way back to the English Channel and *Adventure* had a free wind until the last 600 miles to the finish. But had these two met head winds it could well have been a different story.

Alain Gliksman, one of the most experienced of French ocean sailors, summed up his views on navigation in some notes published in *Neptune Nautisme*.

'When there is a swell and you get several miles of difference between the two altitudes taken of a star it is better to make graphs of a series of altitudes taken as closely as possible. Not always easy because you must be at the crest of a wave so that the swell does not hide the horizon. Another problem is the false horizon.

'Twice in the Indian Ocean we were sailing ENE when I thought we were doing ESE. When I took over navigation I found errors in the compass. The next leg the same thing happened, whereas it had been adjusted and checked in Sydney. Some say that the correction by magnets changes in various latitudes. I suspect the generator, working a couple of hours per day. This does not happen in harbour, therefore the phenomenon is only noticed at sea. Anyhow, it is difficult to have a correct compass reading, what with the swell and all, and the stars must be used as a guide to check it.

'This race seems to have disproved what all the manuals with nautical instructions say: wind force and seas increase with the latitudes. The worst weather was found by those who took the most northern routes. Bad weather seems to be between 40° and 45°S, then becomes more cut up but less strong. Of the three oceans the Indian is the most brutal. It is the only one where the wind precedes the fall in the barometer and does not send a single warning cloud. The cold depends on the time of the year and the latitude, but it was better at 62°S in January than at 55°S in December.

'In the Pacific the most southern route was not only the shortest, but also the sea was at its flattest and it avoided sudden squalls. However, there is the problem of icebergs. Not the route to recommended to singlehanded sailors unless they stop in the dark, which lasts for only three hours below the 60° parallel. In the Pacific the worst weather was in the Tasman Sea. Those taking the Cook Strait (*Second Life*) were becalmed but a few weeks later those who went south could have met much worse weather.' The biggest single factor affecting ocean navigation is the facility to obtain accurate weather forecasts. A certain amount of single observer forecasting can be done on board of course but this provides only a relatively short warning of changes in the weather — certainly not enough to plan which side to pass a depression, which can be what decides whether the yacht keeps going with a fair wind or ends up beating against a light wind.

In the Pacific Alain Colas, shadowing the race singlehanded in his trimaran *Manureva*, broadcast weather information obtained from the facsimile equipment he had installed on board. This equipment is a radio receiver which picks up special weather transmissions and reproduces the information as a weather map. Colas passed the information to the French yachts by radio telephone and they in turn made it available to other competitors. The installation of facsimile equipment on board yachts participating in the race was not allowed but it could be a useful thing to bear in mind for future races of this type. After the race *Sayula*'s navigator, Ray Conrady, wrote:

'A closer look should be made concerning use of radio facsimile equipment. Although good weather reports can be received by morse in the North and South Atlantic and, to a lesser extent, in the southern Indian Ocean, the best coverage in the South Pacific is on FAC (station AYM, Australia; polar stereographic of the southern hemisphere). Since all yachts probably could not carry this equipment, those that did could be required to pass the information to the fleet. As Alain Colas said, "It costs about the same as a couple of spinnakers".'

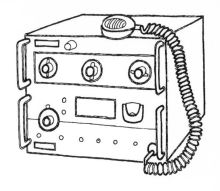

14
Communications

When Sir Francis Chichester broke through the sound barrier by sending radio reports back to London during his attempt to beat the singlehanded trans-Atlantic record in 1962, he confounded the experts by maintaining communication with the UK from beyond 40°W. He had hardly an amp left in his batteries and progress reporting by radio from a yacht was something very novel indeed. In the years that have slipped by since then, radio telephone communication with yachts on ocean passages has all become rather matter-of-fact and is taken for granted. Probably many people think that using a radio telephone from the middle of the ocean is simply a matter of picking up the hand set and drawling 'Hello Portishead. Do you read me?' After all, we do talk to men on the moon these days, so what is so difficult about chatting with yachtsmen in mid-Atlantic or in the Indian Ocean?

Nothing really, provided that the radio is the right type; that the operator really knows how to get the best out of his set; that it has been installed and tuned by an expert, with all that implies with aerial rig – not always so easy or efficient in a sailing craft; and that the correct frequencies are used at the right time of day for the part of the world in which the yacht is sailing.

The matter of frequencies, times and positions is where communications organisation comes in. Paragraph 9.6 of the Special Regulations and Compulsory Equipment (see Appendix 1), details of which were distributed to competitors by the Race Committee early on, stated merely that a participating yacht must be equipped with a 'marine radio transmitter and receiver with minimum transmitter power of 50 watts'. A seemingly innocuous statement but one which would involve the spending of quite a lot of money if the entrant yacht was not already suitably equipped.

That small paragraph was expanded to 12 closely typed pages of Radio Equipment Requirements and 27 pages of Communications Instructions, copies of which were distributed to all entrants.

The principal aim of the Requirements and Instructions was to ensure reliable transmission of distress, emergency and safety signals. Their secondary purpose being to transmit position reports to Race Control via the appropriate coast stations en route round the world. Although the original Compulsory Equipment regulations specified a transmitter output of 50 watts and did not stipulate the incorporation of high frequency facilities for long distance communication, the later Radio Equipment

Requirements recommended, very wisely, a minimum output of 75 watts and a transmitter frequency range from 2MHz to 22MHz, single sideband on high frequency and double sideband or compatible single sideband in the medium frequency range.

The difficulty in complying with these recommendations was twofold. First, buying and installing a suitable set was likely to cost something in the region of £3,000; second, the sets were in particularly short supply because the marine radio industry was over-pressed fulfilling orders for single sideband radio sets for commercial users who needed them to comply with new international regulations. In fact most of the competitors sailed with sets of considerably more power output than the minimum laid down. *Adventure* was fitted with a Redifon GR477 400 watt set with HF as well as MF coverage; the Polish entries, *Copernicus* and *Otago*, the French *Kriter* and Chay Blyth's *Great Britain II* were all fitted with the Marconi Falcon II, also a single sideband set covering HF and MF and with a power output of 150 watts; and the Italian *CS e RB* and the French *Grand Louis* had CRM sets of 400 watts output.

The organisers originally called for a radio position report once a week, but later stipulated two compulsory reports each week on set days. This helped the Race Control organisation and enabled an accurate, up-to-date picture of the progress of the race to be kept.

Transmissions in the medium frequency band usually have a range of 200 to 250 miles – possibly quite a bit more during the hours of darkness – and while yachts outward bound from Portsmouth on the first leg of the course were still within these distances of Land's End radio and Niton radio, their contact calls could be made on 2381 kHz for those of British registry and on 2182 kHz for those sailing under other flags. Medium frequency contact with the coast radio stations at Cape Town, Durban and Port Elizabeth was established on 2182 kHz.

Towards the end of the second leg of the race the Australian coast station group of Perth, Melbourne, Adelaide and Sydney guarded the 2 MHz band and answered calls on 2056 kHz, although calls could also be booked in advance using 2182 kHz. Yachts calling the New Zealand stations at Wellington,

Awarua, Auckland and Chatham Islands on medium frequency used 2182 kHz and the coast stations replied on the same frequency before changing to a working frequency.

When it came to rounding Cape Horn, Falkland Islands radio ran a special service for the yachts keeping a noncontinuous watch on 2182 kHz from 1000 to 0100 GMT daily, but apart from that contact things were not easy on medium frequency during the haul up the east side of the South American coast to Rio. Of the eight Argentine coast stations available, only the principle one, General Pacheco radio at Buenos Aires, presents a 2 MHz service, taking contact calls and answering on 2182 kHz. All the other seven operate in the 4 and 8 MHz bands only and, even for those yachts equipped with high frequency transmitters, there was a language difficulty in communication with these stations. Competitors were warned of this in Captain Norman's comprehensive pre-race documentation.

After Buenos Aires, Uruguay's Punta Carreta coast station affords facilities for communication on 2182 kHz, but, according to the official *List of Coast Stations* compiled by the International Telecommunications Union at Berne, Brazil provides no radio telephone service at all, either on medium or high frequencies, so the next MF contact with a coast station available to the yachts in the race was Lands End radio or Niton again, before the finish.

Those yachts equipped for high frequency radio working who managed to keep their radio equipment operating, had a considerable edge over the others as far as communications were concerned, though the number of crystals they needed to cover all the allocated frequencies of all the coast stations was formidable. In fact, few, if any, of the transmitters were capable of accommodating all the necessary crystals for the whole race in one go, though they should have been able to hold all the crystals needed for one leg. However, this entailed changing crystals with the consequent transmitter re-tuning. Apart from the accommodation and re-tuning problems, transmitter crystals cost over £5 each for the cheapest, so a full outfit tends to be an expensive luxury. The five basic crystals for the Portishead radio long distance family with GKU callsigns were regarded as absolutely essential however, since those yachts with

The skipper of *Second Life*, Roddie Ainslie, sitting at the chart table as he passes a message on the radio telephone.

a sufficiently high power output and efficient aerial installations were able to pass messages through Portishead during most, if not all, of the race. The French yachts reported through their equivalent of Portishead, St. Lys.

Sayula II experienced somewhat unsatisfactory radio performance due to her Northern Radio N550 transmitter being fitted in Finland by Nautor, her builders, when there was no qualified person available to tune the set and the aerial. This job was left until the boat reached England but was overlooked in the busy period of preparation before the race. Furthermore it was found impossible to obtain any performance out of certain channels and this was subsequently attributed to the fact that although a frequency was shown against the channel indicator on the front of the set, there was no crystal in place. Ray Conrady, *Sayula II*'s navigator, commented that he would not recommend the installation of a pre-tuned transceiver of the type they had fitted.

The Secretary's painstaking paperwork gave competitors full particulars of weather broadcasts and time signal transmissions along the race route and allocated 2056 kHz as the frequency for com-munication between yachts and with shipping. Competitors were advised to use this frequency for listening and transmitting for half hour stints between 2100 and 2130 GMT and between 0900 and 0930 GMT during the first leg from Portsmouth to Cape Town; between 1900 and 1930 GMT and 0700 and 0730 GMT on the second leg to Sydney; between 1000 and 1030 GMT and 2200 and 2230 GMT on the leg from Sydney to Rio; and also on the home-ward leg to Portsmouth. Yachts, like other vessels with radio telephones, have to observe the inter-national distress periods by keeping a listening watch on 2182 kHz for three minutes starting on every hour and on every half hour and refraining from transmitting during these periods. They are allowed to use 2182 kHz if they fail to make contact with a call on 2056 kHz which could let them get in touch with a merchant or naval ship or a coast station if there is one within range.

After the race had left Cape Town on the second leg a complaint was made to the organisers that Portishead radio was experiencing interference by special radio weather broadcasts being beamed out over the Indian Ocean by the South African Naval

Authorities. Although this was a directional transmission it was coming all the way round the world and was picked up by Portishead. South Africa was informed and the transmissions ceased on the frequency.

When yachts failed to make a report at the prearranged time this naturally gave rise to concern amongst the race organisers and the families and friends of the crews. The organisers anticipated, quite correctly, that the most likely reason for no report would be the failure of radio equipment but they had to be prepared to instigate a search if they had reason to believe that the missing yacht was in distress. In fact, despite a number of quite serious incidents resulting in damage, especially during the second leg, and the loss of three crew members, the yachts were always able to continue under their own power and never required outside assistance. If no report was received from a yacht for seven days the organisers informed Lloyds, who passed out a message to merchant shipping, and also the BBC World Service, which mentioned that a report was overdue. In many cases the appeal through Lloyds brought a response within a few days and although a yacht may have been out of radio contact with the shore, its whereabouts was known.

The BBC World Club, which has members who listen to worldwide radio transmissions in the hope of finding something unusual, also agreed to report any signals they heard from the yachts, but despite the undoubted 'scoop' appeal no reports were forthcoming from this source.

There were few sighting reports from merchant ships simply because for much of the race the course followed by the yachts was well away from normal merchant ship routes. When the yachts were in contact with merchant shipping – at the beginning of the first leg and during the final stages of the last leg – they were in areas of good radio communication. In the South Atlantic the yachts were spread between the normal shipping lanes which follow the west coast of Africa and the east coast of South America; only two or three merchant ships a month sail between Cape Town and the southeast ports of Australia; and there is virtually no traffic from Sydney round the Horn.

For most of the race, the yachts made every effort to comply with the communication and reporting rules. When the race became tactical on both the first and last legs, Race Control had reason to believe that some of the positions reported lacked something in accuracy but there was never any evidence to show that a failure to report was the result of a deliberate breakdown.

The technical causes for failure will doubtless be investigated thoroughly by the makers of the various sets, but, in broad terms, the most frequent cause was dampness, either from condensation, which in the cold areas of the Southern Ocean was at a very high level, or by salt spray through open or damaged hatches. In some cases the actual siting of the set may well have contributed to the failure.

Whenever a set was working, whether it was a MF set with comparatively short range, or one of the long range MF/HF sets, it is believed that the yacht managed to pass its position report, which was sometimes relayed by more than one yacht before it reached Race Control. Tribute must be paid to all the yachts which relayed messages and particularly to *British Soldier* which did a magnificent job in this respect. The introduction of an inter-yacht frequency (the chatter net) and the establishment of inter-yacht schedules was proved to be of considerable morale value, particularly on the two southern legs. At least one yacht reported that the improvement in morale resulting from regaining touch after a break of nine or ten days was remarkable.

Several of the yachts reported difficulty in making initial contact with shore stations but that once established and a schedule or timing call arranged there were few problems. This is an area calling for further investigation as there is obviously scope for improvement. It would appear that the majority of radio failures were the result of expecting the set to stand up to conditions for which it was not designed. The yachting fraternity is increasing in numbers and voyaging further and further afield. Design techniques and miniaturization are improving continually. We can send television pictures in colour from the moon and yet are still prevented by known conditions from communicating over relatively short distances on the surface of our own earth. Perhaps one day we shall get the answer.

15
Organiser's Comments
by Rear Admiral Otto H.M.St J.Steiner KB RN

Many lessons have been learned from the race which will be of enormous benefit, not only when planning and conducting future ocean races, but also to all those who sail in long distance cruises. In retrospect, even before a full analysis has been carried out, certain factors and happenings stand out loud and clear and I will try and summarize them, in a logical sequence.

The importance of forming a Race Committee with wide experience cannot be over-emphasized and that procured by the RNSA was tolerant, firm and respected by all. This committee and band of volunteers who manned Race Control was the backbone of the whole organisation and the months of patient, detailed work before the race started paid dividends. Without this detailed work, communications would have been far less reliable than they were – and this is not to say that they were as good as they could or should be. They will be better next time.

Nor could advance arrangements have been made at the stopping points unless the speed of advance of the yachts had been very carefully calculated from all the statistics available on wind, weather and currents. Even so, some of our predictions, based on statistics, did not come up to expectations. But in spite of this, they averaged out and the overall timing was maintained.

Chairman of the Race Committee, Rear Admiral Otto Steiner holds the premier award for the race, the Whitbread Challenge Trophy, which was won by *Sayula II*.

There was considerable discussion on the best handicapping system to adopt and there was a large body of opinion, including some of the competitors, which did not favour time on distance. I believe that it proved itself – its effect on the overall results was no greater than time on time would have produced but it is far simpler and competitors know exactly where they stand throughout a race. The critical factor is the handicap distance, easy on a short race but more difficult over very long distances unless yachts are encouraged to cut corners. We chose what we considered to be the 'prudent' navigator's course to discourage unnecessary risks. I would certainly recommend time on distance in any future long distance races, in preference to time on time or to using the performance factor system.

Communications are dealt with in detail elsewhere but one thing seems clear. They will never be reliable until radio sets are impervious to condensation, salt and salt water. They must be watertight like electrical instruments.

Position reporting was distasteful to many at the start of the race and some were loath to use the inter-yacht routine chatter net. But conditions are quite different in the broad oceans to those in the purely tactical races in the Channel – and it is mighty lonely in the Southern Ocean. It was interesting to see how chatter increased as the race progressed and how keen competitors became to make known their positions. We started off insisting on position reports every seven days – on any day chosen by individual yachts – and ended by making reports compulsory twice a week on set days. This helped Race Control enormously and also gave a more accurate picture of the progress of the race.

The RNSA with its world-wide connections, sister associations and local officers is probably in a better position to organise this type of event than any other club in the world. But no club can afford to organise current events of such proportions unless subscriptions are increased to such an extent as to be counter-productive. We are lucky to have formed such a friendly and close association with Whitbread & Company Ltd. We trust them and they trust us, so the future looks good.

Was the race a success? To my mind it was without doubt, and the most successful aspect was the genuine links of friendship regardless of race, creed or politics that have been forged amongst fifteen nationalities sailing in yachts from seven countries. This in itself makes another race worthwhile in this violent, strife-ridden world.

Our next venture is the Whitbread Multihull Race in the North and South Atlantic – then another WRTWR in 1977, and I feel sure that we can count on the world-wide support from navies, clubs and the public that was accorded to us in the first ever Round the World Race for fully crewed yachts.

Race Secretary Dudley Norman leaps over the guard rail to shake Chay Blyth by the hand when *Great Britain II* arrived at Portsmouth after the race. Already on board and with two feet firmly on the deck is Race Chairman, Otto Steiner.

16
Reflections

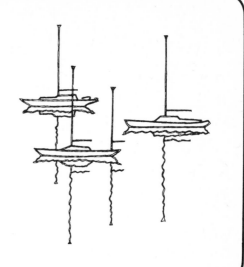

There can be no doubting the success of the race or the fact that this success has slammed the critics. True it took its toll of human life, but every sport is dangerous and this race compared well to an Everest expedition. There was every bit as much of the unknown and when dealing with the elements man is always vulnerable. In each case the death of a competitor could have been avoided by the prudent use of adequate safety equipment. Carelessness in mountaineering leads to loss of life, and so it is in ocean racing.

Before the Whitbread race, offshore racing had been measured in hundreds of miles. Apart from events like the Cape Town – Rio and the Transpac, 700 miles was considered a major distance. The classic Fastnet of 605 miles is run only on alternate years and 50 years ago when it was started, marked the beginning of ocean racing in small yachts. Now after 27,500 miles these races seem puny to the men and women who have raced around the world. The singlehanded circumnavigators proved that it was possible, although they weren't driving their boats against the clock. A fully crewed race seemed inevitable once Chichester, Rose and Knox-Johnston had completed their adventures. It proved the seaworthiness of the modern ocean racing yacht. Gear failures were slight and yet in eight months

Jean Pierre Millet, skipper of *33 Export*, washes down a lump of cheese with wine soon after his arrival at Portsmouth. It was his first real food for four days.

these boats completed more racing miles than the average ocean racer would in 7 years. The capsize of *Sayula II*, by a freak wave, and her subsequent recovery with only minor damage shows how much inherent safety there is built into the latest designs. Builders are aware of the immense strains on hulls and there are safety factors calculated to be well in excess of requirements. It mustn't, however, lead to a re-think in terms of scantlings and the stringent standards imposed by Lloyds will ensure that. Boats of glassfibre, aluminium alloy, steel and wood all came through the race and only the rushed *Burton Cutter*, whose hull was always too frail, met with severe structural problems. The inexperience of her builders led to bad welding of the plates and stringers in her aluminium alloy hull. It is nevertheless true to say that even so the weld failure rate was extremely low, but it did lead to major distortion. In contrast the aluminium alloy hull of *Pen Duick VI* appeared exactly the same afterwards as it did the day she arrived at HMS Vernon to take part. Both of these were specially built for the race but the German entry, *Peter von Danzig*, was far from new. Her steel hull and all her gear were nearly 40 years old, yet she came through the race with only minor superficial damage. Few would deny that the Southern Oceans were particularly kind in the southern summer of 1973/4.

There was one repeated gear failure which surprised all the competitors as well as most yachtsmen all over the world. The dismasting of Eric Tabarly's *Pen Duick VI*, the pre-race favourite, on the first leg came as a shock. When it happened again two days out on the third leg it caused incredulity. The most competitive skipper was out of the race because of lack of sailing experience with his yacht. It's not the first time this sort of thing has happened to Tabarly. He had failure with the trimaran *Pen Duick IV* in the 1968 Singlehanded Transatlantic Race because of the rush to complete her on time, yet four years later Alain Colas won that race and went on to sail the boat around the world without incident. The number of training miles put in by the Royal Navy crews in *Adventure* were laughed at by many whilst they were being done, but all paid their dividends. The yacht, from an already proven design, was tested in every way. Each piece of gear was intricately examined to see if it could be improved and all failures replaced with something stronger and more efficient. Even so, the southern Indian Ocean claimed the winning chances of *Adventure* when her rudder failed, but it was the hours and hours of experience of her crew which kept *Adventure* going hard by steering her on the trim tab.

The strain on crews was harder than most of them are prepared to admit. Living in cramped and often uncomfortable conditions with a handful of other people whose only common factor is yacht racing, was bound to produce friction. Its manifestation was generally light in terms of frayed tempers and any greater incidents were covered by crew loyalty, but they did occur. The strains were only mental, the race, whilst physically demanding, was not unduly arduous; the limb breakages were limited to an arm and a foot. The desire to communicate by radio and to give true positions to the rest of the competitors increased as the race progressed. The knowledge that if something went radically wrong, there was a better chance of being found caused this. Fear was

Chay Blyth, united with his wife Maureen and daughter on the foredeck of *Great Britain II* after the race.

Finale. Prince Philip presents the Whitbread Challenge Trophy for the first yacht on handicap to Ramon Carlin, skipper and owner of the Swan 65 *Sayula II*.

not uncommon and though many crew members laugh about it now the race is over, many admitted, particularly in Sydney and Rio, that there were times when they were scared stiff. It took *Sayula II*'s crew the best part of a week to return to racing her to her limit after her second leg capsize, and this was purely due to human attitude and not gear failure.

The success of the race was in no small part due to the organisation. Only the RNSA have the sort of contacts which proved valuable assistance through the race. Many of the world's navies monitored the communications and provided help at the ports of call and even the 'old boy' net was stretched at times. Getting certain alien nationals into certain countries happened as blind eyes were turned at ambassadorial level after the right approaches had been made. All the wheels were greased and the clockwork-like smoothness reflects the club's thoroughness in preparation. Nothing went wrong and that in itself is a fair measure of the success.

Inevitably the question of doing it again arises. In answer to it in Portsmouth, within minutes of the race finishing, Keith Lorence, the Californian sailmaker on *Sayula II* said, 'No way. No one is going to get me down into those Southern Oceans ever again. They are cold and unfriendly and they frighten me

to death.' Yet on *Sayula II* he had been part of a group which had discussed the ideal way of doing it again, a group of which one member said 'I don't know whether we would want to do it again, but we don't like the idea of another race taking place without us.' For Tabarly the decision is obvious — he has to go again — it is a matter of honour. Leslie Williams had only financial reservation. To go again for him would have to be a fully sponsored effort, the strain on personal resources was too great this time and in future with tougher competition, it is bound to be more expensive. For the happy amateurs like the crew of *Second Life*, the way they say 'I've done it *once*' conveys the message with conviction. There is no need for them to add 'and that's enough.'

The British Navy and Army are now firmly committed to an adventure training programme in yachts and both Services have disclosed their intentions of competing in future marathon ocean races.

There will be other races around the world because this Whitbread/RNSA event was a success. It was a milestone and it was enjoyed by those who raced in it. It produced friendships and it proved that the spirit of adventure is still as high in matters maritime in the reign of Queen Elizabeth II as it was in the previous Elizabethan era.

Appendix I
General Conditions of Entry

1 Management

The Race will be under the management of the Royal Naval Sailing Association.

The Race Committee will be assisted by The Royal Naval Club and Royal Albert Yacht Club, the Cruising Association of South Africa, the Cruising Yacht Club of Australia and the Iate Clube do Rio de Janeiro. The Headquarters of the Race Committee is in Portsmouth England, and subsidiary offices will be set up in Cape Town, Sydney and Rio de Janeiro.

The Race Committee reserves the right to use as it thinks fit any information in competitors' ships logs (Special Regulation 4.1). The logs and all written, recorded, and photographic material gathered during the race by competitors will remain their property for use by them as they wish.

2 Rules

The Race will be sailed under current International Yacht Racing Union racing rules subject to modifications imposed by the General Conditions of Entry and Sailing Instructions.

3 Eligibility

A yacht must be entered for the race, and owned by, or on charter to, a yacht or sailing club recognized by a National Authority, or a member or members thereof. She must

    (a)   have a valid IOR rating of not less than 33 feet nor more than 70 feet.

    (b)   be single hulled.

    (c)   conform with Safety Regulations prescribed for the race.

Ownership of Yachts. The Race Committee may at its discretion take no action under IYRU rule No. 20.2. A charterer shall be regarded as the owner during the charter period, except that where the owner is a Yacht Club, Sailing Association or similar body, the charterer shall be regarded as sailing that yacht on that body's behalf.

Owner Steering Another Yacht. The Race Committee may at its discretion take no action under IYRU rule 55.

4 Entry Forms

Each entry must be made on an official entry form, obtainable from the Secretary of the Race Committee. A yacht may enter for the whole race or for any number of legs of the race.

5 Copy Rating Certificate

An official copy of the yacht's IOR certificate must be lodged with the Race Committee not less than 72 hours before the start of each leg.

6 Race Entry Fee

An Entry Fee of £150 for the whole race or £50 per leg must be paid before the closing date for entries.

7 Closing Date for Entries

An entry for the whole race or 1st leg of the race must be received not later than the 1st June 1973. Entries for the 2nd, 3rd and 4th legs must be received by 1st August, 1st October and 1st December respectively. A late entry may be accepted up to 72 hours before each leg of the race, at the discretion of the Race Committee, upon payment of an additional fee of £25.

An entry will not be considered to be complete, nor will it be finally accepted, until receipt of the Entry Fee.

8 Refund of Entry Fee

75% of the Entry Fee will be refunded, provided that the yacht gives notice of withdrawal not less than 24 hours before it is due to start.

9 Refusal of Entries

The Race Committee reserve the right to refuse any entry without giving a reason.

10 Rating and Handicap System

Rating   IOR.

Handicap   Time-on-Distance.

11 Crew and Crew List

The minimum number on board shall be 5. A crew list on the form which will be provided (together with a passport photo of each member) must be handed in to the appropriate Race Control office not less than 24 hours before the start of each leg. Corrections will be accepted up to 2 hours before the starts.

12 **Sail Numbers and Letters**

Sail numbers must be carried as prescribed in IYRU Rules but must not be less than the following dimensions:

Height	Width	Thickness	Space between
21 in	14 in	3 in	4 in

13 **Flags**

Racing flags are to be worn for at least 1 hour after the start of each leg. Ensigns may be worn throughout.

14 **Use of Engine**

(a) An engine may be used for bilge pumping, or for supplying power for weighing anchor or hauling off or for charging batteries, but when the main engine is used for these purposes a part of the shaft between the gear box and stern tube must be held stationary.

(b) If the engine is run for the purpose of picking up a man overboard or rendering assistance, or in any other emergency, the circumstances must be reported on the Declaration.

15 **Self Steering**

Automatic steering by mechanical or electrical means or by wind vanes is prohibited.

16 **Inspection – Equipment Declaration**

The Equipment Declaration form which will be provided must be completed and returned to the Race Committee not less than 48 hours *before the start of each leg*. An inspection will be carried out before each leg of the race and possibly after. Attention is drawn to para 17 below of these regulations.

17 **Rule Infringements**

(a) If the Race Committee consider that a breach of the rules has been committed it may impose a time penalty by decreasing the yacht's time allowance for that leg or the race by up to 5 per cent, or disqualify the yacht, or refer the matter to the RYA for action under IYRU racing rule 74.

(b) If a yacht incurs a time penalty under this regulation and subsequently might qualify for a prize based on elapsed time, her elapsed time shall be increased by the same percentage as under (a) above before deciding whether she has won a prize.

18 **Declaration**

During this race competing yachts will inevitably sail for lengthy periods out of sight of one another, and the person in charge may be the sole judge of fair play. When signing his Declaration he must be either entirely satisfied that the race has been sailed in complete obedience to all the rules for the race or he must qualify his declaration suitably.

19 **Assemblies**

Competitors for the 1st leg of the race must arrive in the Solent area by 1st September 1973 and notify the Race Committee of their whereabouts.

Assembly dates for subsequent legs will be one week before the start and will be notified.

Special Regulations and Compulsory Equipment

1.1 *These special regulations are based on the Offshore Rating Council's Special Regulations. Additions or Amendments to the ORC Special Regulations are printed in italics.*

1.2 It is the purpose of these special regulations to establish uniform minimum equipment and accommodation standards for yachts racing under the International Offshore Rule.

1.3 These regulations do not replace, but rather supplement, the requirements of governmental authority, the Racing Rules, and the International Offshore Rule. The attention of owners is called to restrictions in the rules on the location and movement of equipment.

2.0 **Owner's Responsibility**

2.1 The safety of a yacht and her crew is the sole and inescapable responsibility of the owner, who must do his best to ensure that the yacht is fully found, thoroughly seaworthy and manned by an experienced crew who are physically fit to face bad weather. He must be satisfied as to the soundness of hull, spars, rigging, sails and all gear. He must ensure that all safety equipment is properly maintained and stowed and that the crew know where it is kept and how it is to be used.

2.2 Neither the establishment of these special regulations, nor the inspection of a yacht under these regulations in any way limits or reduces the complete and unlimited responsibility of the owner.

2.3 It is the sole and exclusive responsibility of each yacht to decide whether or not to start or continue to race.

3.0 Basic Standards

3.1 Hulls of offshore racing yachts shall be self-righting, strongly built, watertight and capable of withstanding solid water and knockdowns. They must be properly rigged and ballasted, be fully seaworthy and must meet the standards set forth herein.

3.2 All equipment must function properly, be readily accessible and be of type, size and capacity suitable and adequate for the intended use and the size of the yacht, and shall meet standards accepted in the country of registry.

4.0 Inspection

4.1 *Each entry will be inspected before the start of, and possibly on finishing, each leg.* If she does not comply with these special regulations her entry may be rejected, or she will be liable to disqualification or such other penalty as may be prescribed.
The entrants must keep a ship's log which is to be made available to the Race Committee for inspection on demand at any time during or after the race.

5.0 Structural Features

5.1 HATCHES, COMPANIONWAYS AND PORTS must be essentially watertight, that is, capable of being strongly and rigidly secured. Cockpit companionways, if extended below main deck level, must be capable of being blocked off to main deck level.

5.2 COCKPITS must be structurally strong, self draining and permanently incorporated as an integral part of the hull. They must be essentially watertight, that is, all openings to the hull below the main deck level must be capable of being strongly and rigidly secured.

5.21 COCKPIT VOLUME. Except for boats built before 1.1.73, the maximum cockpit volume below lowest coamings shall not exceed 6%L times B times FA. The cockpit sole must be at least 2%L above LWL.

5.3 Yachts must have:

5.31 COCKPIT DRAINS. With a combined area (after allowance for screens, if attached) of not less than the equivalent of four 3/4 inch (2.0 cm) drains.

5.4 STORM COVERINGS for all windows more than two square feet in area.

5.51 SEA COCKS OR VALVES on all through-hull openings below LWL, except integral scuppers, shaft log, speed indicators, depth finders and the like, however a means of closing such openings, when necessary to do so, shall be provided.

5.52 Soft wood plugs, tapered and of various sizes.

5.6 Life Lines and Pulpits

5.61 Fixed bow pulpit (forward of headstay) and stern pulpit (unless lifelines are arranged so as to adequately substitute for stern pulpit). Pulpits and stanchions must be thru-bolted or welded, and the bases thereof must not be further inboard from the edge of the working deck than 5% of B max. or 6 inch (15 cm), whichever is greater. The head of a stanchion must not be angled from the point of its attachment to the hull at more than 10 degrees from vertical. Taut double life lines, with upper life line of wire at a height of not less than 2 feet (60 cm) above the working deck, to be permanently supported at intervals of not more than 7 feet (2.15 m). A taut lanyard of synthetic rope may be used to secure life lines provided that when in position its length does not exceed 4 inch (10 cm). Life lines need not be affixed to the bow pulpit if they terminate at, or pass through adequately braced stanchions 2 feet (60 cm) above the working deck, set inside of and overlapping the bow pulpit, provided that the gap between the upper line and the bow pulpit shall not exceed 6 inch (15 cm).
A lower life line must be rigged around the bow and stern pulpits if the pulpits are not manufactured with an intermediate rail.

6.0 Accommodations   Yachts must have:

6.1 TOILET, permanently installed.

6.2 BUNKS, permanently installed.

6.3 COOKING STOVE, permanently installed with safe and accessible fuel shutoff control.

6.4 GALLEY FACILITIES, including sink.

6.5 WATER TANKS, permanently installed and capable of dividing the water supply into at least two separate containers. *20 gallons of potable water for each member of the crew must be embarked at the start of each leg of the race and carried in the tanks and in additional water containers if necessary. Adequate arrangements are to be made for collection of rainwater and/or to distill desalinate sea water so as to provide at least ten gallons more per man of potable water on each leg of the race unless this extra is carried in water containers from the start.*

7.0 **General Equipment** Yachts must have:

7.1 Fire extinguishers, *at least three fire extinguishers are to be carried each of 3 lbs weight of dry powder or equivalent. One fire blanket must be carried in a stowage close to the galley.*

7.2 BILGE PUMPS, at least two, manually operated, one of which must be operable with all cockpit seats and all hatches and companionways closed.

7.3 ANCHORS, two with cables.

7.4 FLASHLIGHTS, one of which is suitable for signalling, water resistant, with spare batteries and bulbs.

7.5 FIRST AID KIT and manual, *also one "Monoject" morphia per crew member is to be carried in a separate locked container.*

7.6 FOGHORN.

7.7 RADAR REFLECTOR.

7.8 SET OF INTERNATIONAL CODE FLAGS and international code book.

7.9 SHUTOFF VALVES on all fuel tanks.

8.0 **Navigation Equipment.**
Yachts must have:

8.1 COMPASS, marine type, properly installed and adjusted.

8.2 SPARE COMPASS.

8.3 CHARTS, LIGHT LIST AND PILOTING EQUIPMENT.

8.4 SEXTANT, TABLES AND ACCURATE TIMEPIECE.

8.5 RADIO DIRECTION FINDER.

8.6 LEAD LINE OR ECHO SOUNDER.

8.7 SPEEDOMETER OR DISTANCE MEASURING INSTRUMENT.

8.8 NAVIGATION LIGHTS to be shown as required by the International Regulations for Preventing Collision at Sea, mounted so that they will not be masked by sails or the heeling of the yacht.

8.9 General note: – *Radar, hyperbolic navigational aids except Consol and pre-arranged radio transmissions for the use of individual competitors are prohibited. If any device other than those permitted is installed for use when not racing, such device must be provided with a clear and positive means by which it is rendered inoperable and thus sealed throughout the race.*

9.0 **Emergency Equipment** Yachts must have:

9.1 SPARE RUNNING LIGHTS and power source.

9.2 SPECIAL STORM SAIL(S) capable of taking the yacht to windward in heavy weather.

9.3 EMERGENCY STEERING EQUIPMENT.

9.4 TOOLS AND SPARE PARTS, including a hacksaw *and heavy wire cutters.*

9.5 YACHT'S NAME to be marked on miscellaneous buoyant equipment, such as life jackets, oars, cushions, etc. A portable sail number for display horizontally and vertically.

9.6 MARINE RADIO TRANSMITTER AND RECEIVER with minimum transmitter power of 50 watts. If the regular antenna depends upon the mast, an emergency antenna must be provided.

10.0 **Safety Equipment**   Yachts must carry:

10.1 LIFE JACKETS, one for each crew member.

10.2 WHISTLES (referee type) attached to life jackets.

10.3 SAFETY BELT (harness type) one for each crew member.

10.41 LIFE RAFTS. Two are to be carried having the combined rated capacity to carry the whole crew. They must have a valid certificate that they have been inspected and tested within 4 months of the start of the race. Each raft must be marked with the sail number and name of the yacht so as to be visible from the air. They are to be capable of meeting the following requirements:

Must be carried on deck (not under a dinghy) or in a special stowage opening immediately to the deck, containing life raft(s) only.
Must be designed and used solely for saving life at sea.
Must have at least two separate buoyancy compartments, each of which must be automatically inflatable.
Each raft must be capable of carrying its rated capacity with one compartment deflated.
Must have a canopy to cover the occupants.

Must have the following equipment appropriately secured to each raft:

1 Sea anchor or drogue
1 Bellows, pump or other means for maintaining inflation of air chambers
3 Hand flares
1 Repair kit
1 Signalling light
1 Knife
1 Bailer
2 Paddles

10.42 Provision for emergency water and rations to accompany raft.

10.52 At least one horseshoe type life ring equipped with a high intensity water light and a drogue within reach of the helmsman and ready for instant use.

10.53 At least one more horseshoe type life ring equipped with a whistle (referee type), dye marker, a high intensity water light, and a pole and flag. The pole is to be attached to a ring with 25 feet (8 m) of floating line and is to be of a length and so ballasted that the flag will fly at least 8 feet (2.45 m) off the water.

10.61 DISTRESS SIGNALS to be stowed in a waterproof container and meeting the following requirements:

10.62 Twelve red parachute flares.

10.63 Four red hand flares.

10.64 Four white hand flares.

10.7 HEAVING LINE (50 feet (16 m) minimum length floating type line) readily accessible to cockpit.

Extracts from Sailing Instructions

Provisional Sailing Instructions

Start

September 8th 1973 at Portsmouth England.

Course

From Portsmouth to Cape Town, Sydney, thence via Cape Horn to Rio de Janeiro and back to Portsmouth. The race will be stopped and re-started at Cape Town, Sydney and Rio de Janeiro.

Massed re-starts at Cape Town and Sydney will take place at the discretion of the Race Committee between 7 and 12 days after the finish of approximately 70% of the yachts which have also entered for the next leg of the race. When this number have finished, the Race Committee will, within 24 hours, announce the actual date of the start of the next leg.

The final leg of the race from Rio de Janeiro will be a PURSUIT race, so that yachts should arrive back at Portsmouth together. The start date of the lowest handicap yacht will be about 7 to 12 days after the finish of approximately 70% of the yachts which have also entered for the final leg of the race. When this number have finished the Race Committee will, within 24 hours, announce the actual dates and times of the starts of the competitors on the final leg.

As a planning guide, start dates are expected to be approximately as follows:

Cape Town	during 1st week in November 1973
Sydney	during 2nd week in December 1973
Rio de Janeiro	during last week in February and early March 1974
Finish	Early April 1974

Joining, leaving and storing whilst racing

Any crew member may be disembarked on to a passing ship or helicopter, or leave by other means, but may not be replaced except at Cape Town, Sydney and Rio de Janeiro.

Should this result in the number of the crew being reduced below 5 this fact is to be reported on the Declaration Form. The decision as to whether to continue the race rests solely with the skipper.

Apart from fishing, a yacht may not embark food, drink or equipment at sea without penalty. Any such action must be reported in the yacht's Declaration.

Emergency Stops

Yachts may stop at any port on the globe. They may land crewmen who are injured or unwell, but replacement crew may not be taken on (see above para). Food, drink and equipment may be embarked and repairs may be made.

Carrying and Setting Sails

(a) Sails shall be set only in those areas which have been declared for inclusion in the sail area and must not exceed the limit specified.

(b) A device for keeping the spinnaker clear of the shrouds shall not be regarded as a second spinnaker boom.

(c) Two sails may be carried set on spinnaker booms forward of the mast, provided that:

    (i) Neither sail exceeds the area of the biggest jib for which the boat is measured.

    (ii) The mainsail is not set at the same time as the leeward running sail, except when shifting sail.

    (iii) Neither spinnaker boom is longer nor mounted further forward than is permitted by the rules of measurement for the yacht's rating.

Note: These Sailing Instructions are for planning purposes. Detailed Sailing Instructions and Regulations for Radio Communication will be provided to intending competitors at a later date.

Sailing Instructions. Leg 1

Start: Saturday, 8th September, 1973

PORTSMOUTH – CAPE TOWN

Flags

Racing flags are to be worn while IYRU Racing Rules govern. (See Right of Way) Ensigns should be worn at the start and may be worn throughout. Sail numbers must be displayed on life lines at the start and at the finish.

Alterations

If it is necessary to make a last-minute alteration in the Sailing Instructions, International Code Flag 'L' will be hoisted at the starting point (Southsea Castle) and at HMS Vernon before 1100. It is then the responsibility of owners to acquaint themselves with the alterations before starting.

Start Local Time

Warning	1145	Gun
Ten Minutes	1150	Class flag broken and gun
Preparatory	1155	BLUE PETER broken and gun
START	1200	ALL FLAGS HAULED DOWN AND GUN

Tides at Portsmouth

LOCAL TIME		HEIGHT
High	0939	12 ft 2 in
Low	1459	6 ft 3 in

Starting Line

Chart No 2625
A line drawn approximately 220° (True) from the flagpole on Southsea Castle to east side of Spitsand Fort which is the outer distance mark. Transit marks: diamond and triangle, on Southsea Castle. A buoy will be anchored off the castle approximately on the one fathom line. Start: NW to SE

Recalls

Recall numbers will not be issued or displayed. When a yacht starts prematurely, a gun will be fired or a suitable sound signal made as soon as possible after the starting signal, and numeral pennant 'O' will be broken out.
A premature starter shall return in accordance with IYRU racing rule No 51.1 but the Race Committee will not inform her that she has wholly returned to the right side of the starting line.

Course

From PORTSMOUTH by any route seaward to Cape Town, leaving Bembridge Ledge buoy to STARBOARD.

Handicap Distance

6650 nautical miles.

Finishing Line

The finishing line is on a bearing approximately 047° (True) from the main flag staff of the South African Merchant Naval Academy, Granger Bay, to the No 1 Main Channel arrival buoy (conical white flashing).
The line will be limited by an inshore conical buoy distance 2 cables from the main flag staff of the South African Merchant Naval Academy and an outer can buoy distance 4 cables from the main flag staff. Both buoys will display quick flashing amber lights during hours of darkness. Yachts finishing are to cross between the inner and outer buoys leaving the outer buoy to port. (see Chart SAN 1014)

Finishing Time

Each competing yacht must take her own finishing time accurately. The GMT of finishing must be entered on the Declaration Form and verified by another member of the crew BOTH OF WHOM must sign the Declaration Form. The ship's watch should be corrected before and as close to the finish as possible.

Finishing at Night

When finishing at night the yacht's Sail Number must be illuminated while crossing the line.

Retirements

Yachts retiring from the race or putting into any port must notify Race Control Portsmouth as soon as possible, using radio message, cable or telephone.

Racing Rules and Regulations

The race will be started and sailed under IYRU Rules subject to RYA Prescription, modifications imposed by the General Conditions of Entry and Special Regulations for the race, and these instructions.

Right of Way

For determining the Right of Way between contestants, the IYRU Racing Rules shall govern while yachts are NORTH of Bembridge Ledge Buoy. Thereafter IYRU rules 36–43 will cease to be applicable and will be replaced by International Regulations for the Prevention of Collisions at Sea, until yachts have entered within a circle, whose centre is the flagstaff at the South African Merchant Naval Academy and radius 5 miles, when IYRU Racing Rules will again govern.

Declaration

A Declaration Form, completed and signed by the person in charge when the yacht has finished the course, must be handed to the Duty Race Control Officer at Race Control, Cape Town, as soon as possible after arrival.
If no Declaration is made, a yacht may be treated as having failed to complete the course.

Protests

Protests arising out of the race must be made in writing within 24 hours of arrival, accompanied by the protest fee of £10 or equivalent, to the Secretary, Cruising Association of South Africa, Room 1815, Sanlam Centre, Heerengracht, CAPE TOWN.

Leg 2

Start: Wednesday, 7 November, 1973

CAPE TOWN – SYDNEY

Start Local Time

Warning	1315	Gun
Ten Minutes	1320	Class flag broken and gun
Preparatory	1325	BLUE PETER broken and gun
START	1330	ALL FLAGS HAULED DOWN AND GUN

Tides at Cape Town

LOCAL TIME		HEIGHT
High	1251	1.768 m
Low	1911	.671 m

Starting Line

The START will be conducted from a Naval vessel which will be anchored close to No. 1 Fairway buoy.
The line will be a line joining No. 1 Fairway buoy to the outer limiting mark of the finishing line, which is a buoy flying a yellow flag in position approximately 047° (True) distance 4 cables from the main flag staff on the Merchant Navy Academy. The Naval vessel must be left to starboard.
The Naval vessel will leave after the start. Late starters must leave No. 1 Fairway buoy to starboard.

Yachts Arriving Late

A yacht which has been delayed and has not been able to arrive in the vicinity of the starting line when the signal is made five minutes before the start, may use her engine or be towed towards the vicinity of the starting line for the purpose of enabling her to cross the starting line, and afterwards under sail alone compete in the race. But a delayed yacht availing herself of this privilege shall cease to use her engine or be towed and then complete a 360° turn before she crosses the starting line. A yacht so competing shall report the circumstances to the Race Committee after arrival in Sydney, who shall decide whether she is a bona fide starter.

Scrutineering Dead Time

Scrutineering times of late arrivals from Portsmouth after OFFICIAL START TIME of the second leg will be considered as SCRUTINEER-ING DEAD TIME. This will be the time from when a late yacht crosses the finishing line at Cape Town until the completion of pre-start scrutiny. Scrutiny will be immediate on arrival and replacement of missing items and other work will not be included in dead time.
The SCRUTINEERING DEAD TIME is to be subtracted from ELAPSED TIME for the second leg commencing at the OFFICIAL START TIME of the leg.

Course

From CAPE TOWN by any route seaward to SYDNEY.

Handicap Distance

6600 nautical miles.

Finishing Line

A line joining HORNBY Lighthouse and the vertical face of OUTER NORTH HEAD.

Finishing

After finishing yachts should proceed to anchor in WATSONS BAY (see Chart No. AUS. 200 or 201) until cleared. No yacht shall pass to the westward of a line between BRADLEYS HEAD and DARLING POINT.

Right of Way

For determining the Right of Way between contestants the IYRU Racing Rules shall govern until yachts have left a circle, whose centre is the flagstaff at the South African Merchant Naval Academy, radius 5 miles. Thereafter IYRU Rules 36–43 will cease to be applicable and will be replaced by International Regulations for the Prevention of Collisions at Sea, until yachts have entered within a circle, radius 5 miles, whose centre is HORNBY Lighthouse, when IYRU Racing Rules shall govern.

Leg 3

Start: Friday, 28th December, 1973

SYDNEY–RIO DE JANEIRO

Start Local Time

Warning	1145	Gun
Ten Minutes	1150	International Pendant No. 1 broken and gun
Preparatory	1155	BLUE PETER broken and gun
START	1200	ALL FLAGS HAULED DOWN AND GUN

Tide at Sydney

LOCAL TIME	HEIGHT
High 1120	1.6 m
Low 1757	0.3 m

Starting Line

The START will be conducted from Hornby Light on Inner South Head.
The line will be between Hornby Light and the Western extremity of Cannae Point.

Course

From the starting line to RIO DE JANEIRO, leaving CAPE HORN to port.

Handicap Distance

8370 nautical miles.

Finishing Line

The transit of the two towers on Pta. do Arpoador bearing approximately 352° (True) length about 0.5 miles. To be crossed from west to east.

Finishing

After finishing, yachts should proceed to IATE CLUBE DO RIO DE JANEIRO in GUANABARA BAY.

Right of Way

For determining the Right of Way between contestants the IYRU Racing Rules shall govern until yachts have crossed a line drawn between Macquarie Light and Outer North Head. Thereafter IYRU Rules 36–43 will cease to be applicable and will be replaced by International Regulations for the Prevention of Collisions at Sea, until yachts have entered within a circle, radius 5 miles, whose centre is Pta. do Arpoador, when IYRU Racing Rules shall govern.

Leg 4

Start: March 1974

RIO DE JANEIRO–PORTSMOUTH

ALL TIMES LOCAL

Starts

Warning	1245	Gun
Ten Minutes	1250	International Pendant No. 1 broken and gun
Five Minutes	1255	BLUE PETER broken and gun
START	1300	ALL FLAGS HAULED DOWN AND GUN

Starting Line

The transit of two triangles on ARPOADOR ROCKS. CROSS THE LINE FROM WEST TO EAST. A buoy will be moored approximately 1/2 miles from Punta do Arpoador, on or near the line. This buoy must be left to starboard.

Course

From the starting line to PORTSMOUTH, ENGLAND.

Handicap Distance

5500 nautical miles.

Finishing Line

At the Royal Albert Yacht Club Signal Station on SOUTHSEA beach, immediately in front of the War Memorial. The line is marked by the transit of an orange Diamond and an orange Triangle. CROSS the line from South to North, leaving Elbow Spit and No. 2 Channel Buoys to port.

Finishing

After finishing proceed to the basin at H.M.S. VERNON in Portsmouth Harbour, where the yachts were berthed before the start of the race.

Racing Rules and Regulations

Right of Way

For determining the Right of Way between contestants the IYRU Racing Rules shall govern until yachts have passed beyond a five mile circle whose centre is Punta do Arpoador, and then will be replaced by International Regulations for the Prevention of Collisions at Sea, until yachts are north of a line joining St. Catherines Light, the Needles Light and Hengistbury Head, or north of a line joining St. Catherines Light, The Nab Tower and Selsey Bill, when IYRU Racing Rules shall govern.

Appendix III

Crew List

(These lists have been drawn from the most accurate information available but certain anomalies in the spelling of names may have arisen due to handwritten source material)

Adventure	Leg 1	Leg 2	Leg 3	Leg 4
Lt Cdr J. P. G. Bryans RN	X			
CPO M. Bird	X			
Capt J. H. Wiltshire RM	X			
Lt P. Wykeham-Martin RN	X			
Lt S. van der Byl RN	X			
Lt Cdr S. Gray RN	X			
PO M. J. Trotter	X			
Ch Tech P. N. Chowns RAF	X			
CEA M. Rose	X			
MEA T. J. Sales	X			
Lt Cdr E. M. R. Skene RN		X		
Lt Cdr C. P. E. Brown RN		X		
Lt A. Higham RN		X	X	
CEA C. Abrahams		X		
Lt D. Budge RN		X		
Cdr M. K. Matthews RN		X		
Lt A. W. Netherclift RN		X		
Sgt G. Norman RM		X		
Surg Lt S. Ormerod RN		X		
Leading Airman D. Thompson		X		
Lt Cdr F. S. Owens RN		X		X
CPO W. E. Porter			X	
Lt M. C. Shirley RN			X	
Cdr C. F. Seal RN			X	
Lt C. F. F. Watkins RN			X	
Capt G. M. F. Vallings RN			X	
Lt R. A. S. Turner RN			X	
CPO R. Mullender			X	X
CPO M. Forrest			X	
Lt Cdr T. Laycock RN			X	
Sub Lt R. A. G. Clare RN				X
Sub Lt H. L. Trotter RN				X
Sub Lt R. J. Kingsnorth RN				X
CPO H. J. Hyland				X
Inst Lt K. Richardson RN				X
Lt Cdr A. A. M. Johnstone RN				X
LS P. J. Long				X
Lt A. J. Bolingbroke				X

British Soldier	Leg 1	Leg 2	Leg 3	Leg 4
Maj J. T. Day	X			
Maj R. J. Knox	X			
Capt D. T. I. Glyn Owen	X			
Flt Lt T. W. Rimmer RAF	X			
Lt R. A. L. Hill	X			
WO II J. B. Rosson	X			
Staff Sgt P. J. C. Green	X			
Staff Sgt P. D. Phillips	X			
Cpl P. Waterhouse	X			
Cpl G. S. Marshall	X			
Maj G. C. Philp		X		
Maj R. G. Barton		X		
Maj S. A. Edwards		X		

Name	Leg 1	Leg 2	Leg 3	Leg 4
Maj J. A. Cuthill		X		
Lt P. R. G. Ash		X		
Maj C. Davies		X		
Cpl G. Marshall		X		
Cpl A. C. Badrick		X		
Cpl M. E. Cox		X		
Lt R. A. Hill		X		
Maj A. N. Carlier			X	
Maj R. S. P. Tamlyn			X	
Capt A. W. D. Edsor			X	
Capt D. M. Gill			X	
Capt A. E. Truluck			X	
FO M. J. Hayman RAF			X	
Lt R. J. Little			X	
WO II(CSMI) J. A. Bullock			X	
L Cpl A. M. Hogton			X	
L Cpl J. R. Le Maitre			X	
Lt Col J. E. Myatt				X
Maj L. D. Edinger				X
Maj J. J. J. Phipps				X
Maj M. C. Lewin Harris				X
Sqd Ldr R. K. Webster RAF				X
Maj A. G. Whitfield				X
Capt G. I. Bye				X
Staff Sgt J. Doherty				X
Staff Sgt D. A. Leslie				X
L Cpl C. Edge				X

Burton Cutter	Leg 1	Leg 2	Leg 3	Leg 4
J. F. B. Buchanan	X			
P. F. Rosser	X			X
P. J. Blake	X			X
N. R. D. Rowe	X			
D. Alan Williams	X			X
C. G. Edwards	X			X
Jacques R. Redon	X			X
A. Smith	X			X
Leslie Williams	X			X
Ricardo Villarosa	X			
Marco Chiara	X			X
J. Tanner	X			X
W. Elgie	X			X
S. Berkeley				X
A. Culley				X
T. W. Moore				X
C. Forbes				X

CS e RB	Leg 1	Leg 2	Leg 3	Leg 4
Doi Malingri di Bagnolo	X	X	X	X
Christina Monti	X			
Alberto Passi	X			
Paolo Bertoldi	X			
Riccardo Tosti	X			
Constance Imbert		X		
Alessandro Lojacono	X	X	X	X

	Leg 1	Leg 2	Leg 3	Leg 4
Maurizio Curci		X		
Franco Malingri		X		
Paolo Grazioli		X		
Carla Malingri			X	X
Michele Meda			X	
Carlo Mauri			X	
Francesco Longanesi Cattani				X
Paolo Mascheroni				X

Concorde	Leg 1	Leg 2	Leg 3	Leg 4
Pierre Chassin		X		
Christian Aguesseau		X		
Graeme Corlett		X		
David Dean		X		
Colin Berry		X		

Copernicus	Leg 1	Leg 2	Leg 3	Leg 4
Zygfryd Perlicki	X	X	X	X
Bogdan Bogdzinski	X	X	X	X
Mackiewicz Ryszard	X	X	X	X
Bronislaw Tarnacki	X	X	X	X
Zbigniew Puchalski	X	X	X	X

Grand Louis	Leg 1	Leg 2	Leg 3	Leg 4
André Viant	X	X	X	X
Bruno Lunven	X	X	X	X
François Thepaut	X	X	X	
Philippe Facque	X	X	X	X
Gilles Berthelin	X	X	X	X
Loïc Caradec	X	X	X	X
Patrice Carpentier	X	X	X	X
Jean Michel Carpentier	X			
Jean Michel Viant	X	X		X
Michel Vanek		X	X	X
Sylvie Vanek		X	X	X
Gérard Beck		X		
Franck van Beuningen			X	
Pieta Rens			X	
Patrick Elies				X

Great Britain II	Leg 1	Leg 2	Leg 3	Leg 4
Chay Blyth	X	X	X	X
Alec Honey	X	X	X	X
Mike Thompson	X	X	X	X
Len Price	X	X	X	X
Brian Daniels	X			
Len Robertson	X	X	X	X
John Rist	X	X	X	X
Bernard Hosking	X	X	X	
Eddie Hope	X	X		
Pete Bates	X	X	X	X
Eric Blunn	X	X	X	X
Alan Toones	X	X	X	X

Guia	*Leg 1*	*Leg 2*	*Leg 3*	*Leg 4*
Giorgio Falck	X		X	
Nino Pecorari	X	X		
Piero Bianchess	X			
Gigi Vaicava	X			
Luciano Ladavas	X	X	X	X
Giovanni Verbini	X	X	X	
Giorgio Pecorari		X		
Franco Pecorari		X		
Jerome Poncet		X	X	
Toio Piegieggoli			X	
Conrad Burge			X	
Pierre Dagreves				X
Piero Bianchessi				X
Michel Drouart				X
Luigi Arzenati				X

Jakaranda	*Leg 1*	*Leg 2*	*Leg 3*	*Leg 4*
John Goodwin	X			
Gerhard Last	X			
Wilhelm Griitter	X			
Yvonne van de Byl	X			
W. J. Damerell	X			
M. Avery	X			
P. Koehurst	X			
C. Smith	X			

Keewaydin	*Leg 1*	*Leg 2*	*Leg 3*	*Leg 4*
Victor Renstrom	X			
Kerstin Jensen	X			
Nils-Arne Jensen	X			
Per Jangen	X			
Tage Nilsson	X			
Karl-Olof Elmdahl	X			
Thomas Andersen	X			
Hakan Olsson	X			
David Sundbaum	X			
Bertil Lundin	X			
Harry Gedda	X			
Jan-Erik Lindgren	X			
Gosta Werner	X			

Kriter	*Leg 1*	*Leg 2*	*Leg 3*	*Leg 4*
Jack Grout	X	X		
Oliver Stern-Veyrin	X	X		
Alain Gliksman		X	X	X
Patrice Quesnel	X	X	X	X
Hughes Lallement	X	X		
Gilles Vaton	X	X	X	X
Bernard de Guy	X			
Michel Girard	X	X		X
Michel Malinovsky	X		X	X
Philippe Bayle	X	X		
Bernard Lauvray	X			X

Jean Louis Duboc	X			
Georges Commarmond	X	X	X	X
F. A. de la Noe		X		
Joel Charpentier		X	X	
Jean Claude Montesinos		X	X	X
Armand Broyelles			X	
Didier Roquet			X	X
Pierre Lenormand			X	X
Michael Austin			X	
Guy Schwartz			X	
Alain D'Auzac				X
Pierre Bonnet				X
Alain Benech				X

Otago	*Leg 1*	*Leg 2*	*Leg 3*	*Leg 4*
Zdzislaw Pienkawa	X	X	X	X
Iwona Pienkawa	X	X	X	X
Witold Ciecholewski	X	X	X	X
Bohdan Berggrun	X	X	X	X
Kazimierz Kurzydlo	X	X	X	X
Edwin Trzos	X	X	X	X
Adam Michel	X	X	X	X
Stanislaw Jakubczyk	X	X	X	X
Zygmunt Choren	X	X	X	X

Pen Duick III	*Leg 1*	*Leg 2*	*Leg 3*	*Leg 4*
Nicola Egger				X
M. C. Cruz				X
Jean Claude Grigaux				X
J. Nebout				X
J. Pommaret				X
E. Riviere				X
Y. Allemand				X
M. Cuiklinski				X

Pen Duick VI	*Leg 1*	*Leg 2*	*Leg 3*	*Leg 4*
Eric Tabarly	X	X	X	
Pierre Leboutet	X	X	X	
Patrick Meulemeester	X			
Bernard Rubinstein	X	X	X	
Pierre Monsaingeon	X	X	X	
Marc Pajot	X	X	X	
Patrick Phelipon	X	X	X	
Michel Barré	X	X	X	
Olivier de Kersauson	X	X	X	
Jean Philippe Chaboud	X	X	X	
Antoine Croyere	X	X	X	
Arnaud Dalhenx		X		
Jean Pierre Dagues	X	X	X	
Patrick Tabarly	X			
Francois Bessieres	X			
Bernard De Guy		X		
Michel le Barre		X	X	
Charles Bonnay			X	
Patrice Madillac			X	
Thierry Vanier			X	

Peter von Danzig	Leg 1	Leg 2	Leg 3	Leg 4
Tomas H. Rüter	X	X	X	X
Thomas Weber	X	X	X	X
Uli Blank	X	X	X	X
Aki Müller-Deile	X	X	X	X
Volker Mackeprang	X			
Reinhard Laucht	X	X	X	X
Achim Meyer	X	X	X	X
Jürgen Meyer	X	X	X	X
Fredrich-Karl Heinemann	X	X	X	X
Maximilian Heinemann	X	X	X	X
Hein Anhold		X	X	
Gert Findel				X
Jan Peter Jamaer			X	
Wilfried Kollex				X
Rüdiger Steinbeck				X

Sayula II	Leg 1	Leg 2	Leg 3	Leg 4
Ramon Carlin	X	X	X	X
Paquita Carlin	X			
Francisco Carlin	X	X	X	X
Enrique Carlin Torios	X	X	X	X
Roberto Cubas Carline	X	X	X	X
Adolfo Orinday	X	X	X	X
Ray Conrady	X	X	X	X
Keith Lorence	X	X	X	X
Robert C. Martin	X	X	X	X
David Bowen	X	X	X	X
Tjerk M. Romke de Vries	X	X	X	X
Butch Dalrymple-Smith	X	X	X	X
Yvonne van de Byl		X		
John Hutchinson			X	
Lawrence Wale				X

Second Life	Leg 1	Leg 2	Leg 3	Leg 4
Charles I. Butterworth	X	X	X	X
Christopher A. J. Lord	X	X	X	X
Alan Taphouse	X	X	X	X
Dr Robin Leach	X	X	X	X
Robert A. James	X	X	X	X
Wendy Hinds	X	X	X	X
W. B. Moulsdale	X	X	X	X
Geoffrey Bush	X	X	X	X
Michael R. Ainslie	X	X	X	X
Timothy A. Kershaw	X	X	X	X
John R. Whitfield	X	X	X	X
F. P. Sheehan	X			
Capt A. W. King-Harman RA			X	
John Stapleton			X	X
Richard Carlyle				X

Tauranga	Leg 1	Leg 2	Leg 3	Leg 4
Erik Pascoli	X	X	X	X
Guy Piazzini	X	X		X
Paolo Chamaz	X	X		
Patrick Diebolt	X	X	X	X
Jean Noel Durand	X	X	X	
Thierry Vanier	X	X		
Serge Bays	X			
Robert Girardin	X			
Livio Caputo	X			
Pascal Emeriau	X			X
Michel Ribet		X	X	
Paul Waterhouse		X		
Zara Pascoli	X	X	X	X
John Dean			X	
Edoardo Guzzetti			X	
Marco Galimberti			X	
Louis George Baitier				X
Patrice Ducourtioux				X
Yvon Redier				X
Vittorio Reggazola				X
Yves Olivaux				X

33 Export	Leg 1	Leg 2	Leg 3	Leg 4
Jean Pierre Millet	X	X		X
Daniel Millet	X	X	X	X
Philipe Viellescase				X
Dominique Guillet	X	X		
Jacques Redier	X	X		
Yvon Redier	X	X		
Tom Addeson	X	X	X	X
Peter Addeson	X	X	X	X
Richard Heberling			X	X
Oliver Stern-Veyrin			X	X
Bruno La Salle			X	
Paul Audoire			X	X
Jose Le Deliou			X	
Patrick Ferre	X			
Roch Pescadere		X		

Results and Prizes

Results Leg 1

Yacht	Elapsed Time in Hours	Finishing Order	Corrected Time in Hours	Position	Overall Position
Adventure	1034	2	873	1	1
British Soldier	1180	11	1045	14	14
Burton Cutter	1008	1	988	6	6
CS e RB	1230	13	1044	13	13
Copernicus	1240	14	1016	8	8
Grand Louis	1159	9	1021	9	9
Great Britain II	1037	3	1037	12	12
Guia	1183	12	977	5	5
Jakaranda	1112	7	967	4	4
Kriter	1113	8	1021	10	10
Otago	1251	15	1101	15	15
Pen Duick VI	1377	17	1368	17	17
Peter von Danzig	1260	16	1113	16	16
Sayula II	1061	4	950	2	2
Second Life	1097	6	1034	11	11
Tauranga	1176	10	1006	7	7
33 Export	1087	5	955	3	3

Results Leg 2

Yacht	Elapsed Time in Hours	Finishing Order	Corrected Time in Hours	Position	Overall Position
Adventure	942	8	781	9	3
British Soldier	967	10	833	10	9
CS e RB	945	9	760	8	8
Concorde	1202	15	980	15	—
Copernicus	1101	14	879	11	11
Grand Louis	766	6	637	2	2
Great Britain II	713	2	713	6	7
Guia	918	7	714	7	5
Kriter	733	4	642	3	4
Otago	1067	12	919	13	12
Pen Duick VI	704	1	673	5	14
Peter von Danzig	1071	13	925	14	13
Sayula II	734	5	624	1	1
Second Life	729	3	666	4	6
Tauranga	1049	11	880	12	10
33 Export	1387	16	1256	16	15

Results Leg 3

Yacht	Elapsed Time in Hours	Finishing Order	Corrected Time in Hours	Position	Overall Position
Adventure	1081	4	877	1	2
British Soldier	1193	7	1023	9	9
CS e RB	1241	9	1006	7	8
Copernicus	1381	12	1099	12	11
Grand Louis	1094	5	921	4	3
Great Britain II	976	1	976	6	7
Guia	1230	8	971	5	5
Kriter	1024	3	909	3	4
Otago	1405	13	1216	13	13
Pen Duick VI	Did not sign declaration				
Peter von Danzig	1272	11	1087	11	12
Sayula II	1022	2	882	2	1
Second Life	1098	6	1018	8	6
Tauranga	1250	10	1035	10	10
33 Export	1407	14	1240	14	14

Appendix IV

Results Leg 4

Yacht					
Adventure	850	4	717	1	2
British Soldier	976	10	864	10	9
Burton Cutter	792	2	775	7	
CS e RB	1072	13	917	13	8
Copernicus	1194	15	1009	14	11
Grand Louis	870	6	756	5	3
Great Britain II	741	1	741	2	6
Guia	936	8	766	6	5
Kriter	888	7	813	8	4
Otago	1169	14	1045	15	13
Pen Duick III	1023	12	906	12	
Peter von Danzig	1308	16	1187	16	14
Sayula II	840	3	748	4	1
Second Life	942	9	890	11	7
Tauranga	986	11	845	9	10
33 Export	857	5	748	3	12

Results Summary

Yacht	Elapsed Time in hours	Finishing Order	Corrected Time in hours	Position
Adventure	3907	6	3248	2
British Soldier	4316	8	3765	9
CS e RB	4488	10	3727	8
Copernicus	4916	14	4003	11
Grand Louis	3889	5	3327	3
Great Britain II	3467	1	3467	6
Guia	4267	7	3427	5
Kriter	3758	3	3386	4
Otago	4893	12	4281	13
Peter von Danzig	4912	13	4311	14
Sayula II	3657	2	3205	1
Second Life	3866	4	3608	7
Tauranga	4461	9	3766	10
33 Export	4738	11	4198	12

PRIZE WINNERS

Yacht	1st Leg	2nd Leg	3rd Leg	4th Leg	Overall
Adventure	1,2,9.		19,20.	28,29.	38,47.
Burton Cutter	7,8.				
British Soldier			27.		47.
Copernicus					44.
CS e RB					46.
Grand Louis		12,13.			39.
Great Britain II			25,26.	30,31,34,35.	42,43,47.
Guia					46.
Kriter		14,15,18.	23,24.		40.
Otago					
Pen Duick VI		16,17.			
Peter von Danzig					45.
Sayula II	3,4.	10,11.	21,22.		37.41.
Second Life					
Tauranga				36.	46.
33 Export	5,6.			32,33.	

First Leg

Trophy No.	Achievement	Trophy
1	1st on Handicap	City of Cape Town Stinkwood Trophy
2		Whitbread Gold Medal
3	2nd on Handicap	Cruising Association of South Africa (Silver Tray)
4		Whitbread Silver Medal
5	3rd on Handicap	Royal Cape Yacht Club Trophy
6		Whitbread Bronze Medal
7	LINE HONOURS	Cruising Association of South Africa (Silver Tray)
8		RNSA Dolphin Trophy
9	BEST PASSAGE	Ocean Cruising Club Plaque

Second Leg

Trophy No.	Achievement	Trophy
10	1st on Handicap	City of Sydney Trophy
11		Whitbread Gold Medal
12	2nd on Handicap	Nestle (Australian) Trophy
13		Whitbread Silver Medal
14	3rd on Handicap	Cruising Yacht Club of Australia, Plaque
15		Whitbread Bronze Medal
16	LINE HONOURS	Port Jackson Trophy
17		RNSA Dolphin Trophy
18	BEST PASSAGE	Ocean Cruising Club Plaque

Third Leg

19	1st on Handicap	Brazilian Ocean Racing Association Trophy
20		Whitbread Gold Medal
21	2nd on Handicap	Iate Clube do Rio de Janeiro Trophy
22		Whitbread Silver Medal
23	3rd on Handicap	Brazilian National Council of Sport Trophy
24		Whitbread Silver Medal
25	LINE HONOURS	The Iate Clube do Rio de Janeiro Plaque
26		RNSA Dolphin Trophy
27	BEST PASSAGE	Ocean Cruising Club Plaque

Fourth Leg

28	1st on Handicap	RORC Silver Trophy
29		Whitbread Gold Medal
30	2nd on Handicap	Rod Rigging Trophy
31		Whitbread Silver Medal
32	3rd on Handicap	Camper and Nicholsons Trophy
33		Whitbread Bronze Medal
34	LINE HONOURS	Henri Lloyd Trophy
35		RNSA Dolphin Trophy
36	BEST PASSAGE	Ocean Cruising Club Plaque

FOR THE WHOLE RACE

37	1st on Handicap	WHITBREAD & CO., TROPHY
38	2nd on Handicap	Royal Naval Club and Royal Albert Yacht Club. Trophy
39	3rd on Handicap	Royal Thames Yacht Club "VELSHEDA" Trophy
40	4th on Handicap	Italvela Trophy
41	1st on Handicap for Legs 2 and 3	RNSA "ROARING FORTIES" Trophy
42	LINE HONOURS	Portsmouth City Council Trophy
43		RNSA Dolphin Trophy (Gold)
44	OUTSTANDING SEAMANSHIP	The Lady Swaythling Trophy (on behalf of the Shipwrecked Mariners Society)
45	"BEST LOSER"	Royal Yacht Squadron Trophy
46	Team Award for Lowest Aggregate Corrected Time	Federazione Italiana Vela Trophy
47	The Duke of Edinburgh	Award for Active Service Personnel

Index

ACNAM 45
Addeson, Peter-John 45
Addeson, Tom 45, 96
Adventure 25, 34–6, 53, 56, 84, 85, 88–90, 98, 107, 109, 111, 112, 114–19, 122, 124–7, 135, 152, 153, 155, 157, 160, 166
Ainslie, Roddie 41, 103, 120
Ainslie, Sue 136
Akademischer Segler-Verein 49, 136
Albatross 156
Alspar 103, 104
Angrade do Heroisme 86
Arg dos Abrolhus 113
Arquipélago de Cabo Verde 84
Astro navigation 147
Auzépy-Brenneur, Georges 44
Avery, Warrant Officer Mike 51
Azores 111, 114, 156

Basic speed factor 24
Bass strait 92, 98, 99
Bay of Biscay 84
Bayle, Philippe 88
Baynham, Captain 24
BBC World Service 25, 162
Bell reef 92
Berthing arrangements 27
Bertoldi, Paolo 49
Bester, Theunis 51
Bich, Baron 45
Bingham,   25
Black Pyramid 92
Blyth, Chay 19, 37–9, 58, 83, 86, 88, 93, 95, 96, 105, 108, 114, 118, 136, 141, 164, 166
Boat preparation 33–51
Bongers, Bobby 51
Bowen, Dave 99, 132
Brazil Current 155, 156
British Army 37
British Soldier 25, 37–8, 58, 86, 109, 112, 113, 117, 121, 124, 126, 142, 157, 162

British Steel 37, 38, 58
Browning, Captain 27
Bruce, Commander Errol 21
Bruder, Jorg 45
Brunner, Commander R.H.H. 22
Bryans, Lieutenant Commander Patrick 35, 85, 87
Buenos Aires 103
Burton Cutter 23, 34, 40–1, 53, 54, 60, 83, 85–9, 93, 94, 103, 112, 114, 116, 119, 121, 126, 127, 129, 137, 153, 166
Butane 140

Cabo de Hornos 101
Camper and Nicholsons 34, 36
Cape Horn 101, 102, 108, 109, 148, 155
Cape of Good Hope 85, 91
Cape Otway 92
Cape Pillar 93
Cape Town 29, 85, 89, 91, 93, 144, 153
Cape Verde Islands 84
Capsize 130–4
Carlier, Major Niel 38
Carlin, Ramon 47, 86, 114, 119, 136, 167
CERBOM 45
Chamaz, Paola 94
Chamber of Shipping 24
Chichester, Sir Francis 22, 159
    Gypsy Moth Circles the World 101
Churchill, Anthony 19
Ciecholewski, Witold 50
Clark, Robert 37, 47, 48
Climatic Chart 146
Clothes, wet 140
Coastguard 24, 30
Coeudevez, Albert 88
Colas, Alain 44, 107, 157, 166
Cold problems 144
Coles, Adlard 98, 134
Collins, Commander F. A. 21

Commarond, Georges 44
Communications 24, 159–62, 164
Concorde 53, 54, 93, 96
Conrady, Ray 47, 114, 155, 158, 161
Cooking 140
Copernicus 50, 54, 86, 98, 103, 109, 112, 116, 120, 122, 155, 160
Coriolan 45
Craglietto 47
Crews and crew selection 25, 26, 34, 38–9, 135, 141
Cruising Association of South Africa 29
Cruising Yacht Club of Australia 29, 30
CS e RB 31, 47, 48, 62, 84, 99, 109, 112, 153, 155, 160
Cubas, Roberto 131, 133, 134

Dalling, Bruce 51
Dalrymple-Smith, Butch 47, 96, 99, 116, 130
Damerell, Bill 51, 152
Daniels, Brian 93
Danziger Werft 49
Declaration form 26
Dehydration 143
de Vries, Jjevk Romke 120
Diego Ramirez 108
Djikstra, Gerard 41
Doldrums 152, 153
Dreux, Maurice 138
Dryad, HMS 23
Dyspepsia 142

Edwards, Chris 137
Endurance, HMS 108, 109, 155
Entries, number of 34
Entry enquiries 25, 33
Epoca 48
Equator 85, 87, 137
Equipment 26
Excellent, HMS 28

Facsimile equipment 157–8
Falk, Giorgio 47, 110
Falkland Current 155, 156
Falkland Islands 156
Faux, Georges 46, 86
Fear 136
Finger tips, splitting of 142
Finish 22, 30, 118
'Flu epidemic 144
Food preparation 139
Food supplies 138
Forms 26
Fox, John E. F. 21
Fraser, Dr. 26
Fround, J. H. 22

Galway Blazer 26
Gastroenteritis 143
Gitana 45
Glacer, Horst 51
Gliksman, Alain 45, 80, 108, 157
Godber, Pat 20
Goodwin, John 51
Grand Louis 44, 45, 64, 85, 98, 106,
    108, 109, 112, 114, 115, 119,
    121, 124, 126, 128, 135, 139,
    141, 156, 160
Great Britain 38
Great Britain II 31, 38–40, 53, 66, 86,
    89, 93, 95, 96, 99, 100, 103–5,
    108, 109, 111, 114–18, 120, 121,
    123–6, 129, 136, 138, 141, 143,
    152, 160, 164, 166
Green, Alan 30
Grout, Ariane 88
Grout, Jack 44–6, 88, 126
Gruber, Henry 49
Grütter, Wilhelm 51, 152
Guia 47, 68, 98, 109, 110, 112, 120–2,
    155
Guillet, Dominique 45, 80, 96, 119
Gurney, Alan 38, 39, 66

Hamilton, Captain Hans 21
Handicapping system 23–4, 164
Hayward, Jack 38, 39, 118
Hestia 44
Higham, Tony 98
Hinds, Wendy 41, 109
Honey, Captain Alec 39, 105
Hood Sailmakers 35
Hope, Eddie 95
Hosking, Bernie 89, 105
Hunt, Gina 19

Iate Clube do Rio de Janeiro 29, 30,
    109

Icebergs 92, 106, 107
ICI 38
Illingworth 40
Indian Ocean 91
Infections 144
Insurance 27, 38
International Offshore Rule 23
International Yacht Racing Union rules
    25

Jakaranda 50–1, 53, 54, 86, 93, 152,
    153
Jason West Cay 156

Keewaydin 51, 53
Kelsall, Derek 38, 39
Kia Loa 121
King, Commander Bill 26
King Island 92
Knox-Johnston, Robin 22, 83, 101
Koehorst, Peter 51
Kriter 44–5, 70, 88, 93, 103, 108, 109,
    112, 116, 120, 126, 130, 138, 160
Kujawa, H. 50

Last, Gerhard 51
Laucht, Reinhard 49, 104, 139
Leach, Robin 95, 141, 142, 144
Le Berre, Michael 42
Leg One 83–9
Leg Two 91–9
Leg Three 101–9
Leg Four 111–20
Lelouche, Claude 83
Le Maire Straits 156
Leopard Norman 44
Liaison officers 27–8
Life on board 135–41
Liskiewicz and Rejewski 50
Lively Lady 83
Lloyds 27
Lloyds Intelligence 25
Lorence, Keith 47, 52, 109, 129, 131,
    167
Lucette 26
Lupke, Herbert 51

Mabelle 47
Majot, Marc 86
Malingri, Doi 48
Malinovsky, Michel 45
Manureva 107, 157
Marabu 35
Marchand, Gwénaël 46
Martin, Bob 131, 132, 134

Maupas, Alain 44
Mauric, André 45, 124
Medical problems and precautions
    142–5
Merlin 35
Millet, Daniel 96
Millet, Jean-Pierre 45, 80, 96, 119, 136,
    165
Moksha 46, 86
Morale 137
Mullender, Chief Petty Officer Roy 34,
    35, 112, 114, 115, 118, 152
Müller-Deile, Aki 49, 104
Myatt, James 113

Nai Ut 51
Narragansett 44
Nautor OY 47, 48, 74, 127, 134
Navigation 147–58
Nile Maru 86
Noon positions form 26
Norman, Captain Dudley 20, 21, 164
Noryema 35
Notice to Mariners 24
Nuffield Trust 38

O'Brien, Conor 19
Ocean navigation 147
Ocean Passages for the World 23, 84, 91,
    101, 111, 148
Ocean Racing International (Pty)
    Ltd. 51
Ondine 121
Orinday, Cantis 132
ORPIE 45
Otago 49–50, 53–5, 93, 98, 103, 109,
    112, 116, 120–6, 128, 130, 135,
    160
Overseas organisation 29

Paiko 116
Pajot, Marc 44
Panama Canal 148
Pascoli, Eric 48, 82, 121
Passad 140
Passi, Alberto 48
Paul, Alan 21
Pearse, Guy 19
Pen Duick II 41
Pen Duick III 41, 45, 112
Pen Duick VI 41–4, 53, 72, 85, 87, 88,
    93, 94, 98, 103, 104, 109, 111,
    116, 122–6, 129, 140, 141, 166
Performance of boats and gear 121–9
Perlicki, Zygfryd, 50, 86, 116

Peter von Danzig 34, 49, 50, 53, 71, 93, 96, 98, 103, 104, 109, 112, 113, 120–2, 126, 127, 135–7, 139–41, 143, 152, 157, 166
Petrel 156
Phelipon, Patrick 98
Philip, Prince 167
Phillips 38
Photophobia 142
Pienkawa, Iwona 50
Pienkawa, Zdzislaw 50, 116
Pionier 26
Planning 23
Port Dalrymple 92
Port Elizabeth 94
Portsmouth 28, 30
Portsmouth City Council 28
Position fixing 147
Position reporting 24, 25, 95, 162, 164
Powell, John 39
Presles, Dominique 45
Price, Len 39, 86
Primrose 40
Psychological aspects 145

Race Committee 20, 21, 23, 163
Race Control 163, 164
Race rules 23
Radio equipment 26, 159
Radio failures 25, 162
Radio stations 160
RANSA 22, 30, 99
Raph 45
Rashes 143
Ratsey and Lapthorn 39
Redier, Jaques 45
Reid Rocks 92
Richardson, Keith 116
Ridgeway, Captain John 38
Rio de Janeiro 30, 106, 109, 111, 142
Rist, John 105
RNSA 20, 148, 164, 167
    expertise and world-wide ramifications 22
    membership 21–2
    Portsmouth branch 27
    Race Committee 20, 21, 23, 163
Robertson, Dougal 26

Rose, Sir Alec 21, 83
    My Lively Lady 101
Royal Albert Yacht Club 29, 30
Rulhe, Dominique 45, 136

Sabre 38
Safety harnesses 47, 96
Sailing Instructions 23
St Papa 44
Saiorse 19
Salt deficiency 143
Salt tablets 143
Sayula II 34, 47, 52, 74, 84, 86–9, 93, 96, 98, 99, 103, 104, 108, 109, 111, 112, 114–16, 118–21, 124, 127, 129–31, 135, 136, 138, 139, 153, 155, 157, 161, 163, 166, 167
Scott Bader 38
Second Life 32, 41, 76, 95, 97–9, 103, 109, 112, 116, 120, 121, 124, 127–9, 136, 141, 142, 144, 145, 153, 155, 167
Sextant 147, 152
Sharp, John 40
Shields, Graham 103, 104
Skene, Lieutenant Commander Malcolm 35
Slocum, *Sailing Alone Around the World* 101
Smith, Alan 40, 86
Smith, Charles 51
Southern Ocean Shipyard 41
Southsea Castle 28
Sparkman and Stephens 47, 48, 74
Sparlight 39
Special equipment form 26
Spencers 39
Sponsorship 25
Stage duration, prediction of 149
Start 20, 22, 28, 83
Steiner, Rear Admiral Otto 21, 22, 24, 163
Stern-Veyrin, Olivier 156
Stewart Wrightson 38
Striana 44
Suhali 83
Sun, protection against 144
Surface current circulation 154

Swift, Jonathan 26
Sydney 29, 93, 99, 103, 144
Sydney Heads 99

Tabarly, Eric 41, 45, 46, 85, 86, 88, 98, 99, 103, 109, 116, 122, 123, 166
Tamblyn, Roger 142
Taphouse, Alan 98, 103
Tasman Sea 104
Tauranga 47, 48, 78, 82, 94–6, 99, 109, 112, 116, 125, 127, 138
Terlain, Jean-Yves 45, 83
33 Export 45, 80, 89, 96, 98, 103, 109, 112, 115, 118, 119, 121, 124, 126, 136, 156, 165
Thomas, Freddy 103
Thomson, Mike 39
Three Hummock Island 92
Time correction factor 24
Time prediction 23
Time signal transmissions 161
Tonsillitis 144

Vallings, Captain George 35, 106, 155
van de Byl, Yvonne 51, 152
Vanek, Michel 44
Vanek, Sylvie 44
Vendredi Treize 45, 83
Vernon, HMS 22, 27, 30, 117, 118
Viant, André 44, 46, 85, 108, 119

Waterhouse, Paul 94, 95
Weather broadcasts 161
Weather conditions 23
Whales 26, 106
Whitbread & Company Ltd. 20, 164
Whitbread Multihull Race 164
Whitbread, Sir Samuel 117
Wild Rocket 119
Williams, Captain John 136
Williams, Leslie 40, 83, 84, 85, 86, 94, 114, 127, 136
Windward Marine 41
Windward Passage 66, 93, 121
Windward Spirit 41, 60

Yacht details 53–82